# The Antecedents of Self-esteem

A SERIES OF BOOKS IN PSYCHOLOGY

Editor: *Stanley Coopersmith*

# The Antecedents of Self-esteem

STANLEY COOPERSMITH

*University of California, Davis*

W. H. FREEMAN AND COMPANY

*San Francisco*

*To Alice for what she has meant and what she has given
and to Mark, Erik, and Karen—
in descending order but not significance.*

# PREFACE

More than eight years ago I began a series of studies intended to clarify the antecedents and consequences of self-esteem. Those studies sought to extend research I had initiated in preparing my dissertation at Cornell University and to define more clearly several conceptual and methodological issues that have hindered investigations of self-esteem. The present work summarizes my findings on the background, the personal characteristics, and the parental treatment associated with high, medium, low, and defensive self-esteem. The report is intended to answer the question, "What are the conditions that lead an individual to value himself and to regard himself as an object of worth?" Although the answers to that question can be briefly summarized by the terms "parental warmth," "clearly defined limits," and "respectful treatment," these terms turn out to be more complex and ambiguous than is generally appreciated. In these pages I have sought to clarify the meaning of these terms and to indicate why such parental treatment has the effect it does. I have, at the same time, sought to develop a conceptual framework that might serve as a guide in investigating self-esteem, or a tool for altering it. The model employs four major concepts—successes, ideals, aspirations, and defenses—which are given operational significance in the course of this report. It is my hope that the findings and conceptualizations will be of interest and use to child psychologists and parents as well as to fellow investigators of personality development.

This book includes selected examples of the correlates and consequences of self-esteem, particularly in the realm of social behavior and personal competence. The examples are intended to validate our indices of self-esteem and to indicate some of the important consequences of self-appraisal. The major focus, however, is upon the conditions that contribute to the formation of self-esteem. This separation permitted me to develop more fully the theoretical foundations and to present more extended findings than could otherwise be given in a single work. The results and formulations of the consequences of self-esteem will be presented in a future monograph.

In the course of this study several individuals assumed active and major responsibilities, and I wish to acknowledge their participation and to express my thanks for their efforts. My chief collaborators throughout the project were Betty James Beardslee and David Lowy. They became involved shortly after its inception, assumed major responsibilities for the selection of subjects for the clinical studies, and were my consultants in the experimental, antecedent, and follow-up investigations. I should also like to express my appreciation to Iona Kaplan, Ruth Peoples, Patricia Brodsky, and Alice Coopersmith, who were directly involved in the testing, interviewing, and coding, and in the analyses of the results reported here. Several other persons contributed to particular parts of the study, and their contributions are noted at the appropriate places in the text.

A first version of this manuscript was completed in late 1965, after a year's stay at the Laboratory of Socioenvironmental Studies of the National Institutes of Mental Health. I wish to express my thanks to Melvin L. Kohn, Chief of the Laboratory, to Leonard Perlin, Acting Chief during my visit, and to the other members of the Laboratory for their hospitality, assistance, and suggestions. I am particularly grateful to Morris Rosenberg, a member of the Laboratory, whose comments served to enrich and expedite this report. Other persons who read earlier versions of this manuscript and gave me the benefit of their knowledge are Leonard Perlin, Harry Scarr, M. Brewster Smith, and Morris Parloff. Ermajean Surman typed the first version of this report as well as many of the analyses; Margaret Hill typed the final revised manuscript.

The research reported here was supported by a series of grants from the National Institutes of Mental Health and by grants from the Connecticut Association of Mental Health and the Wesleyan University Research Committee. In the course of my research I held fellowships from the Social Research Council (1960–1961) and the National Science Foundation (1965). These fellowships expedited both my studies and the preparation of this report, and I am grateful for the generous support extended by these agencies. I trust that they will feel the outcome has warranted their concern. The results of this project reflect a joint effort and support, but of course I assume sole responsibility for any errors that may be found in my presentation of the results of the research.

Finally, I should like to express my personal appreciation to my subjects. During this study I have come to look upon them and their families as close friends, for how else can I explain their cooperation and generosity. My thanks to each of them, with the hope that they will not recognize themselves in this report. My thanks also to James Edmondson for his encouragement and his support over the past eight years and for his continued interest during the preparation of this manuscript.

STANLEY COOPERSMITH

*El Cerrito, California*
*February, 1967*

# CONTENTS

*Chapter one*

# INTRODUCTION

For both psychologists and laymen, "self-esteem" has great significance—personally, socially, and psychologically. It is therefore disconcerting that so little is known about the conditions and experiences that enhance or lessen self-esteem. The research presented here constitutes the major part of an intensive study of self-esteem, carried out during 1959–1965, and focuses upon those antecedent conditions that contribute to the development of positive and negative attitudes toward oneself. Since so much of previous theorizing about feelings of personal worth has been largely speculative, the results of this investigation should be of interest and value not only to students of human behavior, but also to those parents and therapists who are concerned with developing and altering an individual's self-esteem.

This report will also attempt to shed further light upon "self" studies and to place them within the general framework of attitude research. Although in recent years there has been increasing attention to cognitive and symbolic processes (Hebb,[1] Heider[2]), the consequences of such processes, in terms of a person's motivation, have been largely bypassed. The work of Newcomb,[3]

---

[1] D. O. Hebb. *The Organization of Behavior*. New York, Wiley, 1949.
[2] F. Heider. *The Psychology of Interpersonal Relations*. New York, Wiley, 1958.
[3] T. M. Newcomb. "Motivation in social behavior." In J. S. Brown et al., *Current Theory and Research in Motivation: A Symposium*. Lincoln, University of Nebraska Press, 1953, pp. 139–161.

Katz and Stotland,[4] and Festinger[5] clearly relates attitude and motivation, yet attempts to explicate the relation between the two have been relatively limited.[6] In the present study I found it clarifying and profitable to define self-esteem in terms of evaluative attitudes toward the self. This conceptual framework offered several advantages over other personality theories that have been employed to examine self-esteem. Through the use of this formulation and related procedures, several thorny problems relating to the study of the "self" were avoided, certain relationships between self-attitudes and motivation were established, and some broad theoretical generalizations were achieved.

In the course of this study several research tools and procedures relating to the investigation of subjective states were developed, which represent attempts to deal with some of the basic problems of "self" research. These tools and procedures will be introduced in their appropriate context. By measuring the same variable—that is, self-esteem—in its various subjective and behavioral expressions, it was possible to determine whether (and to what extent) the subject's responses were related to his actions. This enabled us to deal with the problems of defensiveness and response set, which have long hindered efforts to study subjective states. With knowledge of both the subjective state and its behavioral expression, we proceeded to validate our indices of esteem against a network of variables that are theoretically related to self-esteem. This procedure showed how the two expressions of esteem—subjective and behavioral—were related to the other variables and indicated the specific and relative significance of both. The question of whether a subject was distorting his responses, presenting an acceptable facade, or expressing a genuine statement of his views was thus given an empirical answer. (The topic of defensive responses will be discussed in greater length in Chapter 2.)

The procedures developed to study self-esteem appear to have considerable promise as well for the study of other subjective states. In the light of the marked interest in subjective states that is now being expressed, through existentialism, personal constructs, and phenomenology, we would hope that other investigators would find these procedures of interest and value.

---

[4] D. Katz and E. Stotland. "A preliminary statement to a theory of attitude structure and change." In S. Koch (Ed.), *Psychology: A Study of a Science.* New York, McGraw-Hill, 1959, Vol. III, pp. 423–475.

[5] L. Festinger. *A Theory of Cognitive Dissonance.* Evanston, Ill., Row-Peterson, 1957.

[6] C. N. Cofer and M. H. Appley. *Motivation: Theory and Research.* New York, Wiley, 1964.

The major basis for our study was the widely held belief that self-esteem is significantly associated with personal satisfaction and effective functioning. The achievement of a favorable attitude toward oneself has been regarded as important by a number of personality theorists—Rogers, Murphy, Horney, and Adler—but few have made direct studies of its effects. This belief in the importance of self-esteem is also shared by many clinicians and social psychologists. Since, however, consensus does not constitute proof, this widely held belief is suggestive rather than definitive. In addition, most statements concerning the importance of self-esteem tend to be relatively general in nature. They rarely indicate the *specific* behaviors to which self-esteem is related or *in what way* it is an effective, contributing determinant of personality.

At the time this study was initiated (1959), we were able to identify or infer from the psychological literature several lines of evidence pointing to the importance of self-esteem. These studies, and the considerable number that have since been added, are reviewed in Ruth Wylie's insightful and scholarly monograph.[7] They reveal that persons who seek psychological help frequently acknowledge that they suffer from feelings of inadequacy and unworthiness. These people see themselves as helpless and inferior —incapable of improving their situations and lacking the inner resources to tolerate or reduce the anxiety readily aroused by everyday events and stress.[8] Clinicians observe that persons who are plagued by doubts of their worthiness can neither give nor receive love, apparently fearing that the exposure that comes with intimacy will reveal their inadequacies and cause them to be rejected.[9] They thus avoid closeness in their relationships and feel isolated as a consequence. Still other studies reveal that persons whose performance does not match their personal aspirations evaluate themselves as inferior, no matter how high their attainments. These persons are likely to report feelings of guilt, shame, or depression and to conclude that their actual achievements are of little importance. Unless and until they can attain their desired goals, they regard themselves as unsuccessful and unworthy. Clinical studies repeatedly demonstrate that failures and other conditions that threaten to expose

---

[7] R. Wylie. *The Self-Concept.* Lincoln, Neb., University of Nebraska Press, 1961.

[8] C. R. Rogers and R. F. Dymond (Eds.). *Psychotherapy and Personality Change: Coordinated Studies in the Client-centered Approach.* Chicago, University of Chicago Press, 1954.

[9] E. Fromm. "Selfishness and self-love." *Psychiatry,* **2:**507–523 (1939).

personal inadequacies are probably the major cause of anxiety. Anxiety and self-esteem are closely related: if it is threat that releases anxiety, as appears theoretically essential, it is the person's esteem that is being threatened.

Many laboratory and field investigations tend to support and extend the clinician's impressions of the importance of self-esteem in personal experience and interpersonal behavior. Although the evidence is often merely an inference derived from the study of other topics, these investigations often conclude that self-esteem is a major contributing variable. Motivational research strongly suggests that the striving after social status and social approval stems, in good part, from the desire to maintain a favorable self-evaluation. Experimental studies indicate that a person with low self-esteem is less capable of resisting pressures to conform[10] and is less able to perceive threatening stimuli. They further indicate that a person with high self-esteem maintains a fairly constant image of his capabilities and of his distinctness as a person. Studies of creative persons show that they rank quite high in self-esteem. Presumably, belief in one's perceptions and the conviction that one can force or impose order upon a segment of the universe is a basic prerequisite for major creativity. These persons with high self-esteem are also more likely to assume an active role in social groups and to express their views frequently and effectively. Less troubled by fears and ambivalence, less burdened by self-doubt and minor personality disturbances, the person with high self-esteem apparently moves more directly and realistically toward his personal goals.

Of even greater relevance to our present study are the indirect indications that in children domination, rejection, and severe punishment result in lowered self-esteem. Under such conditions they have fewer experiences of love and success and tend to become generally submissive and withdrawn (although occasionally veering to the opposite extreme of aggression and domination). Children reared under such crippling circumstances are unlikely to be realistic and effective in their everyday functioning and are more likely to manifest deviant behavior patterns.

### DEFINITIONS

The evidence of all these studies on the importance of self-esteem formed the basis for our study of its antecedents, correlates, and consequences. The first essential step was to clarify the meaning of the term "self-esteem." By self-esteem we refer to the evaluation which the individual makes and cus-

---

[10] I. L. Janis. "Personality correlates of susceptibility to persuasion." *J. Personality*, **22**:504–518 (1954).

tomarily maintains with regard to himself: it expresses an attitude of approval or disapproval, and indicates the extent to which the individual believes himself to be capable, significant, successful, and worthy. In short, self-esteem is a *personal* judgment of worthiness that is expressed in the attitudes the individual holds toward himself. It is a subjective experience which the individual conveys to others by verbal reports and other overt expressive behavior. Although the primary focus of this study is upon private, subjective appraisals of personal worthiness, we shall employ other, overt, behavioral indices of esteem to gauge the quality and validity of the individual's reports. These external indices will serve as criterion variables and also serve to indicate the importance of behavioral and unconscious expressions of esteem.

There are certain features of this definition that require elaboration. First, it should be noted that our definition centers upon the relatively enduring estimate of general self-esteem rather than upon more specific and transitory changes in evaluation. There are undoubtedly momentary, situational, limited shifts in self-evaluation, but these are not the concern of the present study. The focal concern of this research is the generally prevailing estimate of self-esteem reported by and for an individual. Both the enduring and the transitory evaluations deal with the level of individual self-appraisal, but the two differ in the generality and reliability of the appraisals and the conditions under which they are made. That the self-esteem of an individual remains constant for at least several years is demonstrated by measurements obtained under similar conditions and with relatively similar instruments. The test-retest reliability obtained for the Self-Esteem Inventory after a five-week interval with a sample of 30 fifth-grade children was .88, and the reliability after a three-year interval with a different sample of 56 children was .70. This would suggest that at some time preceding middle childhood the individual arrives at a general appraisal of his worth, which remains relatively stable and enduring over a period of several years. This appraisal can presumably be affected by specific incidents and environmental changes but apparently it reverts to its customary level when conditions resume their "normal" and typical course. Aronson[11] shows that persons are generally unwilling to accept evidence that they are better or worse than they themselves have decided, and generally resolve any dissonance between the evidence and their judgment in favor of their customary judgment. Prescott Lecky[12] was perhaps the first major theorist who proposed and demonstrated that self-appraisals are

---

[11] E. Aronson and J. Mills. "The effects of severity of initiation on liking for a group." *J. Abn. Soc. Psych.*, **59**:177–181 (1959).
[12] P. Lecky. *Self-consistency, a Theory of Personality.* New York, Island Press, 1945.

relatively resistant to change because of the individual's need for psychological consistency.

A second consideration is that self-esteem may vary across different areas of experience and according to sex, age, and other role-defining conditions. Thus it is conceivable that an individual would regard himself as very worthy as a student, moderately worthy as a tennis player, and totally unworthy as a musician. His over-all appraisal of his abilities would presumably weight these areas according to their subjective importance, enabling him to arrive at a general level of self-esteem. Though this appears to be the case, objective evidence on the method of arriving at general appraisals is sparse. Accordingly, we decided to include questions from several different areas of activity in our test of subjective self-esteem (Appendix A) and determine the extent to which the appraisals for different areas differed. We therefore included statements relative to school, family, peers, self, and general social activities. Analysis of the tests of 56 children (aged 10 to 12) failed to reveal significant differences between the self-appraisals advanced for the different areas of experience. This suggests that either preadolescent children make little distinction about their worthiness in different areas of experience or, if such distinctions are made, they are made within the context of the over-all, general appraisal of worthiness that the children have already made. Despite this indication that appraisals do not vary for different areas of experience, it is our belief that the current study deals largely with esteem related to achievement and family experiences. This is largely a function of the sample we chose to study, the research setting, and the culture in which we live. As we shall describe shortly, we decided to employ preadolescent males as our subjects. The importance of the orientation toward achievement in American society, particularly for middle class males, has been amply reported elsewhere[13] and requires little elaboration on our part. In addition, we should note that much of our testing took place within a school setting, which would tend to enhance the latent and prevailing orientation toward achievement. In studying children of preadolescent age, we increase the likelihood that family experiences will be an important source of self-esteem. These children are still highly dependent upon their parents and are very likely to employ the family context and its values to judge their own worth.

A third feature of the definition that we should like to clarify is the meaning of the term "self-evaluation." In the present research, the term refers to

---

[13] D. C. McClelland, J. W. Atkinson, R. A. Clark, and E. L. Lowell. *The Achievement Motive*. New York, Appleton-Century-Crofts, 1953.

a judgmental process in which the individual examines his performance, capacities, and attributes according to his personal standards and values, and arrives at a decision of his own worthiness. These self-attitudes are what we have obtained in our test procedures and have observed in their behavioral expression. The attitudes directed toward the self may be defined in the same way as attitudes directed toward other objects: an orientation toward or away from some object or event and a predisposition to respond favorably or unfavorably toward these and related objects and events.[14] Attitudes toward the self, like other orientations and dispositions, may be either conscious or unconscious. Presumably they are like other attitudes in carrying positive and negative affective connotations and in being intertwined with intellectual and motivational processes. Thus the individual need not be aware of his attitudes toward himself, but they will nonetheless be expressed in his voice, posture, gestures, and performance. The very process of measuring a given attitude may tend to bring that attitude to the person's attention, and he may become aware of his predisposition when a particular test has been completed. The attitude he holds may surprise him, and he may confess that he had not previously given the subject much attention.

These and other features of our definition of self-esteem will receive more extended treatment in the conceptual analysis and reformulation presented in Chapter 2. At this point let us note that the present study examines the relatively enduring evaluative attitudes an individual holds toward himself as an object. It is our assumption that attitudes toward the self, like other attitudes, carry affective loadings and have motivational consequences. From our results it appears that the evaluative attitudes that preadolescents express for different areas of experience are not appreciably different. Given the context of American culture, the age and class background of our subjects, and the setting in which the studies were conducted, it is likely that the current study deals largely with self-esteem related to achievement and family experience. To study these attitudes objectively we employed a procedure in which we relate verbal expressions of attitude with more overt behavioral manifestations. As the next section indicates, we obtained self-evaluative attitudes from the individual and compared them with behaviors assumed to express self-esteem.

---

[14] C. I. Hovland and I. L. Janis (Eds.). *Personality and Persuasibility*. New Haven, Yale University Press, 1959.

DESIGN

The decision to study the self-esteem of preadolescents rather than any other age group was prompted by several considerations. By this age (10 to 12), the individual appears to have sufficient experience and ability to think abstractly, so that he can make general assessments of his powers. The period follows one of relative stability in academic and social affairs and is marked by fewer stresses and demands than the ensuing period of adolescence. These children are sufficiently advanced in their academic activities to have an idea of their relative competence. They also have had sufficient exposure to competitive standards and achievement that academic performance would probably be reflected in their self-esteem. Parental values and control remain major influences upon their behavior, and may themselves be subjected to observation and study. School conditions for this age group make it generally possible to obtain raters (teachers) who have observed the subject over an extended time in a relatively constant environment, and these raters are in a position to appraise the child's customary assurance, reactions to stress, and other behavioral manifestations of self-esteem.

We decided further to focus our study on preadolescents of middle class background who were male, white, and normal. These restrictions were intended to cut down the sources of variability and thereby to allow intensive studies on a smaller number of subjects. The decision to study the self-esteem of normal subjects derives from our interest in competent and adaptive behavior. (Operationally, the term "normal" means that there were no indications of serious symptoms of stress or emotional disorder revealed in the teacher's rating, the school records, or the screening interview.) Positive self-esteem is generally assumed to have favorable consequences and it was our belief that the benefits it presumably confers could best be observed in subjects who were judged to be within the normal range. This study is accordingly a study of personality development and functioning in subjects who were functioning effectively at the time the study was begun and did not manifest any overt indications of abnormality.

Our over-all design—to investigate the antecedents, consequences, and correlates of self-esteem—was carried out in a series of four interrelated studies. These studies consisted of (1) *selection* of subjects who differed in self-esteem; (2) the *clinical evaluation* of these subjects on a battery of ability, projective and personality questionnaire tests, and a clinical interview; (3) observation and measurement of the subject's behaviors in a series of *labora-*

*tory experiments* that were theoretically related to self-esteem; and (4) ascertaining the *antecedents* of self-esteem by interviews and questionnaires administered to the mother of the subject and to the subject himself. The same subjects were utilized throughout the entire series of investigations. Inasmuch as the present report focuses on the antecedents of self-esteem, we pay greatest attention to that and to the selection of subjects.

### SELECTION OF SUBJECTS

Our method of identifying subjects who differ in self-esteem requires knowledge of the person's subjective estimate of his self-esteem and its behavioral expression. Such knowledge enables us to determine the level of his self-esteem as well as whether his subjective statements are in agreement with an observer's rating of his (theoretically related) behaviors. If there is a great difference between the self-attitude expressed by the subject and the related behaviors, we assume that conscious or unconscious distortion has occurred, either in the self-attitudes or in the behavioral ratings. If there is concordance between self-attitude and behavioral expression, we assume that the behavior pattern is integrated and that the person's responses are genuine—that is, consistent—in all their manifestations. It is our further assumption that the behaviors revealing the self-esteem of the individual mirror his past experiences: confident and assured behaviors presumably reflect prior successes and favorable treatment; hesitant and fearful behaviors reflect failure and maltreatment. Theoretically, we may anticipate that behavioral manifestations of self-esteem will be significantly correlated with unconscious attitudes toward the self. Both are indirect, generally nonverbal forms of expression; both are covert expressions of prior experience; both may be expressed without the subject's awareness. Correspondence between the various expressions of self-esteem signifies experientially based behaviors and perceptions, a state generally acknowledged to reflect an integrated, realistic, and relatively healthy personality.

### MEASURES OF ESTEEM

To select the subjects who differed in self-esteem we developed subjective and behavioral tests of esteem, administered them to samples who met our general criteria, and selected particular groups of subjects. To measure self-esteem from the perspective of the subject, we used a specially developed 50-item Self-Esteem Inventory (presented with its administration and scoring in Appendix A). Most of the items in this Inventory were based upon items selected from the Rogers and Dymond (1954) scale; several original items were also included. All the statements were reworded for use with children age 8 to 10. Five psychologists then sorted the items into two groups—those indicative of high self-esteem and those indicative of low self-esteem. Items that seemed repetitious or ambiguous, or about which there was disagreement, were eliminated. The set of items was then tested for comprehensibility with a group of 30 children. The final Inventory consisted of 50 items concerned with the subject's self-attitudes in four areas: peers, parents, school, and personal interests. (The present report is based upon the total scores for the Inventory. We have already noted that the differences in the self-attitudes expressed by our subjects for these different areas were not significantly different from one another.) The final form of the Inventory was initially administered to two 5th- and 6th-grade classes, of both boys and girls. The scores ranged from 40 to 100, with a mean of 82.3 and S.D. of 11.6. The mean score for the 44 boys was 81.3, S.D. of 12.2; the mean score of the 43 girls was 83.3, S.D. of 16.7. The difference between the mean scores for boys and girls was not significant ($F = .80$; $p < .50$). The form of the distribution was skewed in the direction of high self-esteem. Five weeks later the Inventory was readministered to one of the 5th-grade classes. With a sample of 30 5th-grade children, test-retest reliability after the five-week interval was .88.

The Inventory was subsequently administered to a total of 1,748 children attending the public schools of central Connecticut. These children were more diverse in ability, interest, and social background than the initial sample. They were tested in their classrooms under the guidance and supervision of members of our research staff. The mean for the males was 70.1, S.D. 13.8, which was not significantly different from that of the girls—72.2, S.D. 12.8. The distribution of scores obtained from this sample was also skewed in the direction of high self-esteem. Test-retest reliability after a three-year interval with a sample of 56 children from this population was .70. The sample of 85 subjects employed in the remainder of the study was selected from this large group of public school children.

The teachers of all the 1,748 children tested were asked to rate each child on a 13-item, five-point scale on behaviors presumed to be related to self-esteem. These items constituted the Behavior Rating Form (BRF), whose scoring and administration will be found in Appendix B. Items in this rating schedule referred to such behaviors as the child's reactions to failure, self-confidence in a new situation, sociability with peers, and the need for encouragement and reassurance. The behaviors to be rated were selected after a series of observations of child behavior in and out of the classroom, repeated interviews with teachers, principals, and a clinical psychologist, and evaluations and discussions with a research committee. On theoretical and empirical grounds, the behaviors were assumed to be an external manifestation of the person's prevailing self-appraisal.

In the initial use of the Behavior Rating Form, we were able to obtain two raters for each child so that an estimate of cross-rater reliability could be established. The school selected was a relatively small one in a stable, middle class neighborhood. The teachers and the principal rated the children independently and did not collaborate or consult one another in their ratings. The principal felt capable of making precise ratings for 71 of the 86 subjects and the other 15 were omitted from consideration. Eight weeks after the first rating, one of the teachers was again asked to rate her class of 21 children.

The correlation between the ratings of this teacher and the principal was .73. Since the correlation between the two ratings was high, we concluded that the behavior of the children was being consistently observed, evaluated, and interpreted. In subsequent evaluations only the teacher's rating was obtained. The teacher ratings for our basic sample ranged between 23–100, with a mean of 68.4 and an S.D. of 15.4. The mean rating for the boys was 65.0, S.D. 16.2; for the girls, 71.3, S.D. 13.6. The mean for the girls was significantly higher than that of the boys ($F = 4.2$, $p < .001$). The test-retest reliability by one teacher after an eight-week interval was .96.

We found considerable differences in the scales of measurement used by different teachers. We also found that teachers differed in assigning higher scores to boys or girls, although there was a general tendency for the teachers to rate girls higher. Whether these ratings indicate that preadolescent girls are generally more assured in their behaviors or that the teachers are prejudiced in their evaluations, we are in no position to say. To correct for systematic biases favoring one sex, and to control for differences in range, we separated the scores for boys and girls and established separately scaled scores for the males and females in each class. This provided a measure of position among individuals of the same sex. Similar scaled scores were used to establish the relative position of each subject for subjective self-esteem. By this procedure we established self-appraisal relative to the individual's immediate social reference group. The subsequent selection of groups differing in self-esteem was based upon these scaled scores rather than upon absolute values.

With this information on the subjective and behavioral self-esteem of 1,748 subjects, we were in a position to select groups differing in self-esteem.

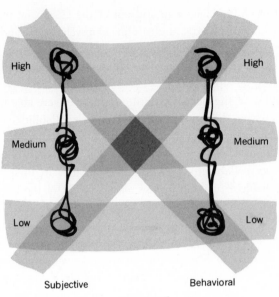

FIGURE 1

Our method of selecting groups required consideration of both the level of self-evaluation and the extent to which subjective and behavioral evaluations were in agreement. Five groups were selected, each representing a particular type of self-esteem. Figure 1 shows how the five groups scored in both the subjective and behavioral expressions of self-esteem.

*Three groups showed agreement in the two expressions: the High-Highs* (H-H), with scores on both the subjective and behavioral rating within the upper quartile of their class; the *Medium-Mediums* (M-M), with both subjective and behavioral evaluations within the interquartile range; and the *Low-Lows* (L-L), with both scores within the lowest quartile of their class. In these descriptions, the first term refers to the self-evaluation and the second to the behavioral rating. *Two groups showed divergent self- and behavioral evaluations:* the *High-Lows* (H-L), with subjective scores in the highest quartile and behavior ratings in the lowest quartile; and the *Low-Highs* (L-H), with low subjective evaluations and high behavior ratings. There were 17 persons in each group for a total of 85 subjects in the five groups.[15] As Figure 1 reveals, with these groups we are able to establish

---

[15] These 85 subjects were selected out of a total of 125 considered. It was our original intention to include 25 subjects in each of the five groups but we decided to study a smaller number more intensively. We therefore selected out of each group of 25 the 17 who best met our criteria. This procedure was adopted before the antecedents study and

three points on each of the subjective and behavioral aspects of self-esteem, and at the same time determine the defensiveness of each group's responses. We are thus in a position to determine the level and quality of self-esteem with a smaller number of subjects than would otherwise be possible.

This procedure of selecting groups to establish several dimensions simultaneously is an example of how experimental types can be of heuristic value. The groups may be ordered along the subjective dimension (HH . . . HL . . . MM . . . LH . . . LL), along the behavioral dimension (HH . . . LH . . . MM . . . HL . . . LL), and along the dimension of discrepancy (HH . . . MM . . . LL; HL . . . LH). In the subjective and behavioral dimensions, there are three points with which to evaluate results and establish linearity; the defensive dimension has the high and low ends to anchor it. Thus, while our focal concern is the subjective, self-evaluating expression of self-esteem, we require the other dimensions to determine the quality of response expressed. By working with our types we can investigate the significance of all three dimensions with no greater effort than would be required to study any single one of them. We may also note that the types selected were found to be significantly different in variables of personality and ability as well as in their self-esteem responses. This leads us to assume that these types represent consistent syndromes of interrelated characteristics. Consolidating the results of our previous studies[16,17] of these characteristics, the five types may be briefly summarized as follows (in order of subjective self-esteem). *High-Highs* are socially and academically successful persons who appear to be relatively content with their situations. *High-Lows* appear to be defensive individuals who maintain a favorable self-regard despite low ratings by teachers, limited acceptance by peers, and relatively poor academic performance. The disparity between self-attitude and external manifestations of acceptance and success presumably reflects defensive distortions against the realities of inferiority. *Medium-Mediums* represent the "average typical" child, who is stable, relatively content, and of moderate capacities and achievements. *Low-Highs* are notable for their extremely low self-evaluation in the face of marked academic and social success. The high levels of anxiety and motiva-

---

before our data had been analyzed. We may note that all of our present results are based upon this same sample of 85 subjects. Some previous reports of our research, with a different number of subjects, have employed similar procedures of selection for other, but similar, groups, who met different criteria of inclusion.

[16] S. Coopersmith. "A method of determining types of self-esteem." *J. Abn. Soc. Psych.,* **59**:87–94 (1959).

[17] S. Coopersmith. "Clinical explorations of self-esteem." In *Child and Education, Proceedings XIV International Congress of Applied Psychology.* Copenhagen, Munksgaard, 1962, pp. 61–78.

tion and the high ideals they set for themselves lead us to assume that these Low-Highs judge themselves in terms of some absolute, personal criteria. Applying these criteria to their present successes, they seem much more negative than they would if they judged themselves by generally accepted social standards. *Low-Lows* are socially and academically unsuccessful children who have accepted the unhappy reality of their inferiority. Mere acceptance, however, does not bring peace since these persons are high in anxiety and other indices of distress and disorder. (We should again note that at the outset of this study, these children were functioning effectively.)

The materials and procedures employed to establish the various aspects and types of self-esteem have been used with two other samples, and the results in both cases have been closely similar to those just presented. The sample employed in this study is not the same as that of our earlier reports,[18] although the characteristics of the various groups are very similar. There were only four groups in the first study, with the Medium-Medium group added in the second sample for purposes of sampling and reliability. It is worth noting that instances of marked discrepancy between subjective and behavioral evaluations were relatively rare. Examination of the scores in our initial sample of 87 subjects and subsequent samples of 74 and 102 indicated that extreme divergence is likely to occur in less than 10 percent of the cases. Substantial disagreement was defined as a difference of more than 20 points in either direction between the reported self-esteem and the observer's rating of behavior. In only 8 of the original 87 cases was there a difference of this magnitude. The distributions for other samples showed similar results and suggested that the use of scaled scores would even further reduce apparent discrepancy. The distribution of differences between self and observer ratings was positively skewed and had a mean of 18.7. Inasmuch as individuals with extreme discrepancy are relatively rare, considerable testing was required to obtain samples of High-Low and Low-High individuals. The Low-High was particularly rare and it was largely to find this and the other type of discrepancy that a population of 1,748 was screened.

Before proceeding to describe the other sections of the study, let us briefly summarize the selection procedure. Five groups of 17 subjects each were selected on the basis of their subjective self-esteem and teacher's ratings of their self-esteem behaviors. Each group represented a particular combination of High-Low self-evaluation and convergent-divergent behavioral evaluations. By using these combinations we were able to determine the defensiveness of each

---

[18] See Footnotes 16 and 17.

subject's response and establish the significance of the two aspects of esteem. The types derived in this procedure are employed as a heuristic device to simplify sampling procedures and reduce sample size. The types appear to manifest consistent patterns of interrelated variables and are themselves of considerable interest.

### CLINICAL STUDIES

In the second part of our study, the 85 subjects selected were individually tested by a battery of clinical tests. These were intended to provide more precise and detailed information on the subject's abilities, affective states, unconscious motives, appraisals and defenses, and characteristic modes of perception and thought. The clinical tests administered to the subjects consisted of the Wechsler Intelligence Scale for Children, Rorschach, Thematic Apperception Test or TAT (selected cards), Figure Drawing, and a specially developed Sentence Completion Test. The subjects were also interviewed and rated by the testing clinician. The clinicians[19],[20] who administered the tests did so without knowledge of the self-esteem of their subjects. The testing session lasted between $1\frac{1}{2}$ to $3\frac{1}{2}$ hours, with an average time of approximately $2\frac{1}{2}$ hours, excluding scoring. Special scoring procedures and indices for evaluating unconscious attitudes toward the self were established. As these procedures and the clinical materials in general are not immediately germane to our discussion of the antecedents of self-esteem, we shall not consider them in this volume.

### EXPERIMENTAL BEHAVIORS

The third section of our study consisted of a series of five experiments to measure behaviors that were presumably related to self-esteem: a task to measure level of aspiration; a variation of the perceptual defense experiment, involving presentation of stimuli of high and low affect; the recall and repetition of success and failure experiences; susceptibility to pressures toward conformity; and motor and perceptual reactions to stress. These tasks were intended to reveal how self-esteem is related to aspirations and expectations, selectivity of perception and memory, constancy and independence of judg-

---

[19] The clinical portion of the study was supervised by Drs. Betty J. Beardslee and David G. Lowy.

[20] We are indebted to Drs. Edward Friedman, William Lesser, Leonard Phillipson, and John Teahan for their skilled participation in this project.

ments, and the ability to tolerate and deal with adversity. The experiments provided specific, overt behavioral expressions of competence, and could be related to the two aspects of self-esteem and the discrepancy between them. (In subsequent studies of these subjects, we administered tests dealing with creativity, prejudice, and social behaviors, some of which will be considered in the present study. We shall, however, examine in Chapter 4 several aspects of the clinical, experimental, and self-report data that bear upon social behaviors. This will provide greater knowledge of the consequences of self-esteem and indicate some of the effects of early social experiences.)

## ANTECEDENTS OF ESTEEM

The fourth section of our study was devoted to a consideration of the various experiences and conditions that were associated with the development of the various levels of self-esteem. The materials gathered in this section form the basis of the present report. The information on antecedents was obtained from three sources. The first of these was an 80-item questionnaire, completed by the mother, that dealt with parental attitudes and practices related to child-rearing. The second consisted of an interview with the mother, which lasted an average of $2\frac{1}{2}$ hours. The third source was the responses of the child to a series of questions on parental attitudes and practices. These disclosed each subject's perceptions of his earlier experiences and provided a different perspective than that obtained from the mother. A related source that we also employed was the subject's attitudes toward his parents as revealed by responses to the Thematic Apperception Test (TAT). These responses presumably revealed less conscious attitudes toward the mother and father than the attitudes disclosed by the questionnaire responses. The father was not directly involved in this study although we did obtain information about him from both the mother and child. The combined information from the mother questionnaire and interview, the child questionnaire, and TAT were used to derive our conclusions on the antecedents of self-esteem. A more extended discussion of the materials and analysis will be presented in Chapter 3.

## THE FOCUS AND PLAN OF THIS BOOK

Our primary concern in this book is to determine the conditions and experiences that are associated with the development of positive self-attitudes. Although our study will also reveal the conditions that produce less favorable self-attitudes, we shall focus our discussion on the conditions that enhance esteem.

This focus is largely a consequence of our interest in psychological health and competence. It also derives, in part, from our belief that these findings may be of considerable interest and value to therapists and parents who are concerned with establishing and raising esteem. We may further note that although this presentation is titled *The Antecedents of Self-Esteem*, that title does not fully represent its contents. Like other investigators of personality development, we are not in a position to determine whether the conditions we find associated with self-esteem are antecedents, consequences, or correlates. Some of the conditions and experiences reported by the mother or child may well reflect the consequences of earlier treatment rather than an initial or precipitating event. It is also likely that some of the conditions we shall consider, such as social class and academic performance, are correlates of other conditions which may precede or follow them in experience. Accordingly, our use of the term "antecedents" implies our focal concern, and "antecedents" will also subsume the correlates and consequences of earlier experience and training.

We should like to note that we have centered our discussions of parent-child relationships and child experiences upon the five-year period immediately preceding the study. One factor that led us to such a focus was consideration of some studies[21,22] which indicate that reports of long-past behavior are frequently erroneous or distorted. Another factor was the relatively limited time available for the mother's interview. In some instances we also obtained information on the earlier years (such as the type of infant feeding employed by the mother and her attitudes toward her pregnancy), but these were points of particular theoretical interest.

The size of the sample is intermediary—considerably larger than the samples generally employed in intensive clinical and laboratory investigations, yet smaller than those employed in large-scale attitude surveys. Accordingly, the sample may be viewed as large or small, depending on the context within which it is judged. The selection procedures and design were intended to maximize the generalizations that could be derived from the sample. Each of the five groups can be considered along the three dimensions employed for selection (subjective, behavioral, and discrepancy), and the extended studies of each subject permit cross-validation and correlational analysis. The selection procedures made certain that the *range* of self-esteem would be covered and that the theoretically crucial issue of defensiveness would be dealt with. It is

---

[21] M. R. Yarrow, J. D. Campbell, and R. V. Burton. "Reliability of maternal retrospection: A preliminary report." *Family Process*, 3:207–218 (1964).

[22] H. K. Pyles, H. R. Stoltz, and J. W. MacFarlane. "The accuracy of mothers' reports on birth and developmental data." *Child Develop.*, 6:165–176 (1935).

certainly clear that a large sample is generally to be preferred to a small one, but the size of any given sample is a matter involving consideration of time, money, and the advantages that might accrue from a markedly larger sample. In this study a large sample would undoubtedly have facilitated generalization —but only if we had continued to obtain the indices of defensiveness and cross-validating behaviors that would give us confidence in the results obtained. Under the circumstances, the question is whether a sample of 85 subjects which has been intensively investigated and which has been subjected to a series of cross-validating studies that provide as broad a basis for generalization as does a larger sample that has been less closely examined. Each reader will have to decide this issue for himself. Our belief that our findings have considerable generality at the theoretical level will be elaborated in the final chapter.

The plan of this book is to proceed from general background conditions that might be associated with the development of self-esteem to specific parent-child relationships that could have a more immediate effect upon that development. We first consider previous formulations and studies dealing with the formation of self-esteem (Chapter 2), and then elaborate upon the methods and materials employed in this study (Chapter 3). In the fourth chapter we examine several social behaviors of our subjects—participation, leadership, and independence—and determine how persons who differ in self-esteem interact with other individuals. Moving to the general conditions that might affect the development of self-esteem and the expression of these social behaviors, we consider the effects of the social background (Chapter 5), and then the relationship between self-esteem and various parental characteristics (Chapter 6) and the characteristics of the child himself (Chapter 7). The next chapter (8) reviews the effects of early incidents and treatment that might conceivably influence the development of favorable self-attitudes. The following four chapters (9 through 12) review parent-child relationships along three dimensions that appear to underlie and be central to those relationships. In Chapter 9 we consider acceptance; in Chapters 10 and 11 we examine permissiveness and democracy—both of which deal with control; and in Chapter 12 we review our findings on the relationship between independence-training and esteem. This is followed by a summary integration of the findings and an appraisal of the implications of our study (Chapter 13).

*Chapter two*

# THEORETICAL FORMULATIONS

T he results of the clinical and experimental studies re-
ferred to in Chapter 1 strongly suggest that self-esteem has pervasive and significant effects. These and similar investigations employing diverse tests,
situations, and interviews provide us with relatively consistent information
regarding the behavior of persons with high and low self-esteem. Though the
findings themselves are not always specific and detailed, they generally indicate that persons high in self-esteem are happier and more effective in meeting
environmental demands than are persons with low self-esteem. The picture
is not a pleasant one for persons with low self-esteem, suggesting as it does
withdrawal from other people and consistent feelings of distress. Although the
consequences of self-esteem are multifaceted in their expression, the results
further suggest that self attitudes are generally integrated with behavior and
only rarely represent an independent, surface defense.

In light of the potential significance of self-esteem and the wide belief that
it is a theoretically central variable, it is surprising to note that the topic has
been barely investigated. There have been theories and speculations in number, but these have not been subjected to more critical empirical analysis and
investigation. The net result is that we have several free-floating hypotheses
regarding the conditions that produce and affect feelings of confidence, superiority, and optimism, but little basis for determining their validity or selecting between contrary claims. Presumably this is another instance where the
theoretical issues and problems of measurement surrounding the study of

subjective experience have resulted in the general avoidance of a significant topic. The next two sections consider some of the issues that have reduced the effectiveness and acceptance of such research and present our definitions and resolutions.

## THE CONCEPT OF SELF

In good part, the avoidance of subjective experience as a topic of study may stem from the varied and uncertain definitions that have been employed in research on the self and the failure to confront basic and confounding issues. We have already indicated that we regard research on the self as falling within the province of attitude studies. This brings us to the question of the object toward which the attitude is being directed. As defined here, "the self" is an abstraction that an individual develops about the attributes, capacities, objects, and activities which he possesses and pursues. This abstraction is represented by the symbol "me," which is a person's idea of himself to himself. This concept is formed in the course of experience by the same process of abstraction employed in other areas of experience. Directed toward self-referent experiences, the process results in abstractions about the self; directed toward external experiences, it results in abstractions about the physical and social world. There is no a priori abstraction made about the self which exists apart from and preceding personal experience; there is no material object which exists apart from such experiences and which must be uncovered, explored, and developed if the individual is to "know" himself and utilize his capacities. The object of observation and appraisal, which we shall call the person, differs from the self, which consists of the abstractions formed about that object. The bases for the abstractions are the individual's observations of his own behavior and the way other individuals respond to his attitudes, appearance, and performance.

During his early years the child develops a concept that the parts of his body, the responses of others to him, and the objects he receives have a common point of reference. With more experience he arrives at an abstraction of what these attributes and events have in common and what they subsume. This abstraction is the "object" to which he refers when he considers his reactions to himself and the reactions of others to him. It is an abstraction that is formed and elaborated in social intercourse, private reactions to himself, mastery in solving developmental tasks, and competence in dealing with life situations.

Inasmuch as young children have little experience and only limited capacity to abstract, they tend to form relatively vague, simple, haphazard abstractions of themselves. Their idea of themselves as an object is sketchy and is likely to be associated with highly localized and specific parts of the body.[1,2] With additional experience and information that give perspective upon the referents of events, and with an increased capacity to abstract, the child's symbolic representation becomes more precise and complex. The concept "self" comes to cover more attributes and experience, while at the same time it becomes more selective as to which features of these experiences are assumed to be self-referring. As with any abstraction, selectivity results in certain attributes being excluded and others being overemphasized. The self—that is, the object a person regards himself to be—is thus selectively weighted according to the individual's abstraction of the common features of his personal experiences. Although the idea of the self is open to change and alteration, it appears to be relatively resistant to such changes.[3] Once established it apparently provides a sense of personal continuity over space and time, and is defended against alteration, diminution, and insult.

The concept of self as an object is inevitably a complex concept. It is formed out of diverse experiences, includes diverse and numerous extensions, is manifest in external objects (the body) as well as internal ones, and is based upon different levels and types of competence in dealing with the environment. The concept of self is thus multidimensional, with the different dimensions reflecting both the *diversity* of experience, attributes, and capacity and different *emphases* in the process of abstraction. Rather than study this multidimensional constellation of concepts in its entirety, we shall focus upon only one dimension—that of evaluation. This will permit more ready cross-comparisons than could be made were the entire complex of dimensions considered. This study is specifically concerned with the evaluative attitude which the individual holds toward himself as an object. In these terms the present work represents an examination of the conditions that produce positive and negative self-attitudes.

Although it is clearly possible to study any particular dimension or group of dimensions of the self-concept, some seem to warrant greater attention than others. Among the reasons for focusing upon a given dimension is the empirically demonstrated importance or theoretical significance of the dimension,

---

[1] E. Horowitz. "Spatial localization of the self." *J. Soc. Psych.*, **6**:379–387 (1935).

[2] T. N. Natsoulas and R. A. Dubanoski. "Inferring the locus and orientation of the perceiver from responses to the stimulation of the skin." *Amer. J. Psych.*, **77**:283–285 (1964).

[3] J. W. Brehm and A. R. Cohen. *Explorations in Cognitive Dissonance.* New York, Wiley, 1962.

the extent to which the dimension is a significant determinant of "important" behaviors, and the frequency with which the particular dimension appears in the population at large. In Chapter 1 we presented some of the evidence indicating that evaluative self-attitudes are significant determinants of several social behaviors and some forms of psychopathology, and suggested the theoretical importance of that dimension. These issues will be more extensively considered in this chapter and the following one. Evidence on the occurrence and pervasiveness of evaluation is available from recent analyses of language.[4] These studies reveal that over one-half of the terms employed in common usage have evaluative connotations. This percentage holds for other languages as well as English, thereby suggesting that the evaluative dimension is widely employed in cultures other than ours. It thus appears reasonable to assume that evaluative self-attitudes are a common and prominent feature of subjective experience and afford a basis for nomothetic generalization.

Our own formulation, in terms of attitudes addressed to the self along one dimension, appears to have several theoretical and practical implications. First, it enables us to draw upon a literature on attitude formation, change, and consequences that is useful in directing and interpreting our study. The extensive research findings on attitudes developed over the last half-century provide several guiding assumptions about evaluative self-attitudes. These findings lead us to believe that these attitudes are intertwined with positive and negative affective states and are likely to have marked motivational consequences. We should also note that the self-attitude formulation relates the study of subjective experience to the study of other cognitive processes as well as of other verbal behavior.

Second, our formulation provides a number of methods, scales, and procedures that are not customarily applied in personality research. Third, it permits a more precise and extended study of the effects of a single dimension than could be achieved by a simultaneous study of complex, multidimensional concepts. Fourth, it permits the application of insights gained by various theories of personality to the context of social and general psychological research. These insights have increased our understanding of human behavior but they have been difficult to translate into experimental terms. The self-attitude formulation and method of study to be described shortly should facilitate the experimental study of personality.

---

[4] C. E. Osgood, G. J. Suci, and P. H. Tanenbaum. The *Measurement of Meaning*. Urbana, University of Illinois Press, 1957.

Other analyses[5] indicate that attitudes engender a readiness to respond to particular stimuli along predetermined lines. Thus a negative self-attitude, reflecting the individual's conviction that he is weak and inferior, may lead him to conclude that his opinions are not worth stating and that he cannot affect the course of group action. Again, attitudes may reflect an individual's expectancies as to what will occur to him in a new situation. Expectations of success or favorable experiences are likely to result in a confident posture, but expectations of failure and rejection are likely to result in apprehension, anxiety, and lack of persistence. The probability estimates of success and failure presumably reflect the individual's conviction that he is or is not able to deal with the situations that he encounters. These estimates have been associated[6,7] with risk-taking, decision-making, and the strategies adopted in problem solving. The adoption of attitudinal orientation to the study of subjective experience also suggests an important association between self-attitudes and the person's needs and values. Other attitude studies have indicated that persons who are hungry are more likely to perceive food-related objects[8] and that personal values are significantly related to what is selectively perceived.[9] The extended studies of the authoritarian personality[10,11] have demonstrated that sociopolitical attitudes are associated with tolerance of ambiguity, the need for order, and feelings of hostility. It appears reasonable to assume that persons with negative self-attitudes would place different values on social participation and enterprise than would persons who held a more favorable view of their worthiness. It is also likely that persons who regard themselves negatively will be inclined to be intropunitive and passive in adapting to environmental demands and pressures. Those who place a higher value upon themselves will adopt a more active and assertive position.

Although this discussion has emphasized the similarities between self-

---

[5] E. M. Siipola. "A study of some effects of preparatory set." Psych. Monogr., 46, No. 210 (1935).

[6] J. W. Atkinson. "Motivational determinants of risk-taking behavior." Psych. Rev., 64:359–372 (1957).

[7] R. M. Thrall, C. H. Coombs, and R. L. Davis (Eds.). Decision Processes. New York, Wiley, 1954.

[8] D C. McClelland and J. W. Atkinson. "The projective expression of needs: I. The effect of different intensities of the hunger drive on perception." J. Psych., 25:205–222 (1948).

[9] J. S. Bruner and C. C. Goodman. "Value and need as organizing factors in perception." J. Abn. Soc. Psych., 42:33–44 (1947).

[10] T. W. Adorno, E. Frenkel-Brunswik, D. J. Levinson, and R. N. Sanford. The Authoritarian Personality. New York, Harper, 1950.

[11] M. Rokeach. The Open and Closed Mind. New York, Basic Books, 1960.

attitudes and other attitudes, it should be noted that there are certain respects in which attitudes toward the self do differ from attitudes toward other external stimuli. With other attitudes, it is possible to establish a common reference that can be separately observed and evaluated by different observers. Thus, we can ask a number of observers to examine and report upon the length, color, size, and value of an object or event. The referent to be judged is commonly available to all observers. This same procedure cannot be employed for self-attitudes, for the object under consideration is totally available to only one person. Thus, only the person who formulates the abstraction appreciates its limits and content and is in a position to define and evaluate its characteristics. Other observers may have considerable knowledge of the subject, but they cannot appreciate those features or persons in the environment he regards as extensions of himself and whose characteristics or responses may affect his own self-regard. Though this feature of self-attitudes appears to distinguish it from other attitudes, recent analyses[12] suggests that the distinction is one of degree rather than kind. They suggest that *all* perceptions and reports are selective and interpretative and that this holds true for the perception of external as well as internal objects. In addition, our formulation, which distinguishes between the self and the person, obviates much of this criticism. It is indeed possible for a large number of individuals to examine the same person, one of these being the individual himself. But although this procedure can be applied to the *person*, it cannot be applied to the *self*, which does not possess any material properties and hence cannot be subjected to common scrutiny. What we can do in studying the self is the same that we do with other abstractions—determine common features of the concept, and then validate these against other behaviors.

Another line of investigation suggests that inferences from an individual's self-attitudes can be made on the basis of his verbal reports and behaviors. These inferences can then be compared with self-attitudes (or independently employed) to validate hypotheses on the experiential determinants of behavior.

Another respect in which self-attitudes differ from other attitudes is that the object under consideration—the self—is different for each individual. This is not true for attitudes expressed toward external objects, in which there can be a common referent point for all persons making assessments. However, though the object of consideration differs in each self-perception, the dimension applied to each (for example, evaluation) may frequently be

---

[12] T. W. Watts (Ed.). *Behaviorism and Phenomenology.* Chicago, University of Chicago Press, 1964.

the same. By focusing upon the end products of the judgmental process, or the self-appraisal, it becomes possible to compare individuals, even though they differ in particulars.

However we view these particular issues, it seems reasonable to assume that self-attitudes are neither more nor less reliable or scientifically meaningful, or less open to experimental study, than are other constructs. The basis of inclusion within scientific bounds is, after all, to be resolved on empirical rather than exhortatory grounds.

### THREE UNDERLYING ISSUES

Given our definition of the self and the proposal to subsume its study under the general category of attitude studies, there still appear to be three major difficulties in studying self-esteem: the distinctions as to the quality as well as the quantity of esteem, the value terms applied to both high and low esteem, and the theoretical superstructure generally invoked in discussing esteem. We shall consider each of these in turn, and follow them with our resolution of the underlying issues.

The qualitative distinctions made in reference to self-esteem reflect uncertainties as to how esteem is expressed, and whether it is genuine in its expression. Does the method employed to measure esteem provide a valid index of the person's confidence and self-appraisal? Individuals may attempt to present a confident and assured facade, but the investigator must decide whether the expression is spurious or genuine. Spurious self-evaluations may express conscious or unconscious distortions from the "true" evaluation. In the first case the individual is aware of the low regard he has for himself and tries to conceal it from others; in the second he is largely unaware of his poor evaluation of himself and attempts to conceal his negative appraisal from himself and others. In either case there is likely to be some external evidence to suggest that the self-evaluation is suspect; the rigorous investigator may even have a blanket suspicion that all evaluations that have not been verified are open to question. Where self-evaluations have been questioned, such terms as spurious and defensive have been applied to the presumably insecure or distorted evaluations.

Another distinction that has been made is between subjective states of self-esteem and their behavioral expression.[13] The behavioral manifestations of high self-esteem have been described by such terms as dominance and

---

[13] A. H. Maslow. "The dominance drive as a determiner of social behavior in infrahuman primates." *Psych. Bull.*, 32:714–715 (1935).

assertiveness, and the subjective state is described by such terms as self-esteem and self-confidence. In addition to these two expressions of esteem there are unconscious appraisals of self-worth that require consideration. Although the subject may consciously make and maintain a favorable appraisal of himself, it is possible that he unconsciously holds a far more negative opinion of his worth. These various aspects and expressions of esteem are related to the quality or genuineness of the subject's response. Genuineness presumes that all manifestations of esteem point in a similar direction; dissimilarity raises doubts on this point as well as presenting difficulties of interpretation.

The second difficulty is the value orientations and preferences that are often applied to self-esteem. Positive self-esteem has been associated with such other terms as self-respect, superiority, pride, self-acceptance, and self-love (narcissism). Negative self-appraisal, or low self-esteem, is often equated with inferiority, timidity, self-hatred, lack of personal acceptance, and submissiveness. Each of these various usages carries connotations of the others and, as we quickly find, the terms are used differently and often interchangeably by different authors.[14] Some investigators believe that persons with high self-esteem are necessarily accepting of themselves and that low self-esteem is associated with the absence of such acceptance. Others appear to attribute negative value to very high self-esteem by associating it with vanity, egotism, pride, narcissism, and arrogance. There appears to be somewhat greater agreement about the terms and usages applied to low self-appraisal, but even at this level the issue is open to varied interpretation. Persons who take a modest view of their worth may be regarded as humble, as more attuned to loftier, less aggrandizing values, or conversely, may be regarded as defeated, passive, and inferior individuals.

The positive and negative values attributed to any given level of self-esteem appear to represent personal values and convictions rather than objective, established data. Though high self-esteem may occasionally be found concurrently with such characteristics as vanity and arrogance, there is no social necessity for their relatedness and no objective evidence that such a relationship exists. It is not that these distinctions as to various concomitants and varieties of high self-esteem are unimportant but rather that their occurrence and significance has not been demonstrated. A similar situation prevails with regard to interpreting the significance of low self-esteem. We may place favorable or unfavorable value on low appraisals, and associate that state with either modesty, detachment, or self-hatred. It should be clear, however, that

---

[14] R. Wylie. *The Self-Concept*. Lincoln, Neb., University of Nebraska Press, 1961.

the value assigned and the behaviors attributed are not an essential part of low self-appraisal. In studying self-esteem, we are interested in that variable and not in any attributed characteristics or value judgments which may be assigned. Such judgments come into play in interpreting our results and implementing their practical consequences, not in establishing the consequences and significance of the determining variable.

The third issue which concerns us is the theoretical context within which self-esteem may be considered. There are several theories of personality that include self-esteem as a significant variable, but only one (Adler) in which it plays a major role. The neo-Freudians—particularly Sullivan, Horney, and Fromm—are highly attentive to the importance of self-esteem but they treat it as a separate topic rather than one central to their own theories. Adler clearly perceived the importance of self-esteem but was more concerned with its implications for therapy than with theoretical explication. The work of such ego psychologists as Hartmann,[15] Erikson,[16] and Jacobson[17] is clearly related to self-esteem, but the relationship is indirect and carries a heavy superstructure of unrelated assumptions. Self-psychologists such as Rogers, and the phenomenologists in general, have been interested in self-esteem but have been more concerned with the general nature of subjective experience and the individual's acceptance of his experiences. These studies have provided an increased understanding of the subjective basis of human behavior and have contributed a number of procedural innovations and refinements which facilitate the study of self-esteem.[18,19,20] However, in their acceptance of experience per se, and its importance in the therapeutic process, they have largely bypassed the issues of defensiveness and external validation.

Earlier psychologists and sociologists such as William James, G. H. Mead, and Charles Cooley provided major insights and guidelines for the study of self-esteem. Their formulations remain among the most cogent on the topic, particularly their discussions of the sources of high and low esteem. Their context is, however, limited and generally not specifically directed toward the investigation of self-esteem. They are likely to be more concerned with the

---

[15] H. Hartman. *Ego Psychology and the Problem of Adaptation.* New York, International Universities Press, 1958.

[16] E. H. Erikson. *Childhood and Society.* New York, Norton, 1963 (rev. ed.).

[17] E. Jacobson. "The self and the object world." *Psychoanalytic Studies of the Child,* 1954, 9:75–128.

[18] C. R. Rogers. *Client-centered Therapy.* Boston, Houghton Mifflin, 1954.

[19] E. T. Gendlin. *Experiencing and the Creation of Meaning:* A Philosophical and Psychological Approach to the Subjective. New York, Free Press, 1962.

[20] W. Stephenson. *The Study of Behavior.* Chicago, The University of Chicago Press, 1953.

origin and nature of the self, and the continuity, consistency, and quality of subjective experience. These early workers, like those who followed them, appreciated the significance of self-esteem but did not possess or propose a specific theoretical framework within which that subject could be discussed and investigated. Our conclusion is that there is no single theoretical context in which self-esteem can be considered without accepting a number of vague and often unrelated assumptions. It is therefore necessary to develop a context from more specific, topical treatments and to integrate these and other concepts into a coherent and testable theory.

## THE ANTECEDENTS OF SELF-ESTEEM: CONCEPTUAL ANALYSIS

The investigation of antecedent factors is essentially a two-step process. We first seek to determine whether certain prior experiences, abilities, and attributes are related to states or conditions that now exist. The search for such relationships is necessarily selective, with the selection guided by some general theory or specific hypothesis—for example, the hypothesis that persons who come from higher social classes or more prestigious occupations are higher in their self-esteem. Without such theoretical guides, the investigation of antecedent, consequent, or any other relationship becomes a meandering, relatively inefficient procedure. The explicit statement of such guides permits generalization to other studies and elucidation of other contributing conditions. Once relationships have been established, the question shifts to *how* the related conditions produce their effects. This is a refined reformulation, which explains the obtained difference in terms of some intervening process. Referring to our example relating social class and self-esteem, we might conclude that such a relationship, if it obtained, would derive from different histories of success or social acclaim. Thus it is clear that both the initial selection of variables to relate to self-esteem and the subsequent explanation of significant relationships stem from the investigator's conceptual framework.

We have reviewed the theoretical and empirical literature dealing with the antecedents of self-esteem, and from it we have derived the major concepts that have guided this study. Inasmuch as the present work is concerned with (1) evaluative attitudes toward the self rather than other attitudes, and (2) the antecedents of such attitudes, our analysis is limited and directed toward concepts dealing with those topics. In this review we shall consider the *general* conditions that previous researchers have hypothesized as being related to the development of self-esteem. *Particular* conditions that have been empirically related to self-esteem—parental interest, precocity of development, and others—will be cited in the context of our results. Our immediate concern is the general conditions that personality theorists, clinicians, and social philosophers have related to positive self-regard. As previously indicated, these ideas constitute the vast bulk of our knowledge on this topic, with empirical studies following far behind. These ideas do, however, provide a guiding and often insightful framework, and will be employed for that purpose. It will, of course, be part of our task to determine whether these guiding ideas are supported by our results.

### WILLIAM JAMES AND G. H. MEAD

Perhaps the most cogent general formulations of the antecedents of self-esteem were expressed by William James and George H. Mead. Both formulations appeared relatively early in the emergence of psychology and sociology, and both were proposed by men who had considerable claim as philosophers. Though neither man devoted himself extensively or specifically to the specific origins of self-esteem, the topic did receive considered attention in their works. William James' analysis, particularly as revealed in *Principles of Psychology* (1890),[21] provides us with three possible influences upon self-esteem. In the course of analyzing subjective experience and the significance of the self, James concludes that human aspirations and values have an essential role in determining whether we regard ourselves favorably. Our achievements are measured against our aspirations for any given area of behavior. If achievement approaches or meets aspirations in a valued area, the result is high self-esteem; if there is wide divergence, then we regard ourselves poorly. "Our self-feeling in this world depends entirely on what we *back* ourselves to be and do. It is determined by the ratio of our actualities to our supposed potentialities; a fraction of which our pretensions are the denominator, and the numerator our success; thus self-esteem $= \dfrac{\text{success}}{\text{pretensions}}$."

James underscores the importance of one's own values in determining which areas will be employed in self-judgment. "I, who for the time have staked my all on being a psychologist, am mortified if others know much more psychology than I. But I am contented to wallow in the grossest ignorance of Greek. My deficiencies there give me no sense of personal humiliation at all. Had I 'pretensions' to be a linguist, it would have been just the reverse. So we have

[21] W. James. *Principles of Psychology* (2 vols.). New York, Holt, 1890.

the paradox of a man shamed to death because he is only the second pugilist or the second oarsman in the world. That he is able to beat the whole population of the globe minus one is nothing; he has pitted himself to beat that one; and as long as he doesn't do that nothing else counts. He is to his own regard as if he were not, indeed he *is* not. . . . Yonder puny fellow, however, whom everyone can beat, suffers no chagrin about it, for he has long ago abandoned the attempt to 'carry that line'. . . . With no attempt there can be no failure; with no failure, no humiliation."

James concludes that achievement is measured against aspiration with valued areas assuming particular significance, but he also believes that men achieve a sense of their general worth by employing communal standards of success and status. "We may weigh our own worth in the balance of praise and blame as easily as we weigh other people—though with difficulty quite as fairly. . . . There is no reason why a man should not pass judgment on himself quite as objectively and well as on anybody else. No matter how he feels about himself, unduly elated or depressed, he may still truly know his own worth by measuring it by the outward standard he applies to other men, and counteract the injustice of the feeling he cannot wholly escape. . . . The normal provocative of self-feeling is one's actual success or failure, and the good or bad actual position one holds in the world. A man . . . with powers that have uniformly brought him success with place and wealth and friends and fame, is not likely to be visited by the morbid diffidences and doubts about himself which he had when he was a boy, whereas he who has made one blunder after another and still lies in middle life among the failures at the foot of the hill is liable to grow all sicklied o'er with self-distrust, and to shrink from trials with which his powers can really cope."

A third source of self-esteem, according to James, is the value placed upon extensions of the self. James views the self as "the sum total of all that he can call his, not only his body and his psychic process, but his clothes and his house, his wife and his children, his ancestors and his friends, his reputation and works, his lands and horses, and yacht and bank account. All these things give him the same emotions. If they wax and prosper, he feels 'triumphant'; if they dwindle and die away, he feels cast down—not necessarily in the same degree for each thing but in much the same way for all." In addition to the material constituents of the self, James proposes a "social self which is the recognition he gets from his peers. . . . A man has as many social selves as there are people who recognize him and carry an image of him in their mind. To wound any one of these, his images, is to wound him." The enhancement of a man's extended self, be it his body, race, father, or reputation, would thus be expected to raise self-esteem, and derogation would be expected to have the opposite effect.

G. H. Mead's (1934)[22] contributions on this topic are an elaboration of what James called the social self. As a sociologist, Mead is concerned with the process by which the individual becomes a compatible and integrated member of his social group. He concludes that in the course of this process the individual internalizes the ideas and attitudes expressed by the key figures in his life—observing their actions and attitudes, adopting them (often unknowingly), and expressing them as his own. This holds true for attitudes and actions expressed toward himself as well as toward external objects. He comes to respond to himself and develops self-attitudes consistent with those expressed by the significant others in his world. Internalizing their posture toward him, he values himself as they regard and value him and demeans himself to the extent that they reject, ignore, or demean him. He thus learns how he appears to specific others, "assumes the attitude or uses the gesture which another individual would use, and responds to it himself, or tends to so respond. . . . He gradually becomes a social being in his own experience and acts towards himself in a manner analogous to that in which he acts towards others." The end result of regarding and speaking to and of himself as others have spoken is that he assumes the properties of a social object. When this occurs he tends to conceive of himself as having the characteristics and value that others attribute to him.

From Mead's formulation we would conclude that self-esteem is largely derived from the reflected appraisal of others. The gauge of self-evaluation is a mirror image of the criteria employed by the important persons of our social world. As children we internalize these criteria, observe how we are regarded, and value ourselves accordingly. Thereafter our responses to our own attributes, abilities, and actions are those we would make to objects outside ourselves. To Mead, no man is an island in his self-appraisal. No matter how isolated and independent he may believe himself to be, he carries within himself the reflecting mirror of his social group. If he places high value on himself, there have been key persons in his life who have treated him with concern and respect; if he holds himself lowly, significant others have treated him as an inferior object. The views of the generalized (significant) others as expressed in their manner of treatment are Mead's key to the formation of self-esteem.

---

[22] G. H. Mead. *Mind, Self and Society*. Chicago, University of Chicago Press, 1934.

ADLER, HORNEY, AND SULLIVAN

Three neo-Freudians—Harry Stack Sullivan, Karen Horney, and Alfred Adler—have theorized on the origins of self-esteem. As clinicians, they appear to have derived their formulations from the retrospective reports of patients in treatment. Sullivan accepts Mead's interpretation of the social origins of personality and then proceeds to a more extended analysis of the interpersonal processes involved. He believes that the awareness of other people is virtually omnipresent and has a large evaluative component. The individual is continually guarding himself against a loss of self-esteem, for it is this loss that produces the feelings of distress that are elsewhere termed anxiety. Anxiety is an interpersonal phenomenon that occurs when an individual expects to be or is indeed rejected or demeaned by himself or others. If we find persons with low self-esteem, we assume that derogation by significant others has occurred in the previous life history of that individual and that he anticipates or perceives derogation in his present circumstances. Sullivan also raises the issue of how the individual learns to diminish or to thwart threats to his self-esteem. Individuals learn to cope with such threats in differing styles and to different degrees. The ability to minimize or avoid loss of self-esteem is important in maintaining a relatively high, acceptable level of esteem. Although Sullivan does not discuss how this ability develops, he does suggest that early familial experiences play an important role. His focus on the interpersonal bases of self-esteem, the particular importance of parents and siblings, and the importance of procedures to minimize demeaning events are Sullivan's general contributions to the study of the origins of self-esteem.

Karen Horney (1945,[23] 1950[24]) also focuses on the interpersonal processes and on ways of warding off self-demeaning feelings. She lists a wide range of adverse factors that might produce feelings of helplessness and isolation. She believes that these feelings, which she terms "basic anxiety," are major sources of unhappiness and reduced personal effectiveness. The conditions that presumably produce anxiety include domination, indifference, lack of respect, disparagement, lack of admiration, lack of warmth, isolation, and discrimination. Though she indicates that the list of specific factors could be virtually endless, the common antecedent of all these conditions is a disturbance in the relationship between parent and child, which is generally associated with

---

[23] K. Horney. *Our Inner Conflicts*. New York, Norton, 1945.
[24] K. Horney. *Neurosis and Human Growth*. New York, Norton, 1950.

parental egocentricity. It is, however, in her discussion of the consequences and defenses against feelings of anxiety that Horney makes her major contribution to the present topic. In speaking of defenses, Horney indicates that one method of coping with anxiety is the formation of an idealized image of one's capacities and goals. This ideal has the effect of bolstering self-esteem by its very loftiness while at the same time leading to dissatisfaction when its unrealistic levels are not achieved. The idealized image thus plays an important role in how the individual evaluates himself. It differs from the ideal of aspiration noted by James in that the idealized image (Horney) necessarily stems from negative feelings, whereas aspirations (James) may arise from either positive or negative sources. In both instances, we would conclude that the level and flexibility of the ideal is an essential component in the self-evaluative process.

Alfred Adler (1927,[25] 1956 [26]) places greater stress on the importance of actual weakness and infirmities in producing low self-esteem than the other theorists do. In his early work Adler proposes that feelings of inferiority may develop around certain organs or patterns of behavior in which the individual is indeed inferior. Such actual impairments as a withered arm or blindness or bodily weakness in breathing or muscular development may produce feelings of inadequacy and insufficiency. Adler terms such deficiencies and disabilities as "organ inferiorities" as distinct from the more socially or individually defined bases of inferiority feelings. He also proposes that feelings of inferiority are an inevitable occurrence of the childhood experiences of every individual. The comparison between relative strengths and sizes that children invariably make leads them to conclude that they are, in fact, weak and incomplete. The result is a feeling of inferiority and insufficiency that goads and motivates the child to achieve greater size and competence.

Adler notes three antecedent conditions that may have unfortunate consequences on the development of self-esteem. The first are the organ inferiorities and differences in size and strength. These conditions are to a great extent unavoidable and, since they do have motivating effects, their presence can also result in a favorable outcome. Whether they do or not depends in good part upon the acceptance, support, and encouragement of the parents and immediate friends. These experiences represent the second major antecedent condition. With acceptance and support, children with inferiorities can

---

[25] A. Adler. *The Practice and Theory of Individual Psychology.* New York, Harcourt, 1927.
[26] H. L. and R. R. Ansbacher (Eds.). *The Individual: Psychology of Alfred Adler.* New York, Basic Books, 1956.

compensate for these weaknesses and turn them into strengths; without such support they become without hope and embittered. Whereas Adler believes in the beneficial effects of support and acceptance, he warns against the destructive effects of overindulgence, the third antecedent. He believes that pampered children come to have an unrealistically inflated value of their worth. They are self-centered and demanding, and are not willing or prepared to engage in mature, reciprocal social relationships.

## FROMM AND ROGERS

There are other personality theorists whose discussions bear less directly upon the development of self-esteem; for example, Fromm, Rogers, and Allport. Insofar as their ideas are relevant, their concepts and formulations should be considered in subsequent, more extended, integrations of self-esteem theory. For the moment let us note here Fromm's[27,28] emphasis upon the possible debilitating effects of social isolation. If the child (and adult) gains freedom from others, he has the opportunity to pursue his own paths. However, if he does not feel confident of his views and exposed position, he may forsake independence. By joining and conforming to a group he enjoys the shelter and privileges they provide, but also obligates himself to their authority. Among the conditions that determine whether he will seek independence or the security of the group are the presence of a stable and consistent frame of reference from which he can view the world, ability to form love relationships marked by understanding and mutual respect, and the conviction that social relationships can be carried on in a spirit of trust and camaraderie. These characteristics, and such others as creativity and individual expression, which have been theoretically related to self-esteem, are formed by social conditions marked by acceptance, respect, concern, freedom of expression, and independence. Fromm discusses these conditions as developed within the total societal framework, but similar conditions could be expected to have similar consequences within the family unit.

Carl Rogers (1951)[29] does not discuss the origins of self-esteem directly, but his discussions of the conditions that facilitate self-acceptance and diminish conflict do contribute to our understanding of that topic. Rogers proposes that all persons develop a self-image of themselves which serves to guide and

---

[27] E. Fromm. *Escape from Freedom.* New York, Rinehart, 1941.

[28] E. Fromm. *Man for Himself.* New York, Rinehart, 1947.

[29] C. R. Rogers. *Client-centered Therapy: Its Current Practice, Implications, and Theory.* Boston, Houghton Mifflin, 1951.

maintain their adjustment to the external world. Since this image develops out of interaction with the environment, it reflects the judgments, preferences, and shortcoming of the particular familial and social setting. Rogers indicates the pernicious effects of self-judgments that the individual as an entity, or in selected components of behavior, is bad. Such harsh, rejecting judgments prevent the individual from accepting himself and therefore cause him suffering. Even though they may be ignored or denied expression, they continue to have a subverting effect by producing underlying doubts of worthiness and competence. Rogers argues that a permissive atmosphere which permits free expression of ideas and affect and does not resort to harsh or frequent evaluative comparisons enables the individual to know and accept himself. Conflicts can be averted if parents and significant others *accept* the views and values of the child, although they need not necessarily *agree* with him. In this way the child can come to respect himself, gain assurance in deriving his own values, and learn to trust himself as a locus of experience. This requires parents who are willing to accept differences and are able and ready to trust their child.

### MORRIS ROSENBERG: SOCIAL ANTECEDENTS OF SELF-ESTEEM

The major previous empirical study of the antecedents of self-esteem is the work of Morris Rosenberg,[30] a sociologist on the staff of the National Institute of Mental Health. Rosenberg's investigation represents a significant step in explicating many of the social conditions associated with enhanced and diminished self-esteem. Information on these conditions and the subjective experience of esteem was obtained from an attitude survey administered to over five thousand high school students. The results of that study, which proved invaluable in interpreting and generalizing the results of the present one, will be described later. There are, however, several general findings in Rosenberg's study that may be profitably employed in this conceptual analysis. First, social class is only weakly related and ethnic group affiliation is unrelated to self-esteem; this finding helped considerably to clarify the norms that the individual employs in self-evaluation. It appears that the broader social context does not play as important a role in interpreting one's own successes as has often been assumed. This is underscored by Rosenberg's finding that the amount of paternal attention and concern, which differs by

---

[30] M. Rosenberg. *Society and the Adolescent Self-Image.* Princeton, Princeton University Press, 1965.

social class, religion, and ethnic group, is significantly related to self-esteem. Adolescents who have closer relationships with their fathers are higher in self-esteem than are those with more distant, impersonal relationships. In thus moving from the more complex and global variable of social class to the specific correlations in the "effective interpersonal environment" that affect self-esteem, Rosenberg has given an indication of those features of his environment that the child equates with "success."

Two further important findings relate self-esteem to religion and to order of birth. In the case of religion, we again find that social prestige in the community at large has little influence on self-esteem. Jews, who are lower in the hierarchy of general social prestige, are more apt to be high in self-esteem than are either Catholics or Protestants. This apparent anomaly seems to be largely a function of the great amount of interest and attention that Jewish children, especially boys, receive from their parents. Within the family itself, only children and particularly only male children are higher in self-esteem. These results provide us with a more concise knowledge of the conditions that lead children to interpret experiences as successes. By showing that broader social forces have little impact (at least until adolescence), Rosenberg's results narrow our focus to the specific parental attitudes and behaviors that can and do influence self-esteem.

The Rosenberg study and the present research represent alternative approaches to investigating the antecedents of self-esteem. The Rosenberg study employed survey research procedures, in which all information is obtained from a single source, by means of a single instrument—an efficient procedure that permits large samples in which more diverse and statistically rarer groups may be examined. This type of investigation allows generalizations on a relatively larger segment of the population—provided that the reader accepts self-reports as a sufficient basis for such generalizations. To the extent that he is doubtful of such reports, the results of the Rosenberg study provide us with a series of findings and insights that require validation and clarification. Our own study represents a more intensive investigation, in which procedures for dealing with defensiveness and cross-validation have been introduced. In addition, our study obtained a wider range of information on childhood treatment and experiences—from the parents of the subject as well as the subject himself. This enabled us to extend and refine the general findings of Rosenberg and to test the hypotheses advanced by earlier theorists.

The views of previous theorists and investigators lead us to conclude that there are four major factors contributing to the development of self-esteem. First and foremost is the amount of *respectful, accepting, and concerned treatment* that an individual receives from the significant others in his life. In effect, we value ourselves as we are valued, and this applies to extensions of ourselves as well as the more centrally experienced aspects of our self-images. A second factor contributing to our self-esteem is our *history of successes* and the status and position we hold in the world. Our successes generally bring us recognition and are thereby related to our status in the community. They form the basis in reality for self-esteem and are measured by the material manifestations of success and by indications of social approval. These indices of success and approval will not necessarily be interpreted equally favorably by all persons. It is by living up to aspirations in areas that he regards as personally significant that the individual achieves high self-esteem. Thus experiences are interpreted and modified in accord with the individual's *values and aspirations.* Success and power and attention are not directly and immediately perceived but are filtered through and perceived in the light of personal goals and values. The fourth factor is the individual's *manner of responding to devaluation.* Persons may minimize, distort, or entirely suppress demeaning actions by others as well as failures on their own part. They may reject or discount the right of others to judge them or, conversely, they may be highly sensitive or aware of other people's judgments. This ability to defend self-esteem reduces the experience of anxiety and helps to maintain personal equilibrium. In the study of how the personality functions, this ability to maintain self-esteem in the face of negative appraisals and discomfiture has been described by such concepts as controls and defenses. These terms refer to the individual's capacity to define an event filled with negative implications and consequences in such a way that it does not detract from his sense of worthiness, ability, or power.

The goal in our present study of self-esteem is to state with some specificity what is meant by the term successes, how and which values and aspirations are transmitted, and how familial and other experiences result in differing responses to devaluation. We shall ascertain whether success history, transmitted values and aspirations, and responses to devaluation occur with different frequency in groups differing in self-esteem. If they are significantly and meaningfully related to self-esteem, we shall seek to establish the specific conditions that affect their development.

Although there have been relatively few studies directly concerned with the antecedents of self-esteem, there have been studies of other personality characteristics that appear germane to our investigation. Using these studies as a frame of reference, we shall attempt to delineate several major conditions and experiences that seem to be associated with the development of positive and negative self-attitudes. We shall consider these in the categories of successes, defenses, values and aspirations, and shall seek to establish more particular relationships between these concepts and the events that occurred in the lives of our subjects.

*Success.* The term "success" has a different meaning to each individual. To some it is represented by material rewards, to others by spiritual satisfaction, and to still others by popularity. There are, in addition, differences in the amount of each of these criteria, such as money or popularity, that would be required before an individual would consider himself to be successful. But despite these differences in value and aspiration, there are certain conditions in our culture that are judged to be more favorable and enhancing than others. Thus, in American society, it would be generally agreed that to be rich, powerful, respected, enfranchised, and autonomous would be more favorable than to be poor, powerless, rebuffed, disenfranchised, and dependent. This is not to say that each person would necessarily assign the same value to each of these conditions, which is clearly not the case, but rather that there are commonly accepted meanings for the term "success" within any given community. On the basis of extended interviews with our subjects and the results of previous studies, we propose that there are four different types of experiences that may be employed to define success. Each provides its own criteria for judging whether the individual has attained a valued objective, but all provide a sense of increased worth when they are attained. These four sources of self-esteem, and the four criteria employed for defining success, are the ability to influence and control others—which we shall term *Power;* the acceptance, attention, and affection of others—*Significance;* adherence to moral and ethical standards—*Virtue;* and successful performance in meeting demands for achievement—*Competence.* We should note that it may be possible for an individual to attain high self-esteem by notable attainment in any of the four areas. This might occur even where attainment in the other areas was mediocre or even poor. Thus an individual might receive great attention and love from important others and thereby develop a highly positive self-attitude even though he was relatively weak, unworthy, and incompetent. Or, he might achieve high self-esteem by great competence without being notably virtuous, significant, or powerful. On the other hand, it is possible for an individual to attain notable success in an area that he does not regard as important, such as competence, and thus conclude he is unworthy because he has not succeeded by the criterion he most values, such as virtue. Thus a man who is extremely capable in performing his occupation may nonetheless conclude that he is not successful because he does not fulfill the precepts he considers to be of major importance. Similarly, the student who is doing very well in his studies may develop negative self-attitudes because he does not have the acceptance, attention, and affection of others. These examples not only indicate the importance of the criteria employed in judging success but also suggest that these criteria may be in conflict with one another. The individual who values and attains power is not very likely to gain affection from his confederates. If he can consider himself a success only if he has affection of the persons he controls, the likelihood of uncertain or low self-esteem is considerable. It therefore appears likely that many individuals are uncertain of the criteria they employ to judge their worth and are apt to employ incompatible criteria or demand attainment in several, if not all. This delineation of the four criteria employed in judging success suggests that further investigation could provide greater understanding of the bases of evaluation and perhaps furnish some indications of how esteem could be rapidly and markedly enhanced.

Although the study of our own subjects tends to indicate that significance and competence are much more important than worthiness and power, this conclusion may be partially a function of the age, class, and cultural backgrounds of these individuals. This analysis of the four sources of esteem suggests one possible basis for the difference between an individual's self-attitude and the appraisals of others. The two appraisals may actually be based upon different criteria, with the external observer unaware of the individual's basis of self-judgment. In such a case the difference would be one of focus rather than evaluation. It is possible that other phenomena related to appraisal are also affected by differential attention to the four general areas of experience. Though our description of a person with high self-esteem suggests that he views himself as competent, powerful, worthy, and significant, we may also indicate that this is not necessarily or invariably the case. The emphasis or blend of these four areas may be expected to show considerable individual variation. In this study we shall focus upon competence and significance, which appear paramount for our subjects. This focus in no way indicates the relative emphasis in other samples or in any particular individual.

If we apply these concepts to the conditions that affect the development of self-esteem, we may inquire as to the particular behaviors associated with experiences of significance, power, competence, and virtue. Success in the area of significance is measured by the concern, attention, and love expressed by others. These expressions of appreciation and interest are subsumed under the general terms of acceptance and popularity, while their polar opposites are termed rejection and isolation. Acceptance is marked by warmth, responsiveness, interest, and liking for the individual as he is. Accepting parents would appear to have enhancing effects in their support and encouragement in times of need and crisis, marked interest in the child's activities and ideas, expressions of affection and comradeship, relatively mild, generally verbal and rational discipline, and more indulgent attitudes toward training and assertiveness. The major effect of such treatment and expressed love is to engender a sense of importance that is a reflection of the esteem in which they are held by others. The more individuals who express such interest and affection, and the more frequent its expression, the greater the likelihood of favorable self-appraisal.

Success in the area of power is measured by the individual's ability to influence the course of action by controlling his own behavior and those of other individuals. In any given situation such power is revealed by the recognition and respect the individual receives from others and by the weight that is given to his opinions and rights. There are guidelines and boundaries within which recognition and control are granted; in the most favorable environment these are clearly and publicly expressed rather than dependent upon the interpretation and discretion of group leaders. The power of the child will vary with age and maturity, and helpful parents will permit greater power as the child manifests greater ability and maturity of judgment. The effect of such recognition is to provide the growing child with a sense of appreciation for his own views and the ability to resist pressures to conform without due consideration of his own needs and opinions. Such treatment is likely to develop social poise and leadership and an independence that may extend at times to extremely assertive, vigorous, exploratory actions. The significance imparted by recognition is enhancing and is experienced as relative autonomy and control over oneself and others.

Success in the area of competence is marked by high levels of performance, with the level and task varying with age. For preadolescent males we would assume that academic and athletic performance are two major areas employed to judge competence. White[31] has proposed that, from infancy onward, the child experiences a biologically given and pleasurable sense of efficacy that accompanies his encounters with the environment and becomes the basis for intrinsic motivation toward achieving further and greater competence. White's proposal stresses the importance of the child's spontaneous activity in deriving feelings of efficacy and suggests that the experiences following independent achievement may be highly reinforcing in their own right and do not depend upon external agents. This formulation does not deny the general importance of social approval and disapproval but proposes that there are innate sources of satisfaction that accompany mastery of the environment and that are independent of extrinsic social rewards and punishments. The sense of efficacy results in striving for competence that appears quite common in infancy, well before social values can be expressed or appreciated. By supporting this sense of efficacy, or at least providing the conditions for its development, parents are presumably more likely to increase strivings for competence. Also, independence and achievement training should increase the likelihood that the individual will take a more active and competitive role in his encounters with the environment. These types of training should presumably result in more frequent feelings of competence, although this may be expected to vary with the individual's ability, values, and aspirations.

Success as judged by the criterion of virtue is marked by adherence to a code of moral, ethical, and religious principles. Parents presumably establish the guiding traditions and philosophies and indicate the behaviors by which they can be realized. These will vary widely and include avoidance of certain actions as well as commission of certain deeds. To cite some of these, we may indicate the frequent don'ts of stealing, aggression, sexual activity and dietary restrictions and the expressive acts of parental respect, regular prayer and obedience. Persons who adhere to ethical and religious codes which they have accepted and internalized assume a positive self-attitude by successful fulfillment of these "higher" goals. Their feelings of esteem may frequently be tinged with sentiments of righteousness, uprightness and spiritual fulfillment.

*Values and Aspirations.* Individuals differ in the importance they attribute to the successes they have in various areas of experience, and these differences are largely a function of the values they have internalized from parents and

---

[31] R. W. White. "Motivation reconsidered: The concept of competence," *Psych. Rev.*, **68**:297–333 (1959).

other significant individuals in their lives. From previous studies[32] we can surmise that accepting and respectful treatment is more likely to result in more flexible values and greater acceptance of the values that the parents espouse and express. This suggests that the conditions that produce self-esteem are also more likely to produce stable and realistic values. There does not, however, appear to be any reason to suspect a systematic relationship between preferences for any given values and esteem. We might expect that individuals would place less value upon areas in which they have failed and greater value upon areas in which they are successful and thus enhance themselves, but evidence on this point is scant. For the age group we are considering, the values of competence (in school and sports) and significance (to parents and peers) appear to be of greatest importance. In general, the relationship between value preferences and experiences of esteem is a point that has been employed as a post hoc explanation but which has not been studied directly.

The relationship between aspiration and esteem has also received little direct attention. There are indications[33] that persons with histories of success respond more realistically than do those with histories of failure, but that the level of aspiration is associated with esteem remains largely theoretical. We might surmise that persons low in esteem would lower their aspirations, but if they did so we could anticipate that their esteem would rise. Thus we are led to assume that there is a considerable gap between aspiration and performance in individuals with low self-esteem and that it is this gap which results in negative self-appraisals. There is, at the same time, some evidence[34,35] that the level of goals and ideals professed by young Americans shows relatively little variation. This holds true for generalized ideals as well as more specific occupational aspirations. Thus, though we may assume that there are wide differences in levels of aspiration, these assumptions have only mixed and uncertain empirical support.

*Defenses.* As we have seen, any experience may be the source of favorable self-evaluation, just as any experience can be the source of devaluating appraisals. The "facts" are not necessarily seen and weighed in the same way by each individual. The "facts" are the raw materials used in making apprais-

---

[32] M. Hoffman. "Child-rearing practices and moral development: Generalizations from empirical research." *Child Develop.*, 34:295–318 (1963).

[33] P. S. Sears. "Level of aspiration in academically successful and unsuccessful children." *J. Abn. Soc. Psych.*, 35:498–536 (1940).

[34] R. Wylie. *The Self-Concept.* Lincoln, Neb., University of Nebraska Press, 1961.

[35] M. Rosenberg. *Society and the Adolescent Self-Image.* Princeton, Princeton University Press, 1965.

als, but their interpretation is not uniform and invariate. The interpretation will vary with the individual's characteristic ways of handling distressing and ambiguous situations and with his goals and aspirations. His manner of dealing with threat and uncertainty represents the individual's way of defending himself against anxiety—or, more specifically, of defending his esteem against the devaluation that would come with feelings of incompetence, powerlessness, insignificance, and lack of virtue. There are a wide number of defenses that can be employed, ranging from massive repressions to dexterous redefinitions and rationalizations. They go beyond those usually described even in comprehensive discussions of defense mechanisms,[36] and represent varied attempts to defend oneself against the distress that follows devaluation.

There is evidence[37] that different social classes characteristically employ different mechanisms to ward off anxiety. This and less formal cross-cultural evidence suggest that characteristic defenses are learned in much the same manner as other behaviors. Thus, though there are undoubtedly individual variations in the type, variety, and effectiveness of defenses that any individual will employ, we may assume that he will generally use defenses similar to those he learns in his immediate environment. Which of these defenses he will find personally effective will undoubtedly depend upon circumstance and their particular reinforcement. That he will employ defenses similar to those utilized by persons emotionally close to him is more likely than that he will employ other means of warding off anxiety. In other words, the models that provide effective ways of warding off anxiety—for example, parents or cultural heroes—contribute indirectly to the development and maintenance of high self-esteem by establishing limits and actions that define and interpret events. These models set bounds upon uncertainty and reduce the personal threat of failure. The individual who can attribute at least part of the failures and deficiencies he encounters to the external world rather than to his own limitations is able to maintain a loftier view of his worthiness. High self-esteem in itself provides some form of defense in giving the individual confidence in his own judgment and abilities and hence increasing the likelihood that he will feel capable of dealing with adversity. It is also probable that persons who feel such confidence and approach situations with assurance and expectations of success are less likely to feel threatened at the outset.

---

[36] A. Freud. *The Ego and Mechanisms of Defense.* New York, International Universities Press, 1946.

[37] D. R. Miller and G. E. Swanson. *Inner Conflict and Defense.* New York, Schocken Books, 1960.

As the preceding discussions make clear we are employing the term defenses in a broader sense than it is traditionally employed in the psychoanalytic literature. For our purposes a defense is not only a means of warding off anxiety, it is also a definition and interpretation that precedes an event and leads the individual to assume a more or less active and assertive posture. We shall have considerably more to say on this subject in our discussion of the theoretical significance of our findings (Chapter 13).

*Chapter three*

# SOME EXPRESSIONS OF SELF-ESTEEM

T he previous chapters considered the substantive and methodological issues that should be considered in any objective study of self-esteem. In them we sought to reveal the major issues that have beleaguered past investigations of self-judgment and indicated how these issues were resolved in the present study. These resolutions represent the theoretical and experimental ground rules for our investigation and guided the various studies we conducted. With this introduction as our guide, we are in a position to begin our specific examination of the antecedents of self-esteem. But we shall first take a more extended look at the subjective experiences associated with different levels of self-esteem as well as some of the social consequences of these experiential states. Such an examination should provide a better picture of the motives, affects, and expectations of persons who are high, medium, and low in self-esteem and should indicate some of the subjective consequences of positive and negative self-appraisals. In addition we shall examine several social behaviors that appear to be theoretically related to self-esteem: independence, leadership, popularity. These discussions of the subjective concomitants and social consequences are intended to clarify and elaborate the theoretical structure we have proposed and also to indicate some of the present consequences of earlier treatment that results in high, medium, and low self-esteem. The discussions are not exhaustive, but they do help to convey the pervasive influence and significance of self-esteem and illustrate the psychological worlds associated with self-respect and self-disdain.

## THE SUBJECTIVE EXPERIENCE OF ESTEEM

The subjects in this study were administered various inventories and projective tests, and participated in several experimental situations and interviews, all of which established differences in individual responses and revealed characteristically different ways of approaching, perceiving, and responding to environmental stimulation. These differences in styles of responding to oneself, to other persons, and to impersonal objects reveal that persons with high, medium, and low self-esteem adapt to events in markedly different ways. They experience the same or similar events differently; they have different expectations of the future and markedly different affective reactions. We shall examine several of the specific responses of our subjects, but we may note at the outset that the responses we consider are particular manifestations of general styles of reaction. This is not to say that the particular responses are unimportant in their own right but rather to indicate that these responses are segments of more comprehensive adaptive reactions. Thus certain findings—that persons with high self-esteem, compared to other subjects, are more independent in conformity-inducing situations, manifest greater confidence that they will succeed, and express more color shadings on the Rorschach—suggest that these individuals respond to internal and external events in a consistent and characteristic style. The over-all pattern and the frequency of results obtained in our study lead us to believe that self-esteem is significantly related to the individual's basic style of adapting to environmental demands. The examination of separate, specific responses will be made within the context of the basic styles characteristic of different levels of esteem and will be integrated and interpreted within that framework.

In the present section we shall offer a general description of the experiences associated with various levels of self-esteem. These abstractions are derived from the study of several individuals at each level rather than from case studies of individual subjects. They represent summary statements that summarize the responses obtained on interviews, questionnaires, and standard personality tests, amplifying the earlier description of the major variable and indicating the consequences of parental treatment. In addition to the general description presented in this section, Chapter 7 will detail some differences in specific responses of our subjects.

To emphasize the experiential nature of these reports we shall present them in the form of self-descriptive statements. Such a hypothetical mono-logue for a person with a positive self-attitude would probably run as follows: "I consider myself a valuable and important person, and am at least as good as other persons of my age and training. I am regarded as someone worthy of respect and consideration by people who are important to me. I'm able to exert an influence upon other people and events, partly because my views are sought and respected, and partly because I'm able and willing to present and defend those views. I have a pretty definite idea of what I think is right and my judgments are usually borne out by subsequent events. I can control my actions toward the outside world, and have a fairly good understanding of the kind of person I am. I enjoy new and challenging tasks and don't get upset when things don't go well right off the bat. The work I do is generally of high quality and I expect to do worthwhile and possibly great work in the future."

A similar monologue by a person with a negative self-attitude would be likely to carry notes of depression and pessimism. This monologue could be expected to proceed along the following general lines: "I don't think I'm a very important or likeable person, and I don't see much reason for anyone else to like me. I can't do many of the things I'd like to do or do them the way I think they should be done. I'm not sure of my ideas and abilities, and there's a good likelihood that other people's ideas and work are better than my own. Other people don't pay much attention to me and given what I know and feel about myself I can't say that I blame them. I don't like new or unusual occurrences and prefer sticking to known and safe ground. I don't expect much from myself, either now or in the future. Even when I try very hard, the results are often poor, and I've just about given up hope that I'll do anything important or worthwhile. I don't have much control over what happens to me and I expect that things will get worse rather than better."

The self-description of the person with medium self-esteem, in its appraisal and associated experiences, falls between these two monologues. It tends to include a number of positive self-statements, but is more moderate in its appraisals of competence, significance, and expectations. Such a self-descrip-tion reflects appreciation of the intermediate position of the subject, but is generally favorable in its assessments and conclusions. The person with medium self-esteem regards himself as better than most but not as good as some select, unusual individuals. In most respects, his opinions are closer to those of persons with high self-esteem than to those of persons with low self-esteem.

There is every reason to conclude that persons with high, medium, and low self-esteem live in markedly different worlds. We find that persons with low self-esteem exhibit higher levels of anxiety,[1] but are otherwise lower in the affect they express,[2] and are likely to exhibit more frequently psychosomatic symptoms[3] and feelings of depression. These descriptions are most immediately relevant to preadolescents in our culture. These preadolescents may differ in the criteria they employ to judge their worthiness, but we would anticipate that they would be likely to employ competence and significance rather than virtue and power. We would further propose that the sources of esteem might vary with age and milieu, but that the affective, anticipatory, and motivational features associated with each level of esteem would remain much the same.

## PARTICIPATION IN SOCIAL GROUPS

Both common observation and theoretical rationale lead us to assume that popularity is positively associated with high self-esteem. The reasoning for this is fairly straightforward: popularity is a manifest indication of social success, and the level of success is presumably related to self-esteem; therefore the more successful person may be expected to be higher in self-esteem. In terms of social success, persons who are accepted and sought after bask in the reflected favorable appraisals of others; those who are ignored or critically received suffer from such ostracism. A number of factors may conceivably alter the relationship between popularity and esteem—age, sex, or the criteria employed for judging success—but there is good reason to believe that a general relationship does indeed exist. This is particularly true in American society, in which participation in social activities and popularity are highly valued and generally desired goals in themselves.

It is, therefore, quite surprising to note (Table 3.1) that popularity is not associated with the subjective experience of esteem, even though it is related to more overt, behavioral indices of assurance. Presumably acceptance by one's peers is not sufficient or closely enough related to self-judgment that it necessarily eventuates in favorable self-appraisal. Such acceptance is revealed by the means in Table 3.1, showing the number of times the members of each group were selected as friends by their public school classmates.

---

[1] See Table 7.9, p. 132.

[2] M. Rosenberg. *Society and the Adolescent Self-Image*. Princeton, Princeton University Press, 1965.

[3] See Table 7.12, p. 136.

TABLE 3.1 *Number of times members in each self-esteem group were selected as friends by their classmates*

| Score | Types of self-esteem | | | | |
|---|---|---|---|---|---|
| | Low-Low | Low-High | Medium-Medium | High-Low | High-High |
| Mean score | 1.47 | 3.47 | 3.35 | 2.41 | 3.53 |
| SD | 1.58 | 2.15 | 2.72 | 1.75 | 2.17 |
| $F = 2.87$  df $= 4, 81$  $p < .05$ | | | | | |

*Source:* Classroom sociogram.

Inspection reveals that the five self-esteem types differ significantly in the number of friends they possess ($F = 2.87$, df$= 4, 81$, $p < .05$).

The differences are not, however, in a regular, descending relationship, as would be the case if popularity were systematically related to subjective self-esteem. Instead, we find that the two groups lowest in behavioral esteem (Low-Low and High-Low) are the least popular, and the two groups highest in such overt esteem (High-High and Low-High) are the most popular. The mean number of friends employed by the Medium-Medium group falls between the means for the high and low behavioral groups, although it is closer to the mean for the highs. This suggests that popularity with one's peers is more likely to be associated with a poised, confident, and forthright exterior than it is with favorable self-attitudes. We have no way of establishing the direction of the relationship—whether greater poise and assurance results in greater popularity or whether it is popularity that leads to assurance. What we can indicate is that such a relationship exists and that popularity is associated with behavioral poise rather than subjective judgments of worthiness.

Another finding that emerges from the data in Table 3.1 is that the popularity ratings of children are remarkably similar to the teacher's behavioral ratings (of esteem). Both teacher and children favor children whose behaviors are poised and assured, but pay markedly less attention to the self-attitudes of the individual. This may be because the self-attitudes are generally unexpressed and hence unappreciated, or because they are perceived but regarded as insignificant. The judgments of teacher and children are probably not fully independent of one another, but both presumably share similar values of what constitutes desirable behavior. Both are observing behavior that occurs within the circumscribed, well-defined setting of the classroom rather than in a more extended or personal social group. The mean values presented in Table 3.1 indicate popularity within the classroom setting, and are not necessarily indicative of acceptance in other social groups. The same consideration applies to the self-esteem behaviors expressed in the classroom, which are presumably the basis for the teacher's ratings. It may well be that in a task-oriented environment, such as the classroom, personal attitudes and judgments assume less importance than overt manifestations of poise and competence. Other environments may provide greater opportunity and encouragement for expressing self-attitudes, regarding them as salient and appropriate of expression. Another question about the mean popularity scores of the self-esteem groups is whether persons tend to have friends with roughly similar levels of self-esteem. From our analysis of the constellations of friendships in several classes it appears that Low-Low individuals are likely to be isolates who select one another, but that individuals in the other groups mix relatively freely. Apparently differences in poise and self-attitude do not make much difference once the individual has reached some relatively low level of assurance and self-respect.

Another problem is whether subjective attitudes, behavioral expressions, or the type of self-esteem is most important in determining social behavior. From the almost endless variety of actions that could be classified under social behavior, we shall only consider a few. We begin with an item included in our questionnaire that deals with the subject's ability to make friends: "Would you say that you are the sort of person who finds it easier or harder to make friends than most other people?" This question requires the individual to appraise his social competence and personal characteristics. The responses of our subjects, summarized in Table 3.2, reveal that persons with subjectively low self-esteem (Low-Low and Low-High) believe they have greater difficulty in forming friendships than do individuals with medium or high self-esteem. The difference between the five groups is statistically significant ($\chi^2 = 9.08$, df = 4, p < .08) with the Low-Low most likely to report that they have difficulty in making friends (87.5 percent). The Medium-Medium group is least likely to report difficulty in this regard (41.2 percent), and only half (52.9 percent) the members of the two groups with subjectively high esteem (High-High and High-Low) believe they have difficulties in forming friendships. Subsequent analysis, in which the groups at the high and low levels of subjective self-esteem were combined, revealed that the differences between the high, medium, and low groups were significantly different ($\chi^2 = 8.17$, df = 2, p < .02). These findings indicate that whereas popularity is associated with overt expressions of confidence, the self-perceptions asso-

TABLE 3.2 *"Would you say you are the sort of person who finds it easier or harder to make friends?"*

| | Types of self-esteem | | | | |
|---|---|---|---|---|---|
| Reply | Low-Low | Low-High | Medium-Medium | High-Low | High-High |
| Easier than others | 12.5% (2) | 29.4% (5) | 58.8% (10) | 47.1% (8) | 47.1% (8) |
| Harder or same as others | 87.5% (14) | 70.6% (12) | 41.2% (7) | 52.9% (9) | 52.9% (9) |
| Totals | 100.0% (16) | 100.0% (17) | 100.0% (17) | 100.0% (17) | 100.0% (17) |

$\chi^2 = 9.08$        $df = 4$        $p < .08$

*Source:* Subject's questionnaire.

ciated with friendship are likely to be associated with subjective perceptions of esteem. In this regard we may say that the hypothesis relating social success and self-esteem are indeed borne out. Persons who perceive themselves as having difficulties in social situations are likely to evaluate themselves poorly, no matter how poised they appear in their overt behaviors. In effect, it is the person's perception of his social success rather than his peers' appraisal of his competence and success that determines how well an individual regards himself. External manifestations of assurance may lead other persons to value and select him as a friend but in his own judgments he may nonetheless regard himself unfavorably. A clear example of this is seen in the responses of the Low-High group. The opposite situation prevails for the High-Lows, who report themselves as having few difficulties and who are high in self-esteem despite relatively low appraisals by their classmates and teacher.

Another expression of the individual's social interest and affiliations is his involvement in group activities and discussions; such involvements may differ in frequency, intensity, variety, and number. Several of our questionnaire items were directed toward clarifying the relationship between self-esteem and these various manifestations of involvement. One of the items asked the subjects to indicate the number of social groups to which they belonged. From their responses we conclude that groups that differ in self-esteem do not differ significantly in the number of social groups to which they belong ($\chi^2 = 2.71$, df = 4, n.s.). There is a tendency for persons high in subjective self-esteem to belong to a somewhat larger number of groups, but this trend does not achieve significant proportions. The absence of a relationship be-

TABLE 3.3 *Role assumed by members of various self-esteem groups in group discussions*

| Role | Subjective self-esteem | | |
|---|---|---|---|
| | Low | Medium | High |
| Generally listener | 56.2% (18) | 41.2% (7) | 25.9% (8) |
| Generally advocate | 43.8% (14) | 58.8% (10) | 74.1% (23) |
| Totals | 100.0% (32) | 100.0% (17) | 100.0% (31) |

$\chi^2 = 6.00$    df = 2    p < .05

*Source:* Subject's questionnaire.

tween self-esteem and frequency of group memberships apparently indicates that persons of all levels of confidence and assurance are equally likely to join social groups. Presumably social needs and interests are sufficiently common and insistent that even persons who lack assurance affiliate regularly. There is, however, a considerable difference in the roles played by persons who differ in self-esteem within the groups of which they are members. Table 3.3, summarizing our subjects' responses to another questionnaire item, indicates the extent to which they were actively involved in group discussions. Inspection reveals that the two groups with favorable self-attitudes are very likely to be active participants (74.1 percent), but those with negative self-attitudes are likely to adopt a quieter, more passive posture (only 43.8 percent are active). The difference between the various levels of esteem are significant ($\chi^2 = 6.00$, df = 2, p < .05), thereby indicating that persons with high self-esteem are able and willing to publicly express and support their opinions.

### INDEPENDENCE AND CREATIVITY

Another indication of this willingness to stand by their opinions is revealed by the responses of our subjects to the conformity-inducing situations developed by Asch (1956)[4] and adapted for use with children by Berenda (1950).[5] In such situations, after seven accomplices of the experimenter have all rendered their opinions, the test subject is required to state his judgment of the relative size of several stimuli. These accomplices are instructed to make

---

[4] S. E. Asch. "Studies of independence and conformity: I. A minority of one against a unanimous majority." *Psych. Monogr.,* **70(9):** 1–70 (1956).

[5] R. W. Berenda. *The Influence of the Group on the Judgments of Children.* New York, King's Crown Press, 1950.

incorrect judgments in over half the comparisons. The individual is confronted with the option of expressing a judgment that accepts the (incorrect) group judgment or that refutes it by expressing an independent opinion. The underlying question is whether the individual will shift his opinions under the pressures of group suggestion. In terms of our study, are persons with high self-esteem more likely to express independent opinions than individuals with lesser self-regard?

The details of the experiment can be briefly summarized. A group of seven preadolescents were gathered together for the presumed purpose of serving as subjects for an experiment in perception—one the test subject and the other six confederates of the experimenter. These confederates were all instructed to give incorrect answers on certain trials. The experimenter, a university student who was unknown to the subjects, instructed them to match a given line with one of three other lines that differed in length. One of the three was the identical length of the standard line and the other two were noticeably shorter or longer. To facilitate responses and reduce ambiguity the comparison lines were numbered 1, 2, and 3. The standard line and the three comparison lines were mounted on separate cards that were changed for each of the thirty-six trials.

The trials were carried out under two separate conditions, of eighteen trials each. Under the first condition the subjects were given paper and pencil and asked to write their judgments on an answer sheet. As each set of lines was presented, the experimenter announced the number of a previous (fictitious) sample of two hundred school children who had judged each of the three comparison lines. For example, he might indicate that six of the two hundred (3 percent) had selected line 1, twelve (6 percent) had selected line 2, and one hundred and eighty-two (91 percent) had selected line 3. The percentages announced to the subjects indicated that between 76 and 99 percent of the previous sample had agreed in their judgment of the line closest in length to the standard.

Under the second condition the subjects were asked to announce their judgments publicly, in the order in which they were seated. The test subject was always seated next to last and thus was required to announce his judgments after almost the entire group had expressed an opinion that was unanimous and, in over half the cases, wrong. He could either deny the evidence of his senses and concur in the popular opinion or state what he believed to be the true judgment despite the unanimous, contrary judgment of his peers. Analysis of the responses under both conditions revealed that conformity to the majority increased markedly when the judgments were publicly an-

TABLE 3.4 *Members of each self-esteem group who always, occasionally, and never conformed*

| Reactions to social pressure | Types of self-esteem | | | | |
|---|---|---|---|---|---|
| | Low-Low | Low-High | Medium-Medium | High-Low | High-High |
| Total compliance | 23.5% (4) | 11.8% (2) | 17.6% (3) | 17.6% (3) | 11.8% (2) |
| Occasional compliance | 64.7% (11) | 41.1% (7) | 11.8% (2) | 35.3% (6) | 23.5% (4) |
| Total independence | 11.8% (2) | 47.1% (8) | 70.6% (12) | 47.1% (8) | 64.7% (11) |
| Totals | 100.0% (17) | 100.0% (17) | 100.0% (17) | 100.0% (17) | 100.0% (17) |

$\chi^2 = 16.08$     df = 8     p < .05

*Source:* Laboratory study.

nounced. Since this increase occurred in groups at all levels of esteem and since there was only a limited number of judgments that could be made, public announcement effectively reduced the differences between the groups. Inasmuch as our present concern is with the social behaviors of persons who differ in self-esteem rather than with the conditions that affect conformity, we shall focus on the first series of comparisons, in which the more notable differences occurred. We simply note here that the group results for the second series were similar to those obtained on the first series.

In Table 3.4 we find the percentage and number of individuals in each self-esteem group who always, occasionally, or totally refused to conform when the majority was wrong. Examination of the responses of each group reveals that persons who are low in both aspects of self-esteem (Low-Low) are least likely to remain independent in all trials, and those who are high or medium in both aspects of esteem (High-High and Medium-Medium) are most likely to resist social pressures. Thus we find that 64.7 percent of the High-Highs and 70.6 percent of the Medium-Mediums are always independent, but only 11.8 percent of the Low-Lows are able to persistently resist group pressures. The two discrepancy groups fall intermediate between the independence of the Medium-Medium and High-High groups and the compliance of the Low-Lows; 47.1 percent of both groups remain independent in all instances. This would suggest that some characteristic associated with their discrepant personality structure affects their reactions to social pressure, so that they are not as independent or compliant as they otherwise would be. In the High-Low group the discrepancy between subjective and behavioral esteem is associated with less independence than that found in the other subjectively high group (High-Low = 47.1; High-High = 64.7), but the Low-High group is markedly *more* independent than the other subjectively low group (Low-High = 47.1; Low-Low = 11.8). This would suggest that *both* aspects of esteem may be called into play by the conformity situation; that is, both the High-Low and Low-High groups, each low in one of these aspects, are caught between widely divergent bases of actions. Independent behavior apparently requires that the individual not only be *convinced* that his judgment is correct, but must also be able to *overtly express* that conviction: the High-Highs and Mediums-Mediums have conviction *and* courage, but the High-Lows and the Low-Highs are limited in the independence they can express. Approximately half of each discrepancy group (47.1 percent) express independent opinions, with the remainder resolving the issue in favor of compliance. This ratio is not markedly different from chance, which indicates that the conformity responses of highly discrepant individuals, as a group, are less predictable than the responses of individuals whose self-attitudes and behaviors are congruent. Given the over-all pattern of results and the significant difference between the groups ($\chi^2 = 16.08$, df = 8, p < .05), it would appear that both the level of esteem and its discrepant-indiscrepant character are important determinants of whether an individual resists or yields to group pressures.

This analysis suggests that there are at least two steps intervening between the presentation of a stimulus and the public statement of a judgment. In the first step, which we have termed conviction, the individual attempts to determine the nature of the stimulus, organize relevant information, and formulate an opinion. In a more general sense this phase of attitude formation deals with information processing and decision making. This phase includes not only the process itself but also the trust and confidence the individual places in his resolution. That is to say, the person not only filters, organizes, and interprets but also has some degree of confidence in the resolution he achieves, resulting in a posture of conviction, vacillation, or lack of trust in his own opinion. Persons with subjectively high self-esteem presumably approach tasks and social situations with the conviction that the opinions they form are likely to be veridical and significant, and believe that what they experience as "real" and "true" is an accurate and reliable appraisal of events. The internal frame of reference of the self-trusting individual provides a constant and consistent orientation, which other experiments[6,7] have revealed to be associated with greater perceptual constancy. Acceptance of the internal frame of reference as the most trustworthy guide of personal behavior relegates other sources to a secondary position; their opinions may be noted but not necessarily attended to. As a result, the individual with high self-esteem is apt to attend to himself most closely and to attend to others only to the extent that he esteems them. This is but another instance of the general finding that the opinions of individuals of high status are more likely to be accepted than are the opinions of unknown individuals or presumed inferiors. The over-all import of this reasoning is that the individual with high self-esteem regards himself as *a* (and presumably *the*) significant source of opinion, and therefore attends to his own judgments and reactions as crucial in making decisions.

The conviction that one is correct appears necessary but not sufficient for the expression of an opinion that differs from that of other persons. This is particularly true when, as in the experiment we performed, such independent opinions run counter to the publicly expressed views of the majority. Under these circumstances the individual must not only be convinced that his opinions are sound and worthy, he must also be able to express those convictions and tolerate the distress and possible ostracism that might eventuate from dissent. It is this latter phase that we have termed courage—an inner strength in behaving consistently with one's convictions in the face of difficulties, distress, and danger. Where courage is lacking, the individual's convictions—strong though they may be—come to nothing; where conviction is lacking, the views that are expressed by dint of courage are likely to lack force and influence. Courage, in our definition, is the attitudinal posture an individual adopts to attain or maintain actions consistent with his beliefs, whether these beliefs deal with his personal view of himself or with more abstract and general values and convictions. It can be the courage of a man whose ideal of himself is that of the staunch, fearless leader, or the courage of a religious figure who is firmly committed to a philosophy and doctrine of faith and observance.

The theoretical context of self-attitudes also provides a meaningful and relatively explicit language for examining such concepts as conviction and courage. By and large, current theories of personality and motivation avoid

---

[6] S. Coopersmith. "The relationship between self-esteem and perceptual constancy." *J. Abn. Soc. Psych.*, **88**:217–221 (1964).
[7] H. Witkin, H. B. Lewis, M. Hertzman, K. Machover, P. B. Meissner, and S. Wapner. *Personality Through Perception.* New York, Harper, 1954.

these and similar concepts because of their presumed ambiguity and because they are not readily reconciled with the concepts commonly employed in other areas of modern psychology. The difficulties of communication and the belief that these concepts are inherently vague have caused most theorists and investigators to avoid the related phenomena altogether or, alternatively, to attempt to subsume them under more general, accepted concepts. For example, there is an inclination to subsume the term "courage" under the more general category of psychological defenses. In such a treatment it can be argued that the capacity to deal with the anxiety attendant upon deliberate and overt deviation is the essential, underlying basis for independent action. Perhaps the greatest difficulty with such a treatment is the dissimilarity between the concept observed or inferred in the study of self-attitudes and the concept transferred from other fields. The concept of defense appears generally relevant to an understanding of courageous behavior, but it is clearly not a sufficient explanation and at best only a partial one.

Another source of difficulty lies in the connotations and theoretical superstructure that generally accompany a concept when it is transferred. The literature and extended studies on the concept will generally invest it with a relatively precise meaning, but one that may be insufficient or inappropriate to the phenomena to which it is applied. Continuing our prior example, the concept of defenses, as traditionally employed, refers to an unconscious process that occurs in response to an anxiety-evoking stimulus. The concept of courage, as here employed, may be applied to either conscious or unconscious processes, and is not as closely related to anxiety as is the concept of defenses. Most personality researchers, recognizing the difficulties involved in transferring concepts and not particularly concerned in behaviors of courage and conviction, ignore the topics and leave the terms out of their professional vocabulary. However, we propose that analysis of such phenomena in terms of self-attitudes and attendant postures provides a language and methodology for investigating a set of relatively unexplored and important behaviors. This language can be relatively precise and parsimonious in dealing with many aspects of subjective experience, and is as open to validation as are other intervening variables.

The concepts of conviction and courage appear equally relevant to the production of creative innovations. The individual who produces new ideas or products or who presents us with a drastically different perspective must be convinced that the fruits of his labor are valuable. He must, at the same time, have the assurance that he can tolerate or cope with any adverse reactions. Without such assurance he would find it difficult, if not impossible, to expose himself and his works to public scrutiny. There thus appears to be an underlying similarity in the processes involved in creative innovation and social independence, with common traits and postures required for expression of both behaviors. The difference is one of product—literary, musical, artistic, theoretical products on one hand, opinions on the other—rather than one of process. In both instances the individual must believe that his perceptions are meaningful and valid and be willing to rely upon his own interpretations. He must trust himself sufficiently that even when other persons express opinions counter to his own he can proceed on the basis of his own perceptions and convictions.

From the self-trust required for social independence and creative expression stems the ability to reject opinions that are popular and to ignore social conventions of correctness. In the self-trusting innovator such acts of rejection are less acts of intentional rebellion than they are a personal affirmation of his own perceptions. This is clearly revealed by the responses expressed in the conformity experiment, in which the persons who resisted group pressures and expressed independent opinions were affirming their perceptions of the line lengths rather than rebelling against popular opinion. In the denial of the emperor's clothes, the child's comment on the emperor's nudity was a personal description, not a clarion call to arms. Presumably this same affirmation is present in acts of creative expression, in which the innovator's actions express his personal perceptions and are not necessarily intended to rebuke or criticize generally accepted views.

There is, at this point, considerable evidence[8,9] that persons judged to be creative by their peers frequently report a sense of "personal destiny" and the conviction that they were and are slated for unusual and significant attainments. Associated with these indirect indices of high self-regard are the studies[10] that reveal the marked social independence of the creative individual. These persons resist strongly any pressures to make them respond along lines that are contrary to their own perceptions and judgments, and will follow their own opinions even where these are markedly different from those that are popularly accepted. Faced with a contrived experimental situation such as the one we performed, they are likely to reject it completely; it is in-

---

[8] D. MacKinnon. "The nature and nurture of creative talent." *Am. Psychologist,* 17:484–495 (1962).

[9] F. Barron. "The disposition toward originality." *J. Abn. Soc. Psych.,* 51:473–485 (1955).

[10] R. Crutchfield. "The creative process." *The Institute of Personality Assessment and Research Symposium on the Creative Person.* Berkeley, University of California Press, 1961.

conceivable to them that there could be such a great disparity between their perceptions and the events that occur in the "real" world. They are, in short, reliant upon their own judgments in determining their course of action and, accordingly, relegate other opinions to a secondary position.

The importance of self-esteem for creative expression appears to be almost beyond disproof. Without a high regard for himself the individual who is working in the frontiers of his field cannot trust himself to discriminate between the trivial and the significant. Without trust in his own powers the person seeking improved solutions or alternative theories has no basis for distinguishing the significant and profound innovation from one that is merely different. To explore ideas and strike out in new directions requires the belief that one can discriminate between sense and nonsense, and that one can impose order where disorder apparently exists. An essential component of the creative process, whether it be analysis, synthesis, or the development of a new perspective or a more comprehensive theory, is the conviction that one's judgment in interpreting the events is to be trusted. Without such self-belief and trust neither the artist, poet, or scientist can play with the full range of possibilities, secure in the conviction that he can select those of greater value. He must also be able to tolerate the unusual and apparently nonsensical ideas that are often required for productive reorganization or valuable innovations. Trust in self is also expressed in the individual's confidence that he can venture into new areas without fear of losing his direction or respectability, particularly since these are largely determined by personal criteria and judgments.

The work of Ernst Kris,[11] one of the most perceptive investigators of ego functions and the creative process, certainly confirms the relationship between creativity and self-esteem. Kris himself did not focus upon self-esteem per se, but many of the attitudes and characteristics he attributes to the strong ego appear characteristic of the individual with high self-esteem. Thus he proposed that only persons who have confidence in their ability to deal with disorder, and are not fearful of being overwhelmed by primitive, disorganized modes of thinking can regularly and voluntarily regress without suffering the debilitating effects of anxiety. His studies of creative persons lead him to conclude that the ability to turn regularly, freely, and fully to the apparent chaos of one's unconscious is frequently found among innovators, and may play a crucial role in their efforts. He termed this ability "regression in the service of the ego," thereby indicating that the person employed and con-

---

[11] E. Kris. *Psychoanalytic Explorations in Art.* New York, International University Press, 1952.

trolled the process of regression rather than being a helpless victim of its occurrence. Other investigators who have made intensive studies of the creative personality, such as Schachtel, Kubie, and Barron, have been similarly impressed by the confidence and self mastery of the creative individual. Their general conclusion is similar to that of Kris'—to be creative an individual must trust his own perceptions of "truth" and "reality" and believe in his capacity to order and deal with uncertainty.

This belief of creative individuals appears quite similar to the concept of conviction that we proposed in interpreting the results of our conformity experiment. Both reflect an insistence that truth is a personal, internal experience rather than something decided by discussion and public opinion; both reflect acceptance and reliance upon one's own personal reactions and perceptions in judging the nature and content of reality. Moreover, to continue the analogy, both independence and creativity require the courage to express or exhibit an unusual or unpopular opinion, as well as the conviction that the opinion is correct. Since creative products, by definition, represent a departure from the conventional and provide an alternative perspective to that which is popularly accepted, their very expression represents an implicit threat to prevailing standards. Such threats arouse a vigorous response, particularly if they challenge long-established and culturally valued assumptions. The knowledge that innovation, like independence, is likely to meet a hostile reception may serve to temper or even totally inhibit its expression. If we observe a new direction of thought being charted and repeatedly and publicly expressed, we may conclude that the individual is able and willing to tolerate the adverse reactions his dissent may arouse. This is as true in the fields of science—the views of Darwin, Freud, and Einstein were initially attacked and rejected—as in the arts and humanities—Picasso, Stravinsky, and Shaw were subjected to harsh critical treatment. But all these men trusted in their judgments, were convinced that their constructions were real and valid, and were willing and able to expose their theories and works to public examination. Without such public exposure there would indeed be nothing to alter and extend our assumptions and conceptualizations. The personal cost may be considerable, as evidenced in the prolonged anguish and procrastination of Darwin, but at least the innovator has had the courage and compulsion of his vision. Creativity, like independence, depends upon a personality structure that seeks to bring public belief in correspondence with private conviction.

Despite these intimations that self-esteem is a significant precondition for creative expression, we could find no studies that directly investigated that hypothesis. In an attempt to do this we administered three tests that are pre-

TABLE 3.5 *Mean scores of self-esteem groups on three tests of creative performance*

| Scores | Types of self-esteem | | | | |
|---|---|---|---|---|---|
| | Low-Low | Low-High | Medium-Medium | High-Low | High-High |
| D.A.P. Talent | | | | | |
| Mean | 1.92 | 1.75 | 1.66 | 1.58 | 1.66 |
| SD | .56 | .68 | .54 | .52 | .48 |
| Unusual Uses | | | | | |
| Mean | 18.33 | 29.83 | 30.17 | 36.92 | 42.33 |
| SD | 14.07 | 10.03 | 22.38 | 23.15 | 18.69 |
| Circles Test | | | | | |
| Mean | 67.33 | 78.25 | 77.58 | 95.17 | 81.58 |
| SD | 30.15 | 19.33 | 28.02 | 30.14 | 27.69 |

*Source:* Laboratory tests.

sumed to measure the creativity of adolescents. The three tests, tapping different aspects of behavior, were Unusual Uses,[12] Circles,[13] and the Draw A Person Test (DAP), employing criteria developed by Brodsky.[14] The Draw A Person provides an index of the individual's creative abilities in art; the Unusual Uses test provides an index of his abilities to provide imaginative variations for common objects and situational changes; and the Circles test indicates how well the individual can employ simple, regular forms to develop an artistic product. We shall give some of the results here. The tests, scoring, and distribution of scores for each of the tests are described in greater detail by Southerly.[14] The mean scores and standard deviations for the five self-esteem groups are presented in Table 3.5, the analysis of variance in Table 3.6. Low scores on the DAP indicate greater originality; higher scores on the Unusual Uses and Circles tests have similar significance.

The analysis reveals that the five groups tend to differ ($F = 2.19$, $df = 4$, 55, $p < .10$). Groups high in subjective self-esteem perform in the most cre-

---

[12] J. P. Guilford, R. C. Wilson, P. R. Christensen, and E. J. Lewis. "A factor-analysis study of creative thinking. I. Hypotheses and descriptions of tests. Los Angeles, University of Southern California, 1951.

[13] K. Yamomoto, Revised scoring manual for tests of creative thinking. (Forms VA and NVA.) Minneapolis, University of Minnesota, Bureau of Educational Research, 1962.

[14] Cited in I. C. Southerly. Origins of Creativity: A Consideration of some Antecedent Factors in Creative Children with Particular Reference to Parental Attitudes and Child-rearing Practices. Unpublished Master's Thesis, Wesleyan University, Middletown, Conn., 1963.

TABLE 3.6 *Analysis of variance of three tests of creative performance*

| Source | df | MS | F |
|---|---|---|---|
| Self-esteem groups | 4 | 1,254.09 | 2.19[a] |
| Tests (T) | 2 | 93,627.26 | 299.13[b] |
| Replicates (R) | 11 | 653.51 | |
| G × R | 44 | 550.81 | |
| G × T | 8 | 462.80 | 1.48[c] |
| R × T | 22 | 459.94 | |
| Residual (G × R × T) | 88 | 277.07 | |
| Total | 179 | | |

[a] $p < .10$    [b] $p < .001$    [c] $p < .10$

ative fashion on all three tests. Groups low in self-esteem, on the other hand, are consistently less original and innovating. These differences are manifest across the different conceptual, linguistic, and artistic skills required in the several tests. This consistency suggests that persons high in their own evaluation are generally more capable of achieving and imposing original solutions than persons who are less confident in themselves. Inspection of Table 3.5 further indicates that the differences in creative ability are as manifest for tasks that appear to be relatively independent of prior training (Unusual Uses and Circles) as in the DAP, in which prior tuition may play a role. On all three tests we find the group low in subjective and behavioral esteem (Low-Low) to be especially poor in performance, and the two groups with high subjective esteem (High-High and High-Low) are either first or second in rank. Inasmuch as the pattern of results suggested that performance on these tests was related to subjective self-esteem, we performed a second analysis in which we combined the groups high in self-esteem (High-High and High-Low) and the groups low in self-esteem (Low-Low and Low-High). This analysis revealed that groups differing in subjective self-esteem were significantly different in their performance (F = 6.90, df = 1, 46, p < .01). The analysis also revealed a significant interaction between the performances of the subjectively different groups on the three tests (F = 3.29, df = 2, 92, p < .05). This interaction approaches significance when the five groups are considered separately (Table 3.6; F = 1.48, df = 8, 110, p < .10) but is accentuated when groups similar in subjective self-esteem are combined.

Taken as a whole, the results presented in this section indicate that persons with high self-esteem are likely to be more assertive, independent, and creative than persons with lower self-esteem. They are less likely to accept social definitions of reality unless these definitions are in accord with their own perceptions of what has occurred. In dealing with the world they appear to be more flexible and imaginative, and capable of more original solutions and interpretations. The impression that emerges is that individuals with high self-esteem listen to themselves more and trust their reactions and judgments to such an extent that they are willing to make them a basis of action. Their attentiveness and respect for their private conclusions enables them to pursue personal inclinations, and because of this their products and opinions often differ from those commonly expressed. From the viewpoint of theory, it is significant that it is the subjective experience of esteem, rather than behavioral assurance or discrepant personality, that is most clearly related to conformity and to creative behavior. Discrepancy between self-attitude and behavior appears to diminish the effectiveness of performance on both the conformity and creativity tasks, but it is not a major determinant in either instance. Inasmuch as the expressions of behavioral esteem, such as poise and assurance, are not significantly related to performance on either set of tasks, it would appear that internal convictions of confidence are more crucial for understanding and predicting independence than are more overt manifestations. In the next section we shall examine some of the personality characteristics (apparently associated with self-esteem) that seem to contribute or underlie such expressions of independence and originality.

### SOME FACTORS CONTRIBUTING TO SOCIAL PARTICIPATION AND INDEPENDENCE

The characteristics we have inferred as basic to social independence and originality—conviction, courage, self-trust, and self-respect—presumably stem from the individual's favorable appraisal of himself. Favorable self-appraisals apparently have the effect of liberating the individual from the demands of social groups and from ordinary ways of responding to stimuli and life situations. By providing the assurance that one's judgment is worthy and one's abilities sufficient to the task, favorable self-attitudes lay the foundation for stable, anxiety-free performance. By generating the expectation that one's efforts will be followed by success and one's judgment borne out by subsequent events, high self-esteem enhances the likelihood of exploratory and independent activities. These convictions and expectations appear to be closely related, if not inherent, in the level of esteem the individual holds of himself. From this theoretical analysis of our findings it would appear that positive and negative attitudinal sets have ramifying consequences that stem from differing assumptions and expectations of how life can and should be confronted. These general attitudinal sets represent self-theories or, more specifically, a set of hypotheses on how to anticipate, initiate, and respond to material tasks and interpersonal events. Evaluative self-attitudes may thus reflect a cognitive style of adaptation as well as a more particular and limited indication of personal esteem.

The existence of such a generalized style would provide a partial explanation of why we obtained similar results in both the conformity and creative tasks. There were, after all, considerable differences in the overt requirements of the creativity and conformity tasks. The creativity tests make virtually no demands for compliance, but the conformity situation is insistent in this regard; the creativity tests permit a wide variety of acceptable solutions, but the conformity situation provides only one solution, clearly veridical; the creativity tests encourage the different, nonconforming responses, but such responses are actively discouraged in the conformity situation. The tendency of the groups with high self-esteem to respond in independent and innovating ways suggests that the two tasks are sufficiently similar in other respects to arouse similar response dispositions. Perhaps the most immediate and striking common feature of the two tasks is that the pressures to comply and the pressures to compete both threaten the sense of adequacy, which suggests that the individual's ability to handle such threats is part of that general style of response associated with self-esteem. This possibility, foreshadowed by the theoretical discussion presented in Chapter 2, implies that persons with high self-esteem are better able to defend themselves against threats to adequacy than are persons who believe they are inadequate and insignificant. According to this reasoning, favorable self-appraisals presume the ability to deal with the anxieties aroused by conflict, ambiguity, and failure and the capacity to resist (but not necessarily deny) the negative implications of difficulties that come from differences of opinion. That is, in the present instances, the individual with high self-esteem is less likely than others to be shaken by either the differences of opinion of the conformity situation or the indefinite responses required by the creativity tests. If a favorable self-appraisal of past behavior is to be achieved, the individual must believe— to his own satisfaction and justification—that his performance was as effective as it could be under the circumstances and that allegations or insinuations to the contrary are not worthy of serious consideration. Thus self-trust provides an effective defense against the insidious negative appraisals of others, and thereby immunizes the individual against rapid or frequent alterations in the level of his self-esteem. Seen in this light, defenses appear to be an integral and essential part of the cognitive style associated with the level of esteem. Persons with high self-esteem have greater confidence in their ability to deal with events—that is, anxiety is less likely to be aroused—and greater ability to resist the negative implications of social judgments.

From this discussion we may infer that persons with low self-esteem are more readily threatened and experience greater difficulty in dealing with threats to their adequacy than are individuals who hold themselves in high regard. This is by no means surprising, since an individual who expresses negative attitudes toward himself thereby indicates that he has little confidence in his abilities to deal effectively with the events that confront him. Such a lack of confidence is likely to become more apparent and critical under conditions of stress, as prevailed in our tests, than under more tranquil conditions. In this same vein, we propose that negative self-appraisals are ipso facto presumptive indicators of limited defensive abilities and are likely to be associated with fearfulness and expectations of failure. Such negative interpretations of one's own abilities to deal with environmental demands is likely to result in cautious, restricted actions, an unwillingness to enter into controversy or otherwise expose oneself to criticism and rebuke, and a ready acceptance of negative judgments. More easily threatened than most, and at the same time less capable of dealing with the anxiety aroused by such threat, persons with low self-esteem apparently have difficulty in resisting actual or implied criticism.

The individual who defends himself against devaluation may be conscious or unconscious of his actions and motives. In that respect, as well as others, the concept of defenses employed here differs from its traditional usage in psychoanalytic theory. From responses to interviews, tests, and questionnaire, it seems clear that persons with high or low self-esteem are aware of their relative abilities to tolerate and counter criticism. Evidence to this effect is revealed by the responses of our subjects to one of the items in our questionnaire: "Would you prefer to say nothing rather than make people angry or would you be outspoken in your opinions regardless of the social consequences?" Such a social dilemma confronted our subject on the conformity task, in which individuals with low self-esteem were more likely than others to profess group consensus as their opinions. The summary of responses to this questionnaire item (Table 3.7) reveals that those low in self-esteem are more likely to report that they remain quiet if dissent might evoke personal attack. The percentage of persons in the Low-Low and Low-High groups who would remain quiet under these circumstances (82.4 and 71.4 percent, respectively) is markedly greater than the percentages for the High-Highs

TABLE 3.7 *"In discussions of public affairs I would prefer to say nothing than something which will make people angry with me"*

| Reply | Types of self-esteem | | | | |
|---|---|---|---|---|---|
| | Low-Low | Low-High | Medium-Medium | High-Low | High-High |
| Quiet | 82.4% (14) | 71.4% (10) | 68.8% (11) | 43.8% (7) | 25.0% (4) |
| Outspoken | 17.6% (3) | 28.6% (4) | 31.2% (5) | 56.2% (9) | 75.0% (12) |
| Totals | 100.0% (17) | 100.0% (14) | 100.0% (16) | 100.0% (16) | 100.0% (16) |

$\chi^2 = 14.46$    df = 4    p < .01

*Source:* Subject's questionnaire.

(25.0 percent) and High-Lows (43.8 percent). Thus, persons who do not esteem themselves and who, as we know, are unwilling to express contrary views even when they are correct, apparently appreciate what they are doing. They may interpret it as tact, moderation, or good citizenship, but they are nonetheless aware that they are unwilling to express unpopular opinions or engage in actions that might bring repudiation and rebuke. The difference in responses between the five groups are well beyond the level that could be expected by chance ($\chi^2 = 14.46$, df = 4, p < .01), as are the differences between groups at high, medium, and low levels of subjective self-esteem ($\chi^2 = 12.06$, df = 2, p < .01).

The unwillingness to express an unpopular opinion, revealed by the responses of those low in self-esteem, sharply limits the issues on which they can speak and the range of postures they can assume. They are restricted to issues on which there is overwhelming consensus or unanimity and cannot take positions which by either word or tone imply differences of opinion. Such individuals cannot serve as leaders who initiate new ideas, or proponents of positions that meet a mixed reaction, or engage in debate that would clarify and seek support for their views. The person of low self-esteem is thus more likely to be a less visible member of the crowd than its leader or the proponent of a dissident, minority position. This finding raises basic questions about the hypothesis that political leaders have underlying low self-esteem[15] and suggests that these leaders cannot be very low in their own estimation or they could not endure the exposure and differences that are inherent in political life.

[15] H. Lasswell. *Psychopathology and Politics.* Chicago, University of Chicago Press, 1930.

TABLE 3.8 *Sensitivity to criticism of members of self-esteem groups*

| Degree of sensitivity | Subjective self-esteem | | |
| --- | --- | --- | --- |
| | Low | Medium | High |
| Extremely, quite sensitive | 54.5% (18) | 35.3% (6) | 17.6% (6) |
| Relatively insensitive | 45.5% (15) | 64.7% (11) | 82.4% (28) |
| Totals | 100.0% (33) | 100.0% (17) | 100.0% (34) |

$\chi^2 = 9.90$      df $= 2$      p $< .01$

*Source:* Subject's questionnaire.

Further evidence on the relative vulnerability of persons who differ in self-esteem was obtained from a questionnaire item dealing with sensitivity to criticism. The subjects were asked to rate themselves on a scale that extended from extremely sensitive to relatively insensitive, with intermediate steps of moderate and mild sensitivity. The responses, summarized in Table 3.8, reveal a linear relationship between subjective self-esteem and sensitivity to criticism. Of the individuals with high self-esteem, only 17.6 percent report that they are extremely sensitive; twice that percentage of persons with medium self-esteem (35.3 percent) and three times that percentage of persons with low self-esteem (54.5 percent) report a similar vulnerability. The frequencies for the two groups with high subjective self-esteem (High-High and High-Low) were virtually identical, as were the frequencies for the two groups low in subjective self-esteem. (Low-Low and Low-High). Comparison of the frequencies obtained at the high, medium, and low levels of subjective esteem revealed significant differences ($\chi^2 = 9.90$, df $= 2$, p $< .01$). These results provide an additional basis for understanding the social behaviors of our subjects. They suggest that persons with low self-esteem are particularly vulnerable to unfavorable opinion and are fearful of evoking anger (Table 3.7). They apparently are greatly distressed by either conflict or personal rejection and prefer to remain silent and passive rather than expose themselves to such exchanges and stimulation. This would provide a further explanation for the conforming and rather unoriginal performance of our subjects with low self-esteem. The sensitivity of these subjects also suggests that such individuals are at the relative mercy of the judgments expressed by the individuals in their social milieu. Their strong reactions to criticism can hardly be overlooked by their peers or by their teachers and parents. This means that those who are concerned for their

TABLE 3.9 *Self-consciousness of members of self-esteem groups*

| Degree of self-consciousness | Subjective self-esteem | | |
|---|---|---|---|
| | Low | Medium | High |
| Relatively self-conscious | 63.6% (21) | 47.1% (8) | 31.2% (10) |
| Barely, if at all, self-conscious | 36.4% (12) | 52.9% (9) | 68.8% (22) |
| Totals | 100.0% (33) | 100.0% (17) | 100.0% (32) |

$\chi^2 = 6.82$      df $= 2$      p $< .05$

*Source:* Subject's questionnaire.

welfare are likely to behave in a constrained and circumspect fashion, avoiding even constructive criticism for fear it may evoke an unwarranted or extreme reaction. Critical of himself, the individual with low self-esteem appears all too ready to believe that others judge him in the same unfriendly fashion. He apparently accepts negative statements about himself in situations where those higher in esteem are more likely to question or reject critical comments. Such acceptance or rejection of criticism is part of the individual's defense against diminished esteem. Those low in their own esteem apparently lack the confidence to reject the critical appraisal of others and thus remain undefended and exposed in their real or imagined deficiencies.

The hypothesis that those low in self-esteem feel more exposed was tested more directly by one of the questions directed to our subjects. The subject was asked to indicate whether or not the following applied to him: "When a number of people are talking I am often self-conscious about talking in front of everyone." Positive responses presumably show that the person feels unusually exposed when faced with the prospect of public conversation. As we might anticipate, individuals with low self-esteem are much more likely (63.6 percent) to feel self-conscious under these conditions than are persons who are medium (47.1 percent) or high (31.2 percent) in self-esteem. The summary of responses, combined along the subjective dimension of self-esteem, is presented in Table 3.9. The differences between the various levels thus ordered is statistically significant ($\chi^2 = 6.82$, df $= 2$, p $< .05$). From this analysis we can infer that persons with low self-esteem are generally more aware of themselves in public situations than are persons who have greater self-appreciation. This awareness does not appear to be limited to situations in which criticism and dispute occur but is a more general reaction to public situations. In effect, the individual with low self-esteem indicates that he finds participation in public events painful and would prefer to avoid exposing himself under those conditions. Presumably he fears that his words and actions will reveal his inadequacies or evoke a situation beyond his (self-defined) limited capacities. The underlying fear is apparently further diminution of esteem and public revelation of the individual's incompetence and helplessness. Being terribly aware of his deficiencies, he assumes that the limelight will always be damaging, and to avoid exposure he stays in the shadows and shrinks from actions that attract attention and criticism.

The greater self-consciousness of the individual with low self-esteem provides another reason why such persons avoid public discussions and positions of leadership. They are very much aware of themselves, and it is an awareness that is colored by feelings of devaluation rather than equally open to all or random thoughts. This is to say that they are very conscious of their inadequacies (real or imagined) and thus their self-appraisals and judgments are likely to be salient and pervasive aspects of their experience. The judgments, being internal, cannot be evaded and hence serve as constant reminders of inferiority. They result in an omnipresent malaise marked by preoccupation with the self and attention to shortcomings and deficiencies. This preoccupation is masochistic in its consequences if not in intent. By dwelling upon their ineptitude and insufficiencies, those low in self-esteem are exacerbating their point of greatest sensibility, and at the same time reducing the opportunities for obtaining successes. They are, in effect, constantly reminding themselves of their failures and lack of power, thereby subverting their own morale and reducing the possibility for effective, real action.

This preoccupation (and one of its consequences) is graphically illustrated by the responses of our subjects to two items included in the questionnaire. The first of these asked them to agree or disagree with the statement "I'm too concerned with inner problems to devote much attention to broader problems of the world." From the responses (Table 3.10), we find that persons with low or medium self-esteem are much more likely to agree with this statement than are those who are high in their own regard. The percentages of those who agree at each level of subjective esteem is 45.5 percent for the low and 47.1 for the medium, but only 9.4 percent of the high self-esteem group say that concern with inner problems interferes with consideration of wider concerns. The differences between the levels, combined by subjective esteem, is greater than could be attributd solely to chance ($\chi^2 = 12.08$, df = 2, p < .01).

Responses to a second question that pursued this issue in another section of the questionnaire provide a very similar picture. This question asked the

TABLE 3.10 *"I'm too concerned with inner problems to devote much attention to broader problems of the world"*

| Reply | Subjective self-esteem | | |
|---|---|---|---|
| | Low | Medium | High |
| Considerable concern with inner problems | 45.5% (15) | 47.1% (8) | 9.4% (3) |
| Little, if any, concern with inner problems | 54.5% (18) | 52.9% (9) | 90.6% (29) |
| Totals | 100.0% (33) | 100.0% (17) | 100.0% (32) |
| $\chi^2 = 12.08$    df $= 2$ | p $< .01$ | | |

*Source:* Subject's questionnaire.

subject to indicate whether he was distracted from public affairs by personal concerns. The responses indicate that approximately two-thirds of those low in self-esteem are distracted by personal concerns, but less than one-fourth of the high self-esteem group reported similar distractions. The medium group (50 percent) falls between those high and low in subjective esteem, with the differences between the various levels of esteem again being greater than could be expected by chance ($\chi^2 = 6.94$, df $= 2$, p $< .05$).

Thus we find that the individual with low self-esteem is more likely to turn inward and dwell upon himself, and those higher in esteem are able to give greater attention to external, public events. Apparently low self-appraisals arouse repetitive and possibly compulsive self-examination, but more positive self-attitudes permit a more expanded perspective. Active and frequent participants in public affairs are thus unlikely to be low in their own esteem, or they could not perform effectively before a public. Such performance requires attention to issues, willingness to expose one's ideas, and a sensitivity to others as well as to oneself. The individual with low self-esteem misses on all counts and is thus restricted in the social actions he can perform.

SUMMARY

The findings presented in this chapter point to pervasive and significant differences in the experiential worlds and social behaviors of persons who differ in self-esteem. Persons high in their own estimation approach tasks and persons with the expectation that they will be well received and successful. They have confidence in their perceptions and judgments and believe that they can bring their efforts to a favorable resolution. Their favorable self-attitudes lead them to accept their own opinions and place credence and trust in their reactions and conclusions. This permits them to follow their own judgments when there is a difference of opinion and also permits them to consider novel ideas. The trust in self that accompanies feelings of worthiness is likely to provide the conviction that one is correct and the courage to express those convictions. The attitudes and expectations that lead the individual with high self-esteem to greater social independence and creativity also lead him to more assertive and vigorous social actions. They are more likely to be participants than listeners in group discussions, they report less difficulty in forming friendships, and they will express opinions even when they know these opinions may meet with a hostile reception. Among the factors that underlie and contribute to these actions are their lack of self-consciousness and their lack of preoccupation with personal problems. Lack of self-consciousness permits them to present their ideas in a full and forthright fashion; lack of self-preoccupation permits them to consider and examine external issues.

The picture of the individual with low self-esteem that emerges from these results is markedly different. These persons lack trust in themselves and are apprehensive about expressing unpopular or unusual ideas. They do not wish to expose themselves, anger others, or perform deeds that would attract attention. They are likely to live in the shadows of a social group, listening rather than participating, and preferring the solitude of withdrawal above the interchange of participation. Among the factors that contribute to the withdrawal of those low in self-esteem are their marked self-consciousness and preoccupation with inner problems. This great awareness of themselves distracts them from attending to other persons and issues and is likely to result in a morbid preoccupation with their difficulties. The effect is to limit their social intercourse and thus decrease the possibilities of friendly and supportive relationships.

These results indicate that individuals who differ in self-esteem behave in markedly different fashions. The behavioral differences are due to differences of anticipation, reaction, and willingness to trust and rely upon personal judgment as a basis for action. They are also attributable to the greater sense of exposure and self-consciousness experienced by the person low in self-esteem and which lead him to turn inward and dwell upon his difficulties. Self-esteem thus appears to have ramifying consequences that vitally affect the manner in which an individual responds to himself and the outside world. We shall next seek to determine the conditions by which self-esteem is established.

*Chapter four*

# PROCEDURES AND MATERIALS

P receding chapters described the conceptual framework of this study and established the differences between the various levels of esteem. With this chapter we begin the actual details of the study itself. Inasmuch as our focus is upon the antecedents of self-esteem we shall not discuss any of the procedures or materials utilized in our clinical or experimental investigations, but rather the methods and materials used to obtain information on the social backgrounds, parental characteristics, and parent-child interaction of our subjects. We shall indicate the methods employed in administering, coding, and analyzing our materials, and the conventions employed to describe and summarize our results.

Before describing the specific procedures we should like to indicate some of the general considerations and precautions involved in developing our procedures. First of all, the subjects whose backgrounds were investigated in the present study had previously been studied by the use of clinical and laboratory procedures. From these studies we had learned much about the capacities, attributes, and characteristics of the children, and this knowledge was used to amplify and interpret the results of our present study of antecedents.

Second, information on the child's experiences and relationships was obtained from both the mother and child. This gave us different perspectives upon the same events and thus provided some corroboration, if not validation, that events had occurred as described. The information from the child came largely through his responses to questionnaire items dealing with parental treatment and his home life. In a few instances we also employed scores derived from the content analysis of projective material (the Thematic Apperception Test), which presumably indicated less conscious attitudes and emotions. The information from the mother came through her responses to a questionnaire dealing with attitudes and practices related to child-rearing. This was followed by an intensive interview covering some of these same areas and extending and defining them in much greater detail.

Third, we employed a number of checks to establish the reliability of our informants' responses. One check consisted of variously worded questions bearing on the same variable within a given interview or questionnaire, as well as across these different sources of data. This enabled us to cross-check responses and determine whether they were consistently expressed despite variations in wording, context, or procedure. Other checks included the comparison of responses that presumably tapped conscious and unconscious levels of expression, and the comparison of responses obtained independently from mother and child. A final check was the interviewer's appraisal of the subject's candor and reliability. Although clearly dependent upon the perceptiveness and skill of the interviewer, the opinions of the person who actually encounters and probes the subject may be of considerable value in identifying defensive respondents. In our study the interviewer's reports and inconsistent responses led us to eliminate three cases from our analysis; this was done before the data had been coded and analyzed.

Finally, we should note that although we obtained information about the father's attitudes and actions from both the mother and child, we did not have any direct contact with the father himself. This was partly because we lacked both the necessary time and money, partly because it was difficult to arrange meetings with fathers. It is worth noting, however, that the mother and son almost invariably agreed in their statements about the father's attitudes and actions. Where we do refer to the father, the source of our information (mother or son) is stated in the context or table heading. Unless specified to the contrary, the term parent refers to the mother, who was the principal source of data on the child's earlier experiences.

MOTHER'S PARTICIPATION:
QUESTIONNAIRE AND INTERVIEW

The mothers were asked if they would participate in our study shortly after we asked their permission to include their sons in our clinical and laboratory studies. The parents were informed at that time, that the study was concerned with the personality traits of normal children, particularly those related to effectiveness of functioning, and that the study would subsequently be expanded to include an examination of parental attitudes and child-rearing practices. Those that let their children participate and agreed to participate themselves were included in the sample; only four persons refused.

Upon agreeing to participate, the mothers of our subjects completed a questionnaire of eighty items taken from the extended list (Parent Attitude Research Instrument, PARI) developed by Bell and Schaefer (1958).[1] The items require that the respondent indicate her agreement or disagreement with statements bearing upon attitudes and practices relating to child-rearing. The eighty items were taken from fourteen scales (PARI) describing attitudes and behaviors that appeared to be most relevant to the formation of self-esteem. The items were selected on the basis or our conceptual analysis, which led us to focus on successes, values, aspirations, defenses, and the specific attributes and experiences that appeared related to these concepts. Two scales of particular theoretical interest, Egalitarianism and Acceleration, contained ten items; the others, five items each. The mothers completed the questionnaires in the privacy of their homes. They did not indicate any difficulties in understanding or responding to the questionnaire items. The items and the scales they came from are presented in Appendix C.

In the light of recent appraisals of the PARI,[2] we may note that its use in the current study is considerably different from those that have received critical attention. As employed here, the PARI is but one of several instruments employed to study parental characteristics and parent-child interaction. The parental attitudes being scrutinized in these questionnaire items are, at the same time, being scrutinized by the more intensive interview and the child's reports of present and previous parental behavior. This use of different informants and different procedures for obtaining information provides corroboration that is unavailable if the PARI items or scales are used as the sole source of information. This multiple-method, multiple-informant procedure makes it unlikely that response biases and self-enhancing facades will remain undetected, and provides external validation of the events and attitudes obtained in response to any one instrument, such as the PARI. In effect, the

---

[1] E. S. Schaefer and R. Q. Bell. "Development of a parental attitude research instrument." *Child Develop.*, 29:339–361 (1958).

[2] W. Becker and R. S. Krug. "Parent attitude research instrument: A research review." *Child Develop.*, 36:329–365 (1965).

responses to the PARI items are but one of several sources of data on parental behavior, and therefore the responses to them can be appraised in a broader and more varied context of parental and child responses.

After the clinical and experimental studies of the children had been completed, an interview study was initiated. Eighty-two of the eighty-five mothers participated in these interviews. One of the families had moved in the meantime, and two others asked to be excused from the interview study. These three were randomly distributed among our self-esteem groups. The interviews were conducted individually by three experienced female interviewers,[3] who had received prior training on the speed, sequence, and kind of approach with which the interview was to be conducted. The interviewers did not know the level of the child's self-esteem or other personality attributes at the time they interviewed the mother. They conducted their interviews "blind" and did not have knowledge or direct contact with the child. The child did know that the interview was being conducted, although we tried to arrange it so that he would be away at the time. The purpose of the interviews, as presented to the mother and child, was to obtain information about those aspects of early experience relating to effective performance.

The interviews were individually conducted in either the home or an office at a nearby university. The interviews lasted between $1\frac{1}{2}$ and 3 hours, with an average length of approximately $2\frac{1}{4}$ hours. The interviewers used a schedule of questions divided into six sections. The general sequence of presentation was (1) social background and family history, (2) pregnancy and infancy, (3) developmental history of the child, (4) current parent-child relationships, (5) parent's appraisal of the child, and (6) interviewer's appraisal of the mother. The interviewers were instructed to adopt a flexible attitude in following the sequence of questions and to adapt their procedures according to the subject and circumstances. The style and content of the questions varied with the topic. The early sections of the schedule contained several factual questions that could be answered by short and simple responses —length of marriage, number of children, and years of schooling. There were other questions that required more extended and considered answers— the mother's responses to her child's failures, and the extent to which the child participated in making family decisions. Although the questions did occasionally veer into attitudes and practices that are often regarded as personal and sensitive, there was little if any probing in these areas. It was our

---

[3] We should like to acknowledge the skilled and careful efforts of Patricia Brodsky, Anne Merritt, and Amanda Roston, who served as our interviewers.

intention and expectation that an interview of this sort, conducted with flexibility of sequence, could retain the good will of the respondent and maximize the quality and amount of information we could obtain.

The interview schedule we devised was the result of our conceptual analysis of those child-rearing practices that appeared related to self-esteem (Chapter 2) and our extensive pretesting of different question and schedule forms. This pretesting enabled us to iron out and clarify ambiguities and difficulties of wording and administration. The theoretical considerations led us to focus on particular areas (decision making, discipline) and dimensions of experience (acceptance, domination). The questions requested information on when certain events occurred, the practices employed in handling these events, and the attitudes and emotions associated with their occurrence—for example, the frequency with which the child differed with his parents' decisions, the mother's characteristic way of responding to such deviation, and her reactions when such differences occurred. The final interview schedule contained a total of 182 questions. There were 116 questions requesting information that was sufficiently straightforward that it could be precoded in the interview schedule.[4] There were 66 open-ended questions for which the range of responses appeared too broad to pre-establish adequate categories of response. The entire schedule is presented in Appendix D.

After the interviews had been completed, the responses to each item were examined and coded independently by two raters who had familiarized themselves with the concepts as well as the questions under consideration.[5] When their codings differed by more than one scale unit, the raters discussed their differences until they were able to achieve agreement as to the most suitable unit. By virtue of prior conferences on the concepts employed, training in the use of categories, and extensive pretesting, it was possible to achieve a high inter-rater reliability. The correlations of their initial appraisal of responses ranged between .62 and .99 for each of the items in the schedule.

Some general description of the mothers may help to identify our sample and facilitate generalization. The mothers were from two middle-sized New England towns in which they had been residing for at least three years. Their children were attending public schools and were in the fifth and sixth grades at the time the study was initiated. The women were all married at the time of the study, although their present husbands were not necessarily the fathers

---

[4] We should like to thank Robert R. Sears and his associates for making their code-books available and the permission to use them.

[5] Alice Coopersmith, Iona Kaplan, and Ruth Peoples served as coders. We express our appreciation to all of them, particularly to Ruth Peoples, who served as supervisor in this task.

of their children. The median age of the mothers was 38.4 years; their ages ranged from 29 to 54, with over 50 percent of them falling between 34 and 42. Their husbands were approximately 3 years older, with an average age of 41.6 years. Fourteen percent of the mothers had graduated from college, but 34 percent had not completed high school. Their husbands tended to be somewhat more educated; 23 percent held college degrees and less than 30 percent had failed to complete high school. Both husbands and wives tended to be upwardly mobile, the husbands being somewhat more mobile than their wives.

The religious backgrounds of the husbands and wives were generally similar and tended to be largely Protestant and Catholic. There were several Jewish mothers included in our sample, but their number was relatively limited in our study, just as it was in their community. The ethnic backgrounds of the mothers tended to be Old American, Irish, Italian, and eastern European. Median family income was between $6000 and $6500 in 1963, with over 40 percent of the families reporting incomes between $4600 and $8400. In terms of social status the group came from the broad range of the middle class. They included some professionals at the upper range of the middle class and some workers at its lower end, but the largest numbers came from the middle of the socioeconomic ladder.

### CHILD'S PARTICIPATION: QUESTIONNAIRE AND TAT

The information from the child came largely through his responses to the Rosenberg Self-Image Questionnaire.[6] The sections in this questionnaire were administered to our subjects in three groups. There were between 25 and 35 in each group, and the total administration time was approximately $1\frac{1}{2}$ to 2 hours. A psychologist on our research staff reviewed the instructions with the respondents and remained in the room during the entire session to answer any questions they might have. His instructions stressed the confidential manner in which their responses would be treated and the importance of candor in answering all questions. In the light of the prior, relatively close relationship we had achieved with our subjects, as well as their reactions to the questionnaire itself, we have every reason to believe that they responded in a serious, sincere fashion. Confirming this impression were their responses to two questions at the end of the questionnaire; their answers indicated that

---

[6] M. Rosenberg. *Society and the Adolescent Self-Image*. Princeton, Princeton University Press, 1965.

they had found the questions interesting and had experienced little difficulty in responding to them.

Other evidence of the son's attitude toward his parents came from the Thematic Apperception Test (TAT). This projective test was included as part of the clinical test battery administered to all the children who participated in our study. This test is intended to measure less conscious affective states and relationships. By presenting ambiguous stimuli, the subject is encouraged and induced to project his own personality characteristics, so that the stories he tells represent him more than the pictures. Our analysis of the TAT protocols utilized the need system developed by Henry A. Murray and his collaborators (1938),[7] and an additional method developed specifically for this study. This second method, developed by Betty J. Beardslee and David G. Lowy, coded the story content in terms of separate, theoretically important experiences and relationships. Examples of such experiences are self-mobilization, dissatisfaction, control, and conflict; examples of the relational codes are the importance and nature of relationships with father, mother, and peers. This method, which we term experiential analysis, involved the application of twenty-six scales, which the raters used on the six stories obtained from each child. These scales, based on cards 1, $A_1$, 1 BG, 7 BM, B1, 13B of the TAT series, were all five-point, unidimensional scales which were applied to each story separately. The scores for all six stories were then combined and an average obtained, and the analyses were performed on these averages. Scores at the upper end of the Importance of Relationship Scale indicate that the relationship is extremely important. Such scores would mean that the story is primarily one that revolves around the child-parent relationship and that the theme is spontaneously and extensively expressed. Scores at the lower end indicate the total absence of references to the relationship. In our study the raters made separate ratings for relationships with father, mother, and peers.

### DATA ANALYSIS AND PRESENTATION

The data obtained from the mother and child were organized into the eight sections around which the present report is organized: Social background, Parental characteristics, Child's characteristics, Early history and experience, Acceptance, Permissiveness and punishment, Democratic practices, and Independence training. These responses were not all variables, nor were they

---

[7] H. A. Murray et al. *Explorations in Personality.* New York: Oxford University Press, 1938.

independent of one another. The responses were analyzed by contingency ($\chi^2$) procedures, which compared the relative frequency of responses for the five self-esteem groups. Where differences were obtained, further analyses were performed by combining groups along the dimensions of subjective, behavioral, and discrepant self-esteem. Thus, for example, if our initial analysis revealed that the five groups differed in permissiveness and that permissiveness was positively related to subjective esteem, we combined the two high subjective esteem groups and two low esteem groups. This was followed by an analysis of the three levels of subjective self-esteem—i.e., high, medium, and low. Combinations of groups along the dimensions of behavioral self-esteem and extent of self-behavioral discrepancy followed the same procedure. Instances of this procedure have already been presented in Chapter 3. Those variables which met our criteria ($p < .05$ significant, $p < .10$ suggestive) were retained for discussion and further analysis. In several instances, negative findings were retained and reported because of their theoretical significance. The tables presented in the text were selected out of a larger number because they appeared of greatest relevance and significance to the specific topic of self-esteem or of general significance to the study of personality formation. In discussing the tables we shall naturally emphasize the dimension that appears most discriminating for that variable or response. Our summary statements for each chapter or section will, however, indicate the positive and negative findings for all three dimensions and for the five self-esteem types. The ordinate of the table will indicate the dimension of self-esteem along which the greatest differences were established. These will be labeled as either subjective, behavioral, discrepancy, or type of self-esteem. Wherever possible we sought information from more than one source. This enabled us to achieve independence from a single response set or methodological procedure.

The tables presented in the text indicate both the percentages and number of persons (in parentheses) in each category. If the total number of cases is less than 80, it means that some persons failed to answer the question or provided an answer that could not be coded. The percentages are calculated by rows—that is, by self-esteem—rather than by column. Inasmuch as our sample was not randomly selected, certain groups may be underrepresented (medium self-esteem) and others overrepresented (discrepancy and low self-esteem). Accordingly, any conclusions on the relative numbers or percentages of persons manifesting those traits in the general population are unwarranted and apt to be misleading. For this reason we shall cite row percentages and indicate column percentages only where they appear meaningful.

After analysis of the individual tables had been completed we examined the over-all pattern of results in each section and chapter. This enabled us to determine whether the results obtained from diverse sources and by different procedures fell into consistent patterns. These patterns are discussed at the end of each chapter, and an over-all integration is presented in Chapter 13.

*Chapter five*

# THE INFLUENCE
# OF SOCIAL BACKGROUND

B̲oth the lay public and social scientists have assumed that feelings of assurance, acceptance, and personal security are associated with certain aspects of the social background. More prestige is accorded some religious groups, such as Protestants, or greater mental power is attributed to some races, such as Caucasians. In these instances and numerous others, we find well-defined hierarchies of prestige that appear to be familiar to the vast majority of people. Studies of occupational, ethnic, and religious stereotypes and rankings of social preferences also reveal that such hierarchies are commonly shared by the community at large. If we assume that greater social honor and material success accrue to persons on the higher rungs of the social ladder than to those below them, we certainly expect the persons on the higher rungs to be higher also in their own self-esteem. The implicit assumptions of this unstated syllogism—that different degrees of honor and success are presumably associated with given social positions and that there is a linear relationship between such success and self-esteem—are virtually untested in either a theoretical or empirical manner. This is intriguing as well as surprising, since aspirants to higher social status or given professions exert great effort, expecting that attainment of these goals will result in more favorable self-appraisals as well as the approval of others.

The reasoning relating social position and self-esteem is most directly relevant to the adult who has known success, status, and privileges. In his case success and the reflected appraisals of the community have a personal significance that is bound into the fabric of life. He has striven for and received the material benefits of acclaim and acceptance that presumably betoken the achievement of his goals. Although this reasoning may apply to the parent, we must consider the more indirect relationship between parental status and the child's self-esteem. The children themselves have not yet known the success and deference associated with status, but they may nonetheless share their benefits. Thus, the children of higher-class parents may gain greater recognition, material rewards, and social acceptance than the children of parents with lesser status. There is some evidence that preadolescent children such as we studied are even at that age already aware of social distinctions.[1]

## SOCIAL CLASS

Perhaps the clearest and most striking index of prestige and success is an individual's social status. Social position is based largely on occupation, income, and residence. Persons higher in the system have more prestigious occupations, have higher income, and tend to live in larger and more luxurious houses located in more desirable neighborhoods. These persons are more successful in the eyes of the community and receive the material and cultural benefits that should lead them to believe that they are generally more worthy than others. This presumed relationship between social prestige and self-esteem would appear to have different significance for children and adults. For one thing, the social status of children is ascribed rather than achieved and hence reveals the consequences of being brought up in a given social position rather than achieving it. We should also note that the child experiences his class position in the neighborhood and school rather than in the occupational context from which his social status is largely derived. Despite this attenuated impact of prestige and attention, we would assume that children from higher status families are more apt to have enhancing material benefits and to receive more respectful treatment.

The index of socioeconomic status employed in the present study is a combined weighted score of the father's income and occupation. Inasmuch as sample selection eliminated both extremes of the distribution, the results are available only for the intervening range of the distribution. For the purposes of our analysis, the class system was divided into three cate-

---

[1] M. Radke, H. G. Trager, and H. Davis. "Social perceptions and attitudes of children." *Genetic Psych. Monogr.*, **40**:327–477 (1949).

TABLE 5.1 *Social status and self-esteem*

| Social class | Subjective self-esteem | | |
| --- | --- | --- | --- |
| | Low | Medium | High |
| Lower middle or working class | 43.3% (13) | 64.7% (11) | 30.3% (10) |
| Middle class | 26.7% (8) | 23.5% (4) | 27.3% (9) |
| Upper middle class | 30.0% (9) | 11.8% (2) | 42.4% (14) |
| Totals | 100.0% (30) | 100.0% (17) | 100.0% (33) |

$\chi^2 = 6.60$    df $= 4$    p $< .15$

*Source:* Mother's interview.

gories. Fathers in the upper middle class have generally had some college, enjoy incomes that are above average for the population, and are frequently in professional and managerial occupations. Fathers in the middle class have generally graduated from high school, receive average incomes, and are frequently in lower managerial, clerical, and skilled semiprofessional occupations. Fathers in the lower middle and working classes have generally had some high school, are below average in income, and are generally engaged in service and manufacturing occupations.

The most striking feature of Table 5.1 is the weak, nonsignificant relationship (p < .15) between self-esteem and social class. There are some interesting and suggestive trends: children in the upper middle class are more likely to have high esteem and those in the lower middle class low or medium esteem, but the effects of differing social position are not very striking. In this regard our results are generally similar to the weak but significant results previously obtained by Rosenberg (Table 5.2). The distribution (for males) revealed by that study, which covered a broader range of social classes, parallels that obtained for our largely middle class (male) sample. Both studies indicate that there is no clear and definite pattern of relationships between social class and positive and negative attitudes toward the self. They further indicate that though persons from the upper and middle classes are more likely to express favorable self-attitudes than persons in the lower group, the differences between groups are neither as large nor as regular as might have been expected. In addition, both studies show that though persons in the lower class are most likely to report lower self-esteem, there are almost as many persons in this class who report high esteem as low esteem.

Rosenberg's distribution does indeed reveal significant differences between

TABLE 5.2 *Social status and self-esteem*

| Social class | Subjective self-esteem | | | |
| --- | --- | --- | --- | --- |
| | Low | Medium | High | Totals |
| Lower class (lower middle) | 39% (65) [38.2%] [a] | 25% (43) [32.3%] | 36% (60) [29.4%] | 100% (168) |
| Middle class (middle) | 28% (387) [38.1%] | 25% (346) [19.1%] | 47% (650) [42.8%] | 100% (1383) |
| Upper class (upper middle) | 28% (25) [36.0%] | 17% (15) [8.0%] | 55% (49) [56.0%] | 100% (89) |

$\chi^2 = 13.96$      df $= 4$      p $< .01$

*Source:* M. Rosenberg. *Society and the Adolescent Self-Image,* p. 40. Princeton, Princeton University Press, 1965. (This table shows percentages by row rather than by column.)
[a] For purposes of comparison, our own percentages are given within brackets.

the esteem of the various classes ($\chi^2 = 13.96$, df $= 4$, p $< .01$), but this appears to be largely a function of his sample size (larger than ours). Both of our results suggest that children in different social classes do not experience as much difference in prestige and success as may popularly be imagined. An alternative interpretation is that success is interpreted differently by the members of the different social groups, and is not as closely related to material benefits as is commonly believed.

### RELIGION

The religious group with which an individual identifies has several immediate consequences. It provides him with a locus for social experiences and a set of acquaintances, if not friends. In most cases it presents a set of moral and ethical rules which the individual may use for his personal and social behavior. Religions also present some solution to the problems of good and evil, and an interpretation of events that exceed sensible or scientific explanation. Co-religionists represent groups bound together by common faith and convictions, who may occasionally join together in more formal associations. They are often regarded by others as sharing certain attributes and behaviors that are not limited solely to their religious beliefs. The social image of a religious group as well as the behaviors attributed to it tend to be placed into a consistent pattern by other (nonreligionist) members of the society.

Given the varied and complex significance of religious group membership, it is not altogether surprising to find that there are several divergent opinions

TABLE 5.3 *Religion and self-esteem*

| Religion | Subjective self-esteem | | | |
|---|---|---|---|---|
| | Low | Medium | High | Totals |
| Catholics | 31% (535) [33.3%] [a] | 26% (449) [27.8%] | 43% (743) [38.9%] | 100% (1727) |
| Protestants | 32% (612) [41.7%] | 25% (478) [16.6%] | 43% (823) [41.7%] | 100% (1913) |
| Jews | 23% [28.6%] | 23% [14.3%] | 53% [57.1%] | 100% (592) |

$\chi^2 = 24.36$      df $= 4$      p $< .001$

*Source:* M. Rosenberg. *Society and the Adolescent Self-Image,* p. 50. Princeton, Princeton University Press, 1965. (This table shows percentages by row rather than by column.)

[a] For purposes of comparison, our own percentages are given within brackets.

on the self-esteem of different social groups. Viewed in terms of social acceptance, there is every reason to expect that Jews, who rank lower in the prestige ladder than Protestants and Catholics, would suffer from fairly negative self-attitudes. Supporting this view is the common conviction that Jews suffer from feelings of inferiority, which they seek to cover by overt displays of material wealth. In contrast to such versions of "what makes Sammy run" are the views that Jews are arrogant in believing themselves to be the chosen people and self-confident in their business ventures. Similar differences of opinion and interpretation are expressed regarding the self-esteem of Catholics. They are, on the one hand, underlings in a relatively inflexible system, and on the other they are offered ready penitence and the likelihood of salvation. Protestants are driven to seek personal redemption by their acts (the Protestant ethic) and, at the same time, occupy the position of the dominant majority in this country. Such admixtures of social, ethical, supernatural, historical, and status considerations make it difficult to predict the nature of the relationship between religion and self-esteem.

Analysis of our data relating religious affiliation and self-esteem failed to reveal any significant differences in the level of esteem reported by members of the three major religious faiths. There was a tendency for Jews to express higher esteem than either Catholics or Protestants. But this was not a trustworthy finding (p < .30) and was based on too small a number of Jewish subjects. Interestingly enough, however, Rosenberg obtained a similar, and significant, relationship with his larger sample (Table 5.3). Both studies indicate that the members of the three major religious groups in America are equally likely to be medium in esteem but that Jews are least likely to express negative self-attitudes. Both results indicate that Jews, who are lower in the hierarchy of general status and who are a minority group, are more likely to have favorable self-attitudes than either Protestants or Catholics. They suggest that religious identification per se is not a salient, or determining influence in personal judgments of worthiness.

Our results on the relationship between self-esteem and social class and religion thus run counter to general expectations. Although our study, like Rosenberg's, indicates some relationship between social class and esteem, the relationship is weaker and less patterned than might have been expected on the basis of differences in status. The findings for religion indicate that the members of a minority group who elsewhere rank lower in prestige ratings are more likely to be high in self-esteem than are the members of more numerous, prestigious, or dominant religious groups. These results suggest that the psychological bases of esteem are more dependent on close, personal relationships and the immediate environment than upon material benefits or prestige rankings in the community at large. In effect, they suggest that the definition of success is a matter of personal interpretation rather than a direct and immediate consequence of one's social status and affiliation, and that it is the experiences within one's own social reference group that determine one's social definition of success—not the broader social context.

This leads us to focus greater attention upon the immediate social environment in which the child develops rather than upon more abstract or distant determinants. It may be tempting to consider the significance of theological, historical, or economic influences upon the development of esteem, but factors must ultimately be considered in their everyday social expression. Persons are, after all, affected by the actions that occur in their immediate sociocultural environment rather than by the general concepts employed to describe social phenomena. Social class and religion are both complex and multifaceted concepts and the bases for our findings, or lack of them, must be sought in more particular behaviors. Thus, for example, we have some indications that it is parental interest and concern that differentiates the members of the three religious groups. Utilizing an index of the parental interest experienced by the child, Rosenberg found that "very few parents gave any indication of indifference toward their children; but where such evidence did appear, it was least likely to be found among Jewish parents." He found that Catholic parents were almost twice as likely to express indifference toward their children as were Jewish parents, and that Protestant parents were intermediate between Catholics and Jews. The differences in parental interest among the three religious groups were statistically significant and persisted when controls for the influence of social class were imposed. This finding tends to support the notion that the direct, immediately experienced, explanatory factors are encompassed by broad social categories such as class and religion. We shall examine this effective interpersonal environment in much greater detail to determine the extent and manner in which it produces enhancing and de-valuating effects. Before doing so, it is worth noting that although subjective self-esteem was only weakly related to social class and religion, that relation-ship was much closer than those obtained for behavioral esteem and self-behavioral discrepancy. This would suggest that the factors responsible for expressions of poise and defensiveness are even less directly related to the broad concepts of class and religion.

### FATHER'S WORK HISTORY

Our consideration of social class provided some information about the rela-tionship between father's occupation and self-esteem. Fathers in the upper middle classes, whose children are more likely to be high in self-esteem, are engaged in managerial, professional, and entrepreneurial activities quite dif-ferent from the activities of fathers in other classes. Since these differences in occupation might reflect the personality traits of those who select a given occupation or the consequences of occupational demands, we conducted a more detailed examination, relating self-esteem with specific occupations. These failed to provide any indication that the occupation of the father was related to the self-esteem of his sons. In short, the son of an unskilled ditch digger is as likely to have high self-esteem as is the son of a corporation executive. Children apparently are much more affected by the specific treat-ment they receive than by the prestige generally associated with their father's work. There is one exception to this general finding:[2] the sons of men en-gaged in authoritarian or "violent" occupations, such as members of the armed or police forces, are unusually low in self-esteem.

There are, however, other aspects of the father's occupational background that may have an influence on self-esteem. Inasmuch as American society emphasizes a man's ability to achieve and produce, the father who has diffi-culties in this regard might be considered a failure. There is enough evi-dence of the destructive consequences of long-term unemployment upon

---

[2] M. Rosenberg. *Society and the Adolescent Self-Image.* Princeton, Princeton Uni-versity Press, 1965.

TABLE 5.4 *Regularity of father's employment and child's self-esteem*

| Regularity of father's employment | Subjective self-esteem | | |
|---|---|---|---|
| | Low | Medium | High |
| Occasionally, often out of work | 27.3% (9) | 23.5% (4) | 3.3% (1) |
| Rarely, if ever, out of work | 72.7% (24) | 76.5% (13) | 96.7% (29) |
| Totals | 100.0% (33) | 100.0% (17) | 100.0% (30) |

$\chi^2 = 6.78$    df = 2    p < .05

*Source:* Subject's questionnaire.

personality[3,4] for us to believe that its effects are generally demeaning. There may be subcultural groups in which unemployment is not assumed to reflect on one's competence or worthiness, but these appear to be rare in the general pattern of American society. For the purposes of our study we shall assume that fathers who are unemployed tend to feel they are unsuccessful and are apt to communicate this feeling to their sons. As one test of this hypothesis, we asked our subjects whether their fathers had been and were regularly employed.

The answers to that question, presented in Table 5.4, indicate that fathers of children with high self-esteem are least likely to show irregular employment. The percentage of fathers with histories of unemployment was only 3.3 for children with high self-esteem. This is significantly lower than the percentages obtained for children with low (27.3 percent) and medium (23.5 percent) self-esteem. In interpreting this finding we should note that we are relating the child's perception of whether his father is regularly employed to his own feelings of worth. His father's self-esteem, though of considerable interest and significance, remains unknown. Nor do we have any other way of knowing, at this point, the extent to which the father is or has been unemployed. Whatever the "reality," these findings indicate that if the child perceives that his father is unemployed there is less likelihood of positive self-esteem in the son.

The relationship between self-esteem and regularity of employment suggests that this relationship may at least partially underlie our findings for

---

[3] M. Jahoda, P. Lazarsfeld, and H. Zeisl. *Die Arbeitslosen von Marienthal.* Leipzig, Herzal, 1933.

[4] M. Komarovsky. *The Unemployed Man and his Family.* New York, Dryden Press, 1940.

TABLE 5.5 *Extent of father's job-related absence from home and child's self-esteem*

| Extent of father's absence | Discrepant self-esteem | |
| --- | --- | --- |
| | High discrepancy groups (High-Low, Low-High) | Low discrepancy groups (High-High, Medium-Medium, Low-Low) |
| Father absent frequently | 48.3% (15) | 18.0% (7) |
| Father rarely, never absent | 51.7% (16) | 82.0% (32) |
| Totals | 100.0% (31) | 100.0% (39) |

$\chi^2 = 6.08$      df $= 1$      p $< .05$

*Source:* Mother's interview.

social class. The decreased likelihood of unemployment in the higher classes should provide fewer circumstances in which fathers are perceived as ineffectual. In the eyes of the child, parental failure is likely to be notable when the parent is at home, worried about financial matters, and discouraged or bitter about his inability to find a means to support his family and thereby demonstrate his prowess. Such a situation could conceivably develop at any level of the social structure but it is far more likely to occur, because of differential unemployment rates, to persons lower in the class structure. An unemployed executive, screenwriter, or office clerk is as likely to be uncertain of his adequacy as is a stevedore or assembly-line worker if unemployment extends over months or years. In the effective interpersonal environment of the child, a father's doubt about his powers assumes considerable significance. In addition, extended or frequent unemployment is likely to evoke sympathy, pity, or derision from the broader community, as well as from the father's peers, further subverting the child's confidence in his father's powers.

Another aspect of the father's occupation that may affect his child is his certainty that he can earn a living wage. In some occupations, of which sales work is but one example, the individual may continually have to seek and develop new ideas or clients. Such occupations may provide continual employment but they require constant personal attention. They may also require considerable travel by the individual and, quite often, moves by his family. To determine whether such conditions might affect the child's self-esteem we included two questions on sense of stability in our mother interview schedule. The first question asked how frequently the husband's job required him to travel; the second asked the mother to appraise the sense

TABLE 5.6 *Father's sense of stability in employment and child's self-esteem*

| Father's employment stability | Discrepant self-esteem | |
| --- | --- | --- |
| | High discrepancy groups (High-Low, Low-High) | Low discrepancy groups (High-High, Medium-Medium, Low-Low) |
| Position labile, unsettled | 22.6% (7) | 00.0% (0) |
| Position stable, secure | 77.4% (24) | 100.0% (39) |
| Totals | 100.0% (31) | 100.0% (39) |

$\chi^2 = 7.44$     df $= 1$     p $< .01$

*Source:* Mother's interview.

of stability and permanency in her husband's occupation. The distribution of responses to those questions is presented in Tables 5.5 and 5.6.

The results in Table 5.5 indicate that children who manifest a discrepancy between subjective and behavioral self-esteem are more likely to have fathers whose positions require frequent travel. Whereas 48.3 percent of the children with discrepant self-esteem have fathers who travel, the comparable figure for nondiscrepant children is only 18 percent. This suggests that the father's intermittent absence from home does not reduce the child's estimation of himself but rather results in uncertainty about how valuable he is. This same effect results where the father's occupation situation is labile and unsettled (Table 5.6). In those families where the mother reports that her husband's occupational situation does not provide him with a sense of personal stability, her son manifests discordance between subjective and behavioral self-esteem. Among the nondiscrepant children, we find no cases where the parent feels unstable, but 22.6 percent of the mothers of discrepant children report that their husband's employment is unstable. The resulting uncertainty of the child as to his own value is reflected in disparate ways of behaving and perceiving oneself; it may also be reflected by sensitivity to criticism and public self-aggrandizement. This suggests that defensive reactions are likely to result from uncertain self-esteem rather than a definitely low opinion of one's worth. It also suggests that discrepancy between subjective and behavioral indices of esteem stems from ambiguous and unsettled conditions rather than harsh or rejecting treatment. Defensive—that is, uncertain—self-esteem apparently differs from low self-esteem in its antecedents as well as its consequences.

## MOTHER'S WORK HISTORY

The father's occupation and income is the major determinant of a family's status, but there are a large number of cases where the mother makes a material, if not a major contribution. In over 30 percent of American families, the wife is engaged in part-time or full-time work. The nature and extent of employment tends to vary with class[5] but its prevalence in the middle and upper classes shows definite and regular indications of increase. The motives for working vary with class, region, and individual. The most commonly accepted distinctions are that women in the higher social classes tend to work more for reasons of intellectual stimulation and self-fulfillment, middle class women to improve their standard of living, and lower class women to help provide the basic essentials of life. (There are, of course, the single, divorced, or widowed women who are the sole providers for their family unit. These women exist in all classes and they work, first and foremost, out of necessity.) There has been much argument about the effects of a wife's absence from home upon the personality development of her children. "How is a child affected by his mother's absence?" "What will be the impact upon his present and future mental health?" "Is he more apt to become a delinquent?" The answers to these and similar questions are now beginning to appear. Our own study contributes to this clarification by determining how a child's self-esteem is affected by the mother's work history.

Our discussion will focus upon two aspects of the mother's work history. These deal with the extent to which the mother has been employed either part or full time and the extent to which she gained satisfaction from her work. These questions were asked of both mother and son so that we could compare reports on the mother's work history and the attitudes associated with her employment. Turning first to the question of whether the mother worked since the child's birth (Table 5.7), we find that there is no relationship between the frequency of the mother's working and the child's self-esteem ($\chi^2 = 3.09$, df = 2, p <.30). The percentages of mothers regularly or occasionally employed since the child's birth are 57.6 percent for the high self-esteem group, 82.4 percent for the medium self-esteem group, and 63.3 percent for the low self-esteem group. Thirty-five percent of the mothers report that they have rarely if ever worked since their child's arrival, but these women are almost as likely to be mothers of children with low self-

[5] A. B. Hollingshead and F. C. Redlich. *Social Class and Mental Illness.* New York, Wiley, 1958.

TABLE 5.7 *Extent to which mother has worked since child's birth*

| Extent of mother's work | Subjective self-esteem | | |
|---|---|---|---|
| | Low | Medium | High |
| Never or rarely worked | 36.7% (11) | 17.6% (3) | 42.4% (14) |
| Occasionally or regularly worked | 63.3% (19) | 82.4% (14) | 57.6% (19) |
| Totals | 100.0% (30) | 100.0% (17) | 100.0% (33) |

$\chi^2 = 3.09$     df $= 2$     p $<$ .30

*Source:* Mother's interview.

TABLE 5.8 *Extent to which mother worked while child was in grade school*

| Extent of mother's work | Subjective self-esteem | | |
|---|---|---|---|
| | Low | Medium | High |
| Never or rarely worked | 38.7% (12) | 29.4% (5) | 34.5% (10) |
| Occasionally or regularly worked | 61.3% (19) | 70.6% (12) | 65.5% (19) |
| Totals | 100.0% (31) | 100.0% (17) | 100.0% (29) |

$\chi^2 = .42$     df $= 2$     p $<$ .80

*Source:* Subject's questionnaire.

esteem (36.7 percent) as high self-esteem (42.4 percent). The children's reports of whether their mother worked during their school years (Table 5.8) are similar to those obtained from the mothers. From the results it appears that children whose mothers work do not necessarily feel that they are unimportant or rejected. Presumably it is the way her work is interpreted and the way she and the family evaluate her absence that determine whether her children show any adverse effects.

The length of the mother's employment does, however, tend to be *positively* related to her children's subjective esteem ($\chi^2 = 4.79$, df $= 2$, p $<$.10). The *higher* the child's self-esteem the more probable it is that his mother has been regularly employed for more than one year. This revealing aspect of the mother's work history, obtained during the course of the interview, is summarized in Table 5.9. We find that 33.3 percent of the mothers of children with high self-esteem have been employed for more than one

TABLE 5.9 *Length of continuous employment of mother during child's school years*

| Length of mother's employment | Subjective self-esteem | | |
|---|---|---|---|
| | Low | Medium | High |
| Less than 12 months | 90.0% (27) | 75.0% (12) | 66.7% (20) |
| More than 12 months | 10.0% (3) | 25.0% (4) | 33.3% (10) |
| Totals | 100.0% (30) | 100.0% (16) | 100.0% (30) |
| $\chi^2 = 4.79$  df = 2 | p < .10 | | |

*Source:* Mother's interview.

year. The equivalent percentage for mothers of children with medium self-esteem is 25.0 percent, and that of the low self-esteem group is only 10 percent. As the high self-esteem group has the highest socioeconomic position, the length of employment cannot reflect absolute economic necessity. It may reflect a familial or personal aspiration for a materially enhanced way of life or it may reflect the mother's personal inclinations for independence from her homemaking duties. In either event, it is clear that her working and her necessary absence from home that this signifies, does not lower her child's self-esteem. Not only does the child not interpret his mother's employment as a personal rejection, he appears all the more likely to express a favorable self-regard.

This somewhat surprising finding requires a closer examination. Inasmuch as frequency of employment is unrelated to self-esteem and length *is* related, the mother's mere absence from the home is not, in itself, a sufficient condition for enhancing self-esteem. Presumably there is some characteristic of mothers who seek or engage in regular employment, or some consequences of their employment, that facilitates the development of high self-esteem in their children. Possibly mothers who engage in long-term employment are more assured and reliant, and convey their sense of reliance to their children.[6] Or possibly, if the mother is regularly employed, the child might achieve greater independence and encounter and complete a greater number of tasks. Underlying both these possibilities is the mother's attitude toward her work. If she is dissatisfied with her work and desires to stay at home, she is likely

[6] Though it might be possible that mothers who engage in long-term employment are more educated than others, our findings indicate that the extent of the mother's education is unrelated to her employment history. Further, the extent of her education is unrelated to the child's self-esteem.

to convey her dissatisfaction to her children. The facilitating effects of her absence might remain, but might also be deliberately or unconsciously subverted. As an indirect index of the mother's attitude, we asked the mothers whether they would stop working if they had the opportunity or if they would continue. More mothers of children with high self-esteem responded that they wanted to continue (45.5 percent) than did mothers of children with medium or low self-esteem. Over 70 percent of the mothers of children with lesser esteem indicated that they would prefer to stop if the opportunity arose. Although the differences between the groups are not striking ($\chi^2 = 3.89$, df = 2, p < .15), the results do suggest that the mothers of children with high self-esteem are more satisfied with their work.

The positive attitude of these mothers and the greater regularity of their employment suggest that these women are relatively independent persons who wish to establish lives of their own. They apparently enjoy their work and have few anxieties about its consequences for themselves or their children. These speculations, advanced as hypotheses in the present context, will be subjected to critical examination in our next chapter, Parental Characteristics.

In summary, we can cite several positive and negative findings in the relationship between self-esteem and social background. Social class appears to be positively related to self-esteem, even though the relationship is weaker than had been expected. Persons in the higher (upper middle) social classes are more likely to have high self-esteem than persons in the middle-middle or working classes. Jews are more likely to report high self-esteem than are Protestants or Catholics. This finding appears to be related to differences in parental attention provided by members of the different faiths. The father's work history is related to his son's self-esteem in two ways. Children with low self-esteem are likely to have fathers who have been unemployed for extended periods; children whose expression of self-esteem is not integrated (discrepant groups—High-Low and Low-High) are more likely to have fathers whose jobs require frequent absences and whose positions are regarded as unstable. There is no relationship between the child's self-esteem and the extent to which the mother is presently employed or was employed during his earlier childhood. The mothers of children with high self-esteem are likely to have worked for long periods and to express more favorable attitudes toward their work. The results indicate that broad social contexts and prestige hierarchies do not have as pervasive and significant effects upon self-esteem as is generally assumed, but suggest instead that conditions in the effective interpersonal environment are employed to judge whether one is appreciated and respected. Reflected appraisal apparently is given an immediate social context, with such conditions as parental interest and father's occupational success assuming personal significance. The general social definition of success, which William James assumed to be commonly shared and accepted by the members of any given society, does not appear to be as common and potent an influence as he believed.

# Chapter six

# PARENTAL CHARACTERISTICS RELATED TO SELF-ESTEEM

The individuals in any given social position share many values, experiences, and activities, but each is nonetheless unique in his characteristics. Possessing differing abilities, manifesting different appearances, and backed by their individual childhood experiences, they are a highly varied lot. The regularities we note by virtue of cultural and social definitions form outer limits and channels within which individual expression takes place. We have, to this point, emphasized those regularities, since they provide an individual's anchoring points in his social world. Guided by the knowledge that many of these anchoring points are related to self-esteem, we can take a more considered look at more specific, individual sources of variation. In the present chapter we shall examine several parental characteristics which, we hypothesized, were related to self-esteem. These will deal largely with the mother's characteristics, although we do have some limited information also on the fathers of our subjects. Following this discussion of the parents individually we shall examine several indices of mother-father interaction, such as decision making and conflict, and determine how these are related to self-esteem.

TABLE 6.1 *Rating of mother's self-esteem: assurance, poise, reactions to sensitive and confidential materials*

| Rating of mother's self-esteem | Child's subjective self-esteem | | |
|---|---|---|---|
| | Low | Medium | High |
| Below average | 63.3% (19) | 35.3% (6) | 24.3% (8) |
| Average and above average | 36.7% (11) | 64.7% (11) | 75.7% (28) |
| Totals | 100.0% (30) | 100.0% (17) | 100.0% (36) |

$x^2 = 10.22$     df $= 2$     p $< .01$

*Source:* Interviewer's report.

## THE MOTHER'S SELF-ESTEEM AND STABILITY

Although the mothers of our subjects were not formally tested, our interviewers rated them on a number of personality characteristics; the ratings were made after completion of the mother interview, which averaged over 2 hours. We should again note that the interviewers were experienced psychologists and social workers who had been trained in the use of these procedures and scales. They were unaware of the child's self-esteem or other of his personality characteristics at the time the interview was conducted. They were asked to rate the mother's self-esteem and her emotional stability, and to note any indications of unusual or interesting behavior.

The most noteworthy feature of the interviewer's rating of maternal self-esteem is the low rating of mothers of children with low self-esteem (Table 6.1). Almost two-thirds of these mothers (63.3 percent) are rated below average in poise and assurance. This compares with 35.3 percent for the mothers of children with medium self-esteem and 24.3 percent for the mothers of children with high self-esteem. Although these ratings indicate that the interviewers did not make a marked distinction between the mothers of these last two groups, their comments indicate that such a distinction was indeed made. In their postinterview statements of personal reactions to the mother, the interviewers indicated negative reactions more frequently toward the mothers of children with medium self-esteem than toward mothers of children with high self-esteem (52.9 percent versus 42.4 percent). The interviewers responded most negatively to the mothers of children with low self-esteem: 56.7 percent of the ratings were negative.

The interviewers were also asked to rate the mother's emotional stability

TABLE 6.2 *Rating of mother's emotional stability:*
*frequency of problems, anxieties*

| Rating of mother's stability | Child's subjective self-esteem | | |
| --- | --- | --- | --- |
| | Low | Medium | High |
| Relatively troubled, insecure, unstable | 43.3% (13) | 35.3% (6) | 15.2% (5) |
| Relatively stable and free of symptoms | 56.7% (17) | 64.7% (11) | 84.8% (29) |
| Totals | 100.0% (30) | 100.0% (17) | 100.0% (34) |

$\chi^2 = 6.22$　　　df $= 2$　　　p $< .05$

*Source:* Interviewer's report.

as manifested in her reactions and responses to the interviewer. A negative rating on this scale indicates difficulty in controlling expressions of anxiety and overt expressions of abnormal or symptomatic behavior. Analysis of these ratings reveals that the mothers of children with high self-esteem are rated negatively in only 15.2 percent of the cases. This compares with 35.3 percent negative ratings for the mothers of the middle group and 27.6 percent for the mothers of children with low self-esteem—a marked and statistically significant difference ($\chi^2 = 6.22$, df $= 2$, p $< .05$).

We conclude that the mothers of children with high self-esteem tend to be high in their own self-esteem. These mothers are regarded as most stable under the relatively trying situation of a personal interview. The interviewers' favorable reactions to them would appear to stem, in part at least, from their calm, poised, and direct responses to the questions and issues posed. The mothers of children with low self-esteem are themselves seen to be low in self-esteem and fairly apt to be emotionally unstable. The over-all impression is that the mothers of children who differ in self-esteem are themselves similarly different in self-esteem. How this sense of self-worth is conveyed from one generation to the next and what forces underlie and contribute to its expression will be explored in the chapters that follow. We may here conjecture—and it is only conjecture at this point—that women with high self-esteem are more likely to marry men who are themselves high in self-esteem; these fathers may thus serve as models of assurance and masculinity for their sons. And if persons who are high in their own esteem have less need to seek secondary sources of gratification and less need to manifest prowess by manipulating others, we may assume that these mothers permit greater independence and latitude to their children.

The use of interviewer ratings raises a methodological issue that has clouded acceptance of other studies. One of the critiques of *The Authoritarian Personality*[1] was that blind ratings of the interviews did not necessarily preclude global judgments on the characteristics of the subject.[2] Possibly the interviewers and raters possessed or formed some common theories about the characteristics and behaviors of mothers who would rear children with high, medium, and low self-esteem. If such global guesses could be accurately made, it is possible that they might account for many of the other, nonrating associations between parental practices and esteem. Though there is no absolute manner of proving or disproving the influence of the interviewers' and raters' intuitive assessments, there are several reasons for believing that these judgments were not a salient factor. Foremost is the consideration that many of our findings run contrary to popular, common-sense interpretations of how self-esteem develops. As later chapters will indicate, we find that certain practices and attitudes generally labeled as autocratic and restrictive are, in fact, associated with high rather than low self-esteem. For the interviewers and raters to associate such practices with the formation of high esteem would mean that they, *as a group,* had a common theory that was at variance with that held by most professionals and (middle class) parents. This might conceivably hold for individual interviewers and raters but it is difficult to believe it could account for such great shifts as would be necessary to achieve statistically significant reverse trends across three interviewers and three raters. In effect, global judgments of respondents and common-sense theories of behavior are less likely to be a significant influence when the ratings of several observers run counter to popular and professional opinion. In addition, there are a large number of instances that show negative results for variables often assumed to be associated with esteem. Thus at various points our findings reveal that self-esteem is unrelated to social class, mother employment, type of feeding, childhood trauma, and delinquency. The frequency of such findings suggests that our raters did not permit much intrusion of convictions and prejudices upon the immediate performance of their duties. There may well have been individual questions on which this occurred for individual interviewers, but the negative results and findings that run counter to prevailing and common-sense theories suggest that there were no systematic biases or preconceptions introduced by our group of raters.

---

[1] J. W. Adorno, E. Frenkel-Brunswik, D. J. Levinson, and R. N. Sanford. *The Authoritarian Personality.* New York, Harper, 1950.

[2] R. Christie and M. Jahoda (Eds.). *Studies in the Scope and Method of "The Authoritarian Personality."* Glencoe, Ill., The Free Press, 1954.

TABLE 6.3 *Qualities parents appreciate most in their sons*

| Parental values | Subjective self-esteem | | |
|---|---|---|---|
| | Low | Medium | High |
| Strength and aggressiveness[a] | 17.9% (5) | 00.0% (0) | 15.0% (3) |
| Achievement[b] | 32.1% (9) | 83.3% (5) | 65.0% (13) |
| Accommodation[c] | 50.0% (14) | 16.7% (1) | 20.0% (4) |
| Totals | 100.0% (28) | 100.0% (6) | 100.0% (20) |

$\chi^2 = 8.73$        df = 4        p < .08

*Source:* Subject's questionnaire.
[a] Defending and asserting one's rights.
[b] Doing well in school.
[c] Attention and concern for others (helpful, kind, obedient).

## PARENTAL VALUES

Parents influence their children not only by what they are and what they believe but especially by what they do. The codes of behavior they set before their children, both by tuition and example, serve as guides to achieving success and power. Parents provide the criteria by which performance is interpreted and courses of action established, revealing what the parents believe to be fitting and proper behavior. As part of the child questionnaire we asked our subjects the values most strongly prized by their fathers and mothers. A large number of children are not sure of the values that would be most important to their parents. Among those who are able to make definitive statements, we find different values emphasized by parents of children who differ in self-esteem. Children with low self-esteem are more likely to claim that their parents emphasize and prize accommodation than are the parents of children with medium or high self-esteem (Table 6.3). Under the term accommodation we include such characteristics as obedience, helpfulness, adjustment to others, kindness, good grooming, and cordial relationships with one's peers. As judged by their son's reports, 50 percent of parents of children with low self-esteem regard accommodation as an important value. This is more than twice the percentage of parents who emphasize accommodation to children in either of the other two groups. The values reported for the parents of these children with higher self-esteem are heavily weighted toward superior achievement. Whether the parental values reported by these children are those their parents would profess cannot be ascertained from our data, nor is it necessarily crucial to our deliberation. These are the values that the

TABLE 6.4 *Incidence of previous marriages and child's self-esteem*

| Previous marriages | Subjective self-esteem | | |
| --- | --- | --- | --- |
| | Low | Medium | High |
| No previous marriages by either partner | 80.0% (24) | 94.1% (16) | 97.0% (32) |
| One or more previous marriages by either partner | 20.0% (6) | 5.9% (1) | 3.0% (1) |
| Totals | 100.0% (30) | 100.0% (17) | 100.0% (33) |

$x^2 = 5.40$  df = 2  p < .07

*Source:* Mother's interview.

children believe their parents favor and that apparently serve as the children's guides. The beliefs may be erroneous or distorted, but nonetheless they exert their influence upon the child. The values stressed by parents of children with low self-esteem are those that make them acceptable and pleasing to others. Judging by their emphasis on accommodation and lack of concern with achievement, these parents and children presumably rely on pleasing others rather than self-competence for their feelings of success.

### MARITAL HISTORY

Our questionnaires and schedule raised several questions on the marital history of our subjects' parents—possible prior marriages by either partner, the conditions following any marital breakup, and whether the marital partners came from different religious backgrounds. Before examining the responses to these questions, we should note that one criterion for inclusion in our study was that the subject be a member of an intact nuclear family at the time he was selected; that is, the family unit consisted of a husband and wife residing in the same household, and the mother was the natural parent of the subject. Analysis of our results on the incidence of previous marriages (Table 6.4) indicates that these occurred with greater frequency in the backgrounds of subjects with low self-esteem. In 20 percent of these families (6 cases out of 30) we find that the mother reports a prior marriage, but the other two groups display only 1 case each.

This finding is consistent with that obtained by Rosenberg, who noted that children from families marked by divorce and separation were lower in self-esteem. He proposed three causes that might underlie the poorer self-appraisal

TABLE 6.5 *Number of stepparents, foster parents, and guardians and child's self-esteem*

| Stepparents or guardians | Subjective self-esteem | | |
|---|---|---|---|
| | Low | Medium | High |
| No stepparents, foster parents, or guardians | 84.8% (28) | 100.0% (15) | 100.0% (33) |
| One or more stepparents, foster parents, or guardians | 15.2% (5) | 00.0% (0) | 00.0% (0) |
| Totals | 100.0% (33) | 100.0% (15) | 100.0% (33) |

$\chi^2 = 7.75$      df $= 2$      p $< .05$

*Source:* Subject's interview.

of children from broken families. These are the significance of divorce in the light of religious and subcultural norms and its indication of prior conflict, the possible negative effects of remarriage upon the child, and the greater financial burdens incurred when the stability of the family is disrupted by the departure of one of its members. Our study reveals that remarriage is indeed associated with lower esteem in the child, although this may be partly a function of the child's age when remarriage occurs. This should not be particularly surprising, since the parent's remarriage generally means that less attention is given the child and he must at the same time share his parent's time and affection. There is also the uncertainty of how he will be accepted by the new parent, with a possible change in established values and patterns of behavior. These changes may bring him into conflict with the memory of his first parent and thereby threaten earlier bases of esteem.

One set of questions included in the child questionnaire allowed us to cross-check the mother's responses on her marital history and elaborate them still further. These questions dealt with the incidence of stepparents, foster parents, and guardians in the child's life history (Table 6.5). Analysis of these responses reveals that such parents are more likely to rear children with low self-esteem than are the natural parents. There were only 5 children in our study who had a substitute parent, and all of them had low self-esteem. The nonparental figures were stepparents (rather than guardians or others); the marital breakup occurred when the children were between four and nine years of age; and there were no instances of multiple remarriage. The sample is too small to warrant generalizations on the effects of remarriage upon children, but they are suggestive. The child's reports on the incidence of step-

TABLE 6.6 *Religious differences of parents and child's self-esteem*

| | Discrepant self-esteem | |
|---|---|---|
| Religious differences | High discrepancy groups (High-Low, Low-High) | Low discrepancy groups (High-High, Medium-Medium, Low-Low) |
| Partners of different religion | 22.6% (7) | 8.2% (4) |
| Partners of same religion | 77.4% (24) | 91.8% (45) |
| Totals | 100.0% (31) | 100.0% (49) |
| $\chi^2 = 2.22$    df $= 1$    p $< .05$ | | |

*Source:* Mother's interview.

parents (Table 6.5) is also consistent with the mother's report on previous marriages.

The final aspect of the marital history we shall consider is the incidence of religious intermarriage. Our results show (Table 6.6) that marriages between persons of different religions occur almost three times as often in the families of children who manifest large self-behavioral discrepancies as among those with little discrepancy. Although this finding does fall short of conventional levels of statistical significance ($\chi^2 = 2.22$, df $= 1$, p $< .15$), it is consistent with previous indications of instability in the families of highly discrepant children. These families are notable for the frequency of the father's absence, the sense of instability surrounding his employment, and, as we now note, differences in the religious backgrounds of husband and wife. The pattern is theoretically meaningful as well as consistent, and suggests that defensiveness is likely to occur when the father model is absent or insecure, or when the models themselves are of disparate backgrounds. Again we note that defensiveness does not stem from low self-esteem but from non-integration of subjective experience and behavioral expression.

## PARENTAL ROLE BEHAVIOR

The behavior of each parent represents a personal expression of the behavior designated as acceptable and necessary by the members of his social group. Although limited to a great extent by the demands of the child and social expectations, definitions of the parental role are neither precise nor all encompassing. They indicate the general limits of acceptable behavior without specifying the exact details of goals and means. This is partially a function of the great social diversity of modern America, which results in differing norms for persons in different ethnic, racial, regional, and social groups. Lower class parents may learn that it is proper for them to punish their children severely; white middle class parents may believe they should be pals to their sons; Chinese fathers are likely to take their familial responsibilities seriously; many Negro fathers assume that their responsibilities are limited and transitory. These social definitions of what parenthood signifies and how it should be conducted play an important role in shaping parental behavior, but there is considerable individual variation in the acceptance and expression of group norms. Here, as in other forms of behavior, we find that social norms are filtered through the prism of individual needs. In this section we shall examine the role definitions of mothers and fathers whose children differ in self-esteem and try to determine whether any systematic relationships exist between those definitions and their children's feelings of personal worth.

A woman's concept of motherhood may differ in several respects from the definitions of other women. She may view the act of having children as self-fulfilling, onerous, or natural; she may assume that the children she bears are an extension of herself, or are independent persons; she may regard the inevitable limitations of childrearing as burdensome, inevitable, or pleasurable. The way she perceives her duties and responsibilities, the assumptions she makes, and the expectations she possesses will have marked influence upon how the mother responds to her children. In this study we are examining the role definitions of women who have been mothers for at least ten years. The definitions reported may have been those present at earlier periods of marriage and childrearing, but we have no assurance that this is indeed the case. All we can say with confidence is that the role definitions reported by these mothers are those they presently hold or believe to be desirable. As such, they represent a belief of what motherhood can offer and how it should be conducted.

The interview included questions on the reasons for having children and on any preferences for children of either sex. Mothers of children with high self-esteem are much more likely to view it as a natural, expected occurrence than mothers in the other two groups (Table 6.7). Both these groups give answers that were more emotional and romantically tinged—in terms of creative expression, self-fulfillment, and the pleasures associated with children ($\chi^2 = 5.61$, df = 2, p < .05). These results suggest that the mothers in the high self-esteem group are less idealistic in their expectations and definitions of what motherhood signifies and involves in their own lives. Another possibility is that these mothers see less need to give the interviewer

TABLE 6.7 *Mother's reasons for having children*

| Reasons for having children | Subjective self-esteem | | |
|---|---|---|---|
| | Low | Medium | High |
| Natural event, part of being married | 38.7% (12) | 47.1% (8) | 67.6% (23) |
| Self-fulfillment, personal needs and expression | 61.3% (19) | 52.9% (9) | 32.4% (11) |
| Totals | 100.0% (31) | 100.0% (17) | 100.0% (34) |

$\chi^2 = 5.61$    df $= 2$    p $<$ .05

Source: Mother's interview.

a romanticized reason for their maternity. In either case, they appear to be more direct and down-to-earth in the reasons they give for bearing children.

Another expression of the reality orientation of the mothers of children with high self-esteem is revealed in their statements regarding preferences for children of either sex. Inasmuch as parents cannot control the sex of a child, the expression of a preference would presumably reflect personal needs rather than realistic expectations. The preference cannot be effected by the mothers' wishes and is certain to fail in half the cases. More mothers of children with high self-esteem express *no* preference for boys or girls (39.4 percent) than do the mothers of children with medium (25.3 percent) or low (26.7 percent) self-esteem. The mothers of children with lesser self-esteem, who themselves appear to be lesser in esteem, apparently cannot tolerate the uncertainty of prenatal development. They seek to circumscribe and structure the uncertainty of sex determination, and thereby try to concretize that which is indeterminate. This suggests a need for definiteness and control that is considerably greater among the mothers of low self-esteem children than it is among the high self-esteem group. The combination of romanticized reasons for having children and early definite sex preferences suggests that these women are not very logical in their interpretation and resolution of everyday issues. The statements of the high self-esteem group, on the other hand, reflect an appreciation of the conditions of life as it must be confronted and lived.

Another aspect of maternal role definition is the mother's interpretation of what happens to her physical stamina and social life as a result of child-rearing. The birth and rearing of an infant inevitably impose restrictions upon the parents' previous activities and freedom. The pregnant woman

TABLE 6.8 *"Taking care of a small baby is something that no woman should be expected to do all by herself"*

| Reply | Subjective self-esteem | | |
| | Low | Medium | High |
|---|---|---|---|
| Agree | 73.5% (25) | 50.0% (8) | 38.7% (12) |
| Disagree | 26.5% (9) | 50.0% (8) | 61.3% (19) |
| Totals | 100.0% (34) | 100.0% (16) | 100.0% (31) |

$\chi^a = 8.21$     df = 2     $p < .05$

*Source:* Mother's questionnaire.

cannot be as active as she previously was; the mother of an infant or young child must adhere to feeding and sleep schedules; and the mothers of older children must still assume responsibility for their safety and well-being. The responsibilities thus imposed may be interpreted and met in various ways. To determine how these mothers viewed the consequences of maternity, we employed two questions from the Parent Attitude Research Instrument (PARI). The first of these stated, "Taking care of a small baby is something no woman should be asked to do all by herself." Table 6.8 indicates the percentage and number of mothers in the subjective self-esteem groups who agreed or disagreed with this statement. Their responses indicate a regular, positive relationship between the mothers' belief that a woman should take care of her child by herself and her child's self-esteem. Sixty-one percent of the high self-esteem mothers disagree with the statement, thereby expressing the belief that mothers *should* be expected to assume their duties of child-rearing without outside assistance. This percentage (61.3 percent) is more than twice that of mothers in the low self-esteem group (26.5 percent) and above that of mothers of children with medium self-esteem (50.0 percent). This suggests that the mothers of children with high self-esteem are more self-reliant and are more willing, and possibly able, to accept the responsibilities and demands of parenthood.

Our second question on the consequences of parenthood stated, "Most women need more time than they are given to rest up after going through childbirth." Agreement with this question indicated the mother's belief that childbirth was a demanding and exhausting experience and that more rest was needed before returning to the demands of child care and homemaking. Our results show (Table 6.9) that mothers in the lowest group are much more likely (82.4 percent) to agree with this statement than are the mothers

TABLE 6.9 *"Most women need more time than they are given to rest up in the home after going through childbirth"*

| | Child's subjective self-esteem | | |
|---|---|---|---|
| Reply | Low | Medium | High |
| Agree | 82.4% (28) | 50.0% (8) | 54.8% (17) |
| Disagree | 17.6% (6) | 50.0% (8) | 45.2% (14) |
| Totals | 100.0% (34) | 100.0% (16) | 100.0% (31) |

$x^2 = 7.53$     df $= 2$     p $< .05$

*Source:* Mother's questionnaire.

TABLE 6.10 *Mother's acceptance of her role as mother*

| | Subjective self-esteem | | |
|---|---|---|---|
| Degree of acceptance | Low | Medium | High |
| Relatively rejecting | 67.7% (21) | 58.8% (10) | 40.6% (13) |
| Relatively accepting | 32.3% (10) | 41.2% (7) | 59.4% (19) |
| Totals | 100.0% (31) | 100.0% (17) | 100.0% (32) |

$x^2 = 4.80$     df $= 2$     p $< .10$

*Source:* Mother's interview.

of children with high (54.8 percent) and medium (50.0 percent) self-esteem. Mothers in the lowest group apparently feel they need more time to recuperate from the physical and psychological consequences of childbirth than do the mothers in the other groups, possibly believing themselves to be less resilient. Together with the findings of the previous question, the results suggest that the mothers of children with low self-esteem believe they are less able to cope with the difficulties of birth and early care than are mothers of children with higher self-esteem.

Our final item on the mother's definition of her role was based upon a scale evaluating the mother's acceptance of her role. The scale was applied to the mother's responses to six interview questions, extending in five steps from extreme acceptance to extreme rejection. Acceptance was indicated by a favorable, agreeable disposition toward the chores, the isolation, and the physical demands imposed by maternity; rejection was indicated by negative attitudes and actions toward these duties and limitations. Table 6.10 indicates the percentage of mothers in each of the subjective self-esteem groups who accept or reject their maternal roles. The mothers in the highest group are most likely to accept their maternal roles (59.4 percent), and the mothers in the lowest group are least likely to accept their roles (32.3 percent). The percentage of mothers of children with medium self-esteem who are accepting (41.2 percent) falls between the other two groups. This finding corroborates our earlier impression that the mothers of children with high self-esteem appreciate the implications of maternity and childrearing and further indicates that these women have accepted the realities of the conditions imposed.

To recapitulate our findings on the mothers' definitions of their roles, mothers in the highest group tend to view childbearing in a direct and realistic manner. They look at childbearing as a natural event, express no preference for children of either sex, and are self-reliant and resilient in dealing with issues surrounding their maternity. They are more accepting of the consequences of maternity for their own social activities and the greater physical efforts and attention it requires. Presumably they see the conditions associated with childrearing as necessary and also see themselves as capable of dealing with them in an effective manner. This logical, straightforward acceptance of the manifold realistic obligations of motherhood might be viewed as acquiescence with social norms, but, as we shall show, these mothers are quite capable of rejecting popular opinion. Their attitudes and behavior in their maternal roles apparently reflect personal convictions about their responsibilities and how they should be carried out.

PATERNAL ROLE

We have no direct evidence on the father's definition of his role, but we did obtain information on this subject from his wife and son. To be sure, these data indicated how the mother and son viewed the father's performance, not how he himself defined it or whether he found his actions satisfying. Accordingly, these inferences on paternal role behavior are more suspect than are those for the mother's role definition. Their acceptability hinges in part upon the cross-validation of the reports of mother and son, and in part upon the conceptual relationship between these and other findings.

Our first information on the father's involvement in childrearing was obtained during the course of the mother interview. One of our questions asked the mother to appraise the father's performance, both in terms of what he did and whether she was satisfied with the outcome. As an index of what we were seeking we asked whether he was spending enough time with the

TABLE 6.11 *Mother's satisfaction with father's performance in rearing child*

| Degree of satisfaction | Subjective self-esteem | | |
| --- | --- | --- | --- |
| | Low | Medium | High |
| Tends to be dissatisfied | 23.3% (7) | 00.0% (0) | 6.1% (2) |
| Generally pleased | 76.7% (23) | 100.0% (17) | 93.9% (31) |
| Totals | 100.0% (30) | 100.0% (17) | 100.0% (33) |
| $\chi^2 = 7.53$    df = 2    p < .05 | | | |

*Source:* Mother's interview.

child, and had established a good relationship with him. In this question, as in all others, we asked the mother to appraise the attitudes and relationships specifically directed toward our subject rather than toward all her children. The mothers' responses reveal that they were almost invariably satisfied with the performance of fathers in the high (93.3 percent) and medium (100.0 percent) groups but frequently dissatisfied (76.7 percent) with the fathers in the lowest group (Table 6.11). The differences between the various levels of subjective self-esteem were large enough to show that they were not a chance occurrence ($\chi^2 = 7.43$, df = 2, p < .05). Although these reactions do not indicate how the father defines his role, they do suggest that the mothers of children with high and medium self-esteem are more in agreement with their husbands' definition of the paternal role than are the mothers of children with low self-esteem. The findings suggest that the fathers in the two highest groups have a closer and more congenial relationship with their sons than do the fathers of children with low self-esteem.

To ascertain how the son viewed this relationship, we asked him to indicate the person in whom he was most likely to confide. Although this question does not reveal the absolute relationship between father and son, it does indicate the relative closeness to father, mother, or other persons, in and out of the family. Thus, a statement that the father is not a confidant would not necessarily signify social distance or discord between father and son. It is quite possible that the two could have a fairly close relationship without the son regarding his father as his major confidant. Following this line of reasoning, we might conclude that a positive statement pointing to the father as major confidant would presumably signify the son's trust and respect for his father. If this is so, it appears that children with high self-esteem enjoy a markedly closer relationship with their fathers than do children with less

TABLE 6.12 *Person in whom subject was most likely to confide*

| Confidant | Subjective self-esteem | | |
|---|---|---|---|
| | Low | Medium | High |
| Father | 16.7% (4) | 15.4% (2) | 52.2% (12) |
| Mother | 33.3% (8) | 15.4% (2) | 21.7% (5) |
| Other | 50.0% (12) | 69.2% (9) | 26.1% (6) |
| Totals | 100.0% (24) | 100.0% (13) | 100.0% (23) |

$\chi^2 = 11.02$    df $= 4$    p $< .05$

*Source:* Subject's interview.

esteem (Table 6.12). More than half of the boys in the high group (52.2 percent) are likely to confide in their fathers; roughly one in seven of those medium (15.4 percent) and low (16.7 percent) in self-esteem have an equally close relationship. Further inspection of Table 6.12 reveals that boys with medium self-esteem are least likely to confide in either their mother or father, and thus most likely to confide in others. The members of the high self-esteem group are far less likely to confide in nonparental figures (26.1 percent) than are those who express medium (69.2 percent) or low (50.0 percent) self-esteem. Members of the low self-esteem group are more apt to confide in their mothers (33.3 percent) than are members of the high (21.7 percent) and medium groups (15.4 percent).

In interpreting these results on paternal behavior there are three independent indications that boys with high self-esteem have a closer relationship with their fathers. (1) The mother reports that she is satisfied with her husband's performance; (2) the son reports that he confides in his father; (3) Rosenberg gives evidence[3] of a close father-child relationship for children high in subjective esteem. The consistent direction of the evidence gives fairly strong support to the view that the fathers of children with high self-esteem take a more active and supportive position in the rearing of their children. We should note that our results apply only to males, particularly those in their preadolescent years. Although similar results might obtain for girls, there are indications that the pattern of familial relationships varies for male and female children.[4] Whatever the parental relationship may be for

[3] M. Rosenberg. *Society and the Adolescent Self-Image.* Princeton, Princeton University Press, 1965.
[4] M. L. Kohn and E. E. Carroll. "Social class and allocation of parental responsibilities." *Sociometry,* 23:372–392 (1960).

girls, the presence of a close and trustworthy father who is willing to spend considerable time with his son promises well for his son's self-esteem and masculine identity.

### INTERACTION OF MOTHER AND FATHER

Parents must define their relationship to one another as well as to their children. They must determine whether expectations of marriage and parenthood are mutual and whether these expectations have a basis in reality. The parents must, for example, learn whether their social and financial aspirations are the same, whether they can live within their income, and whether they share a similar style of life. Husband and wife, father and mother, they must determine whether they agree in their definitions of privileges and responsibilities. These definitions are likely to vary from one sphere of behavior to another, with greater differences in some than in others. Thus, for example, the parents may achieve consensus on financial and religious matters but have markedly different ideas on how their children should be reared. They may agree on their familial goals but disagree on the means by which these goals should be achieved. Inasmuch as perfect and total agreement on all issues is rarely, if ever, achieved, the evaluation of parental interaction must be phrased in more relative terms. The pertinent question is whether the amount of disagreement and attendant tension generated is greater than the agreement and satisfactions achieved. This is the basis on which marriages are largely sustained, and this is the psychosocial environment in which children develop.

The interaction of husband and wife as it pertains to themselves or to their children is a complex issue, which is not in itself a focal concern of our study. We included a limited number of questions on the subject in our interview, and selected two aspects for particularly close examination: First, the amount of tension and conflict existing between the husbands and wives, and second, the methods they employed in decision-making. The amount of tension and conflict that concerned us was not specifically related to childrearing attitudes and practices. It was our assumption that differences between parents, whatever their source, could have an adverse effect upon the child's self-esteem. Considerable conflict could produce a sense of uncertainty of what standards to apply; competition between parents could result in attempts to make the child take sides and thereby suffer ambivalence and guilt; and the child might, falsely, conclude that he was responsible for the discord and thereby feel rejected or guilty. As for the procedures employed in making major and

TABLE 6.13 *Rating of tension and conflict between mother and father*

| Degree of tension and conflict | Subjective self-esteem | | |
|---|---|---|---|
| | Low | Medium | High |
| Considerable and marked tension and disagreement between mother and father | 43.3% (13) | 47.1% (8) | 18.2% (6) |
| Little, if any tension and disagreement; generally harmonious relationship | 56.7% (17) | 52.9% (9) | 81.8% (27) |
| Totals | 100.0% (30) | 100.0% (17) | 100.0% (33) |

$\chi^2 = 6.16$     df $= 2$     p $< .05$

*Source:* Interviewer's report.

everyday decisions that affect the family and children, parental behavior provides some indication of how parents define their roles vis-a-vis one another. They also provide some indication of how, and to what extent, the parents of children in the different self-esteem groups resolve their differences.

Our first indication of parental conflict is based upon a rating by the interviewer. This rating was made immediately after the interview and was based upon the immediate relevant statements of the mother and upon more indirect indications of discord. These included such cues as slurs, inattention to or lack of mention of the father, or greater attention to nonfamilial adult males. These ratings reveal that there is significantly less tension between the fathers and mothers of high self-esteem children than is true in other families (Table 6.13). Specifically, we find marked disagreement and tension in only 18.2 percent of the high self-esteem families as compared to over 40 percent in the medium (47.1) and low (43.3) self-esteem families. Judging by the interviewer's impressions, these latter families are frequently marked by fairly high levels of tension and conflict. We have no indications of the most significant sources of this tension, but the mothers' statements indicate that almost half of the families of children with low and medium self-esteem are marked by bickering and conflict. There is reason to believe that the characteristics of the parents themselves contribute to the tension between them. The mothers of children with low self-esteem are less secure and stable in their own right and appear more fearful and disturbed by the consequences of childrearing. The fathers in these families are less involved and concerned about their sons and this lack of concern is a source of dissatis-

TABLE 6.14 *Parent who more often makes major decisions that affect the family*

| Leader in major decision-making | Subjective self-esteem | | |
|---|---|---|---|
| | Low | Medium | High |
| Father | 45.2% (14) | 64.7% (11) | 57.1% (16) |
| Both equally | 48.4% (15) | 35.3% (6) | 28.6% (8) |
| Mother | 6.4% (2) | 00.0% (0) | 14.3% (4) |
| Totals | 100.0% (31) | 100.0% (17) | 100.0% (28) |

*Source:* Subject's interview.

faction to their wives (Table 6.11). Another possibility is that the mothers in low self-esteem families may be chronically dissatisfied and disappointed women. They express greater dissatisfaction with their husbands' involvement in childrearing—and are also less accepting of their own roles as mothers. Whatever its source, dissatisfaction is greater among the mothers of children with low self-esteem, and conflict is more pronounced among their families.

We now turn to consider the decision-making process employed by the families. Information was obtained from the son's responses to a series of questionnaire items, which elicited the child's perceptions of who wields power in achieving family decisions and who implements these decisions. The perceptions reported are by no means complete, and they may not be exact representations of events as they occur. However, inasmuch as we are interested in how parental decision-making affects the subject, his perceptions of the process may be assumed to be related to his reactions as well as to his reality. They presumably represent his interpretation of events within his household, and are thus the reality that affects his judgments and actions. The first question asked the subject to indicate which parent more often made the major decisions that affected the entire family. The alternatives were the father, mother, or both equally. The responses to this question, presented in Table 6.14, reveal that decision-making in the high self-esteem families is significantly different from that of other families. There is a much greater tendency in the highest group for *either* the father or mother to make major decisions and less tendency for them to share equally in the decision-making process. Thus we find that only 28.6 percent of high self-esteem parents share in decision-making, but 35.3 percent of the medium and 48.4 percent of the low self-esteem parents employ such a procedure. The differences between the three groups do not achieve statistical significance but the results are included because of their theoretical significance

TABLE 6.15 *Parent who more often makes day-to-day decisions*

| Leader in daily decision-making | Subjective self-esteem | | |
|---|---|---|---|
| | Low | Medium | High |
| Father | 32.3% (10) | 23.5% (4) | 21.4% (6) |
| Both equally | 29.0% (9) | 17.7% (3) | 42.9% (12) |
| Mother | 38.7% (12) | 58.8% (10) | 35.7% (10) |
| Totals | 100.0% (31) | 100.0% (17) | 100.0% (28) |

*Source:* Subject's interview.

and consistency with other findings. It is worth noting that though the fathers are more likely to make major decisions in all groups, there are no unfavorable consequences in those families where the mothers assume leadership. More specifically, in the six families where the mothers did make the major decisions, four of the children had high self-esteem. The pattern of results suggests that there is a clear designation of who is to assume leadership in the families of high self-esteem children. In the majority of cases it is the father who makes the major decisions, but it is more likely to be the mother in the high self-esteem family than in the other two groups. This does not necessarily imply that the father or mother makes all the major decisions, since each may assume dominance in different spheres of activity. What it does indicate is that clear and definite lines of power, privilege, and responsibility are drawn for those decisions that most profoundly affect the lives of family members. Such a procedure should make for clearer models and more explicit goals.

Our second question on decision-making asked the child to indicate which of his parents more often made the day-to-day decisions. The subject could again indicate either the father, mother, or both equally. Inspection of the responses (Table 6.15) reveals that day-to-day decisions are made differently in high self-esteem families than in those of other groups. In 42.9 percent of these families, father and mother share equally in making ordinary decisions, whereas only 17.7 percent of the medium and 29.0 percent of the low self-esteem families employ such a procedure. In these medium and low self-esteem families, it is more customary for either the father or mother to assume dominance, with shared decisions the least common mode of action. Comparison of the procedures employed for major decisions (Table 6.14) and day-to-day decisions (Table 6.15) reveals that the mothers are likely to play a much greater role in making day-to-day decisions. Their role is greater in all groups and does not appear to have particularly favorable or unfavorable effects.

TABLE 6.16 *Parent more likely to tell the child what to do*

| Parental authority | Subjective self-esteem | | |
|---|---|---|---|
| | Low | Medium | High |
| Father | 37.9% (11) | 18.8% (3) | 20.7% (6) |
| Both equally | 44.8% (13) | 56.2% (9) | 44.8% (13) |
| Mother | 17.3% (5) | 25.0% (4) | 34.5% (10) |
| Totals | 100.0% (29) | 100.0% (16) | 100.0% (29) |

*Source:* Subject's interview.

The final question we shall consider asked the subject to indicate which parent was more likely to tell the child what to do. The responses to this question, summarized in Table 6.16, indicate that the mothers of children with high self-esteem play a more active and directive role in their sons' lives. In 34.5 percent of their families, the mother is more apt to tell the child what to do; the percentages for medium (25.0 percent) and low (17.3 percent) self-esteem families are markedly lower. Apparently the mothers of children with high self-esteem play a more active role in carrying out the decisions relating to childrearing than do mothers in other families. The families of the high group presumably have achieved a modus operandi in which authority and responsibility are linked. Once major decisions have been made, and the procedures for day-to-day implementation established, the mother is given considerable authority in the daily supervision of the children. Inasmuch as she is the person who is with them throughout the day and is more responsible for the specific details of their well-being, this appears to be an efficient as well as reasonable procedure. It does, however, rest on the premise that the wife's judgment is trusted by her husband or that she insists upon autonomy and prerogatives in her areas of responsibility. The mothers of children with low self-esteem are least likely to tell their children what to do. These women are also lowest in their own self-esteem and apparently do not carry too much weight in their own homes. Judging by the reports of our subjects, these women have considerably less influence and power on major and day-to-day decisions than do the mothers of children with medium and high self-esteem. These children believe it unlikely that their mothers, who spend entire days in home and child care, will be a frequent source of guidance and discipline.

All these results suggest that the parents of subjects in the high self-esteem group go about their decision-making quite differently than do the parents of other children. In these families one individual—generally the father—is empowered to make the major decisions, which lay down the general goals and directions that the family is to follow and establish the authority and responsibility of the dominant family member. Once these general goals are laid down, both parents participate in their day-to-day implementation. The mother, who is more frequently at home and involved in the everyday affairs of the house and children than is the father, plays a more active role in these day-to-day decisions than she does in the major decisions. She is more actively involved in instructing and guiding the children and apparently does so with the father's knowledge and guidance. This pattern of decision-making and implementation requires that the authority of the dominant figure be accepted and that there be trust between the parents to implement the prescribed goals. Such a pattern of dominance, trust, and common action would apparently be most effective where the individuals admire and respect one another. If we recall that the mothers of the high self-esteem subjects were themselves rated highest in self-esteem, we may presume that they will not set aside their own prerogatives lightly. The implications of the pattern here are that the clear delineation of authority and joint implementation bespeak mutual trust and acceptance. Such a strong, clear relationship between parents would appear to provide reassuring experiences and models for their children.

Before concluding this chapter, let us summarize our findings on the relationships between parental characteristics and the child's self-esteem. The mothers of children with high self-esteem are themselves rated as higher in self-esteem and more emotionally stable than are the mothers of children with medium and low self-esteem. The mothers of children with high self-esteem are more self-reliant and resilient in their attitudes and actions concerning maternity and child care. They are also more likely to accept their roles as mothers and carry them out in a realistic and effective manner. Indirect evidence on the fathers of our subjects indicates that the fathers of high self-esteem subjects are more likely to be attentive and concerned with their sons, and that the sons are more likely to confide in their fathers. The inter-action between husband and wife in the families of children with high self-esteem is marked by greater compatibility and ease than is the case in the families of children with less self-esteem. There are more instances of previous marriages and rearing by stepparents in the families of low self-esteem children than there are in either medium or high self-esteem families. From evidence on the decision-making process employed within the family, we gain the impression that the high self-esteem families establish clearer patterns of authority and areas of responsibility.

Our interpretation of these findings revolves largely around the model that the parent provides the child. Thus, although there is no evidence that the mothers of high self-esteem subjects are more successful (and only limited differences in the social and occupational status of their husbands), our results suggest that they are stable, resilient, and self-reliant women, whose actions are likely to convey the sense they know what they are about and are doing it well. Their children are likely to perceive this posture and this conviction of confidence as indications of success. Similarly, while there are only limited differences in the social and occupational status of the farthers, the fathers of high self-esteem subjects appear more concerned and involved with their sons, and have greater authority in their households than do the fathers of children with less self-esteem. The sense of confidence and authority expressed by the parents within the household may contribute materially to the child's conviction that his parents are successful. Thus, we may conclude that children with high self-esteem are more likely to have parents who provide indirect impressions and direct experiences of success.

Our present chapter provides no indications on the concept of aspirations and only indirect data on values. From the son's reports on parental values, it appears that the parents of children with high and medium self-esteem value achievement, but that the parents of children with low self-esteem place great value on making oneself acceptable to others. This suggests that demands for achievement are *greater* for persons with higher esteem than they are for persons with low self-esteem, rather than the reverse. It also suggests that demands for accommodation and compliance may be greater for persons with low self-esteem. Turning to the child's ability to cope with devaluating circumstances, the parents of children with high self-esteem no doubt provide clearer, stronger models on how to deal effectively with everyday problems and decisions. Though we have only limited and secondary data about the father, our evidence on the mothers of children with high self-esteem suggests that they deal with issues directly, realistically, and effectively. They are more poised and assured in dealing with tasks that confront them and less inclined to be shaken or troubled by anxiety. From these characteristics it would appear that they have less need to repress, distort, or avoid issues, and are, indeed, less likely to do so. Such parents are more likely to provide their children with realistic definitions and interpretations of events and more effective means of coping with stresses. By precept and tuition they provide the means of achieving success and of handling adversity in a realistic yet nondestructive manner.

*Chapter seven*

# CHARACTERISTICS
# OF THE SUBJECTS

Previous antecedent studies have generally focused upon the interaction between parents and children, but, as we have already observed, the determinants of this interaction are more varied and complex than such a focus suggests. Social conditions, for example, affect the stability of the home. Parents, too, differ in their expectations, values, and interpretations of appropriate behavior; they are, in effect, not only parents but also workers, mates, and citizens. They act and respond not only on the basis of situational factors but upon their own impulses, convictions, and needs. They and their children alike live in a social matrix, which produces, affects, and alters their values and attitudes as well as the circumstances of their lives. These social conditions and parental predispositions set the stage upon which the newborn infant arrives. He does not, however, come without some distinguishing characteristics of his own. Children differ in a myriad of ways, which cause them to act, think, and feel differently, and which in turn elicit varying responses from parents and friends. They differ in such manifest characteristics as size, energy, and attractiveness as well as in less obvious intellectual capacities and temperament. They may make different demands, respond differently to the same treatment, and require markedly individual schedules and handling. Rather than being passive, neutral participants in familial interaction, children actively contribute to the manner in which they are treated by others. They do this by what they are, by what they do, and by what they require, although just how they do this is not crucial for our purposes. We must assume, however, that the child's personal characteristics contribute significantly to the manner in which he is treated.

In the subjects under study, we are interested in learning how their personal characteristics are related to their self-evaluations and to the manner in which they are treated by others. Inasmuch as we observe and study our subjects at least a decade after birth, we have no way of distinguishing antecedents from consequences. The child who is tall or attractive at ten may have been puny or plain in his earlier years. This same lack of knowledge arises with regard to the child's earlier behavior; we are generally confronted with this problem in establishing prior parental attitudes and treatment. In this case we shall apply the same logic and procedures we have employed in our treatment of parental characteristics and parent-child interaction— varied sources of information, cross-checking of items, and different levels of analyses. Since we cannot reconstruct the past, we shall proceed on two assumptions, which seem to be borne out by the life histories of most individuals. Our first assumption is that the attitudes and behaviors that are reliably established in the present are likely to be the same or similar to those that existed at an earlier period. Second, we assume that generally there is a continuity of traits over the early and middle years of childhood. This second assumption does not apply to all traits but appears to be true for many of those—such as bodily physique, intelligence, performance—that we shall examine in this chapter. Although those assumptions indicate the bases on which we sought to relate the child's attributes and his self-esteem, we should make it clear that our results do not hinge on the earlier state of the child's attributes and behavior. Even if we make the radical assumption that prior and present traits are generally unrelated, there would be good reason to investigate the relationship between the characteristics of the subject and his present level of esteem.

This chapter will consider five categories of personal characteristics that are related to self-esteem: physical attributes, general capacities, ability and performance, affective states, problems and pathology, and personal values. These characteristics were selected from a larger number studied because of their theoretical importance and because of the associations revealed by our analyses. In several instances, findings that were statistically suggestive were included because of such theoretical importance, and others, of greater magnitude but lesser import, were excluded.

## PHYSICAL ATTRIBUTES

There are a number of physical characteristics that could conceivably be related to self-esteem. Some of these characteristics might confer enhancement by their very presence, such as beauty or height, and others might facilitate success in valued activities, such as strength and speed. Both kinds of characteristics are, to a large extent, beyond personal choice or control and both are generally assumed to have marked consequences upon self-esteem. It is, therefore, with some surprise that we found that the child's (present) physical attractiveness is unrelated to his self-esteem ($\chi^2 = 2.10$, $df = 2$, $p < .50$). This negative finding does not indicate whether attractiveness at an earlier period is related to present self-esteem, but this might indeed be the case. It does, however, indicate that a preadolescent boy's self-evaluation is relatively unaffected by other persons' judgments that he is handsome or unattractive.

That physical attractiveness is apparently unrelated to self-esteem runs counter to our expectations on the effectiveness of reflected social appraisal. In interpreting this finding we should first point out that all of our subjects were boys. It is possible that physical attractiveness is not as salient a criterion of appraisal for the males in our culture as it is for females. This may be truer for young boys and preadolescents than would be the case for adolescent or adult males. Both males and females are expected to achieve and possess favorable attributes, but achievement appears to be more heavily weighted for the males in American society. Another possibility is that judgment of physical attractiveness made by others than those in the effective interpersonal environment may hold little significance. Thus, whereas the judgments of attractiveness we employed were made by teachers and interviewers, the more significant opinions for our child subjects were most likely the appraisals of their parents, sibs, and peers. The clinical cases in which persons who are attractive by any objective standards regard themselves as ugly because they are or were so regarded by significant persons in their lives underscore the importance of the reference groups that are most central to the individual.

Another important aspect of the child's physical development is the age at which he initiated certain locomotor activities. We hypothesized that children with high self-esteem were likely to have experienced earlier and more prolonged success in this regard as well as in their social and interpersonal affairs. To test this hypothesis we asked each mother to indicate the age at which her child started walking. From their responses it seems clear

TABLE 7.1 *Age at which child started walking*

| Age | Subjective self-esteem | | |
| --- | --- | --- | --- |
| | Low | Medium | High |
| Fifteen months and under | 32.1% (9) | 66.7% (10) | 60.0% (18) |
| Over fifteen months | 67.9% (19) | 33.3% (15) | 40.0% (12) |
| Totals | 100.0% (28) | 100.0% (25) | 100.0% (30) |
| $x^2 = 6.43$        df = 2 | p < .05 | | |

*Source:* Mother's interview.

that children with low self-esteem generally start walking at a later age than do children who are currently medium or high in self-esteem. Inspection of Table 7.1 reveals that only one-third (32.1 percent) of the low self-esteem children walk on or before fifteen months or younger; almost twice that percentage (60.0 and 66.7 percent) of the children with medium and high self-esteem have already walked by that age. These figures suggest that the children with low self-esteem are not as advanced in their early motoric development as are those who subsequently develop medium and high self-esteem. The reasons for this slower development are still unknown, but may derive from such differing bases as slower maturation, greater weight, and less parental stimulation. If we assume that the mother's reports of physical development are valid, this finding would indicate that the inferior capacities of the group with low self-esteem are revealed at a relatively early age.

Turning next to the relationship between physique and self-esteem, we again find that persons with low self-esteem are apt to be less advantaged than their medium and high esteem peers. As Table 7.2 indicates, only 20 percent of the group with low self-esteem possess a physique that is regarded as above average for their age group. This figure is less than half of what it is for the other two groups: 48.6 percent of the persons with high self-esteem and 52.9 percent of the persons with medium self-esteem have physiques that are above average. These data are based upon ratings of the child's physique made by the clinician during the course of the test session, and simply indicate that the bodies of persons with low self-esteem are less likely to be well formed, robust, and coordinated than are the bodies of persons with more favorable opinions of themselves. We can note the relationship between our subjects' present physiques and their current self-appraisals, but we have no certitude that similar appraisals and physical development existed at an

TABLE 7.2 *Extent to which child's physique is well formed and coordinated*

| Physical rating | Subjective self-esteem | | |
| --- | --- | --- | --- |
| | Low | Medium | High |
| Above average | 20.0% (7) | 52.9% (9) | 48.6% (17) |
| Average and below average | 80.0% (28) | 47.1% (8) | 51.4% (18) |
| Totals | 100.0% (35) | 100.0% (17) | 100.0% (35) |
| $\chi^2 = 10.49$        df = 2 | p < .01 | | |

*Source:* Clinician's report.

earlier period. However, if we restate our assumption of relative continuity over time, we may conclude that persons with a poor physique come to regard themselves less favorably. There is other evidence[1] that body size in males is a significant source of self-esteem. Given the likelihood that physique tends to be associated with physical strength and prowess, the present findings suggest that such strength and prowess are a more significant source of self-esteem for young males than is physical attractiveness. Presumably strength is more admired by others—males in particular, who form the primary reference group for this age group. It is also likely that physical strength will result in more frequent successes in the athletic contests that loom so large in the life of the preadolescent or adolescent male.

The final physical characteristic we shall consider is height. The interviewer rated the relative height of each subject, as compared with the height norms for males between 10 and 12 years of age, rating the subjects along a five-point scale. The topmost point was awarded to those markedly above (2 inches) age norms, the middle point to those at or close to the age norm, and the lowest point to those markedly below (2 inches) average height for this age group. Analysis of these results indicates that height is not significantly related to self-esteem ($\chi^2 = 1.86$, df = 4, p < .70). In view of the widespread belief that short persons tend to be envious of taller persons and are more sensitive to actual or perceived slight, this is certainly an unexpected finding. We must conclude that great height is not necessarily enhancing and that lack of height does not necessarily result in lowered feelings of worth. It is, however, worth noting that we are studying children who differ

[1] S. Jourard and P. Secord. "Body size and body cathexis." *J. Consult. Psych.,* **18**:184 (1954).

markedly in their growth rates and the age points at which they manifest sudden sharp spurts of growth.

There are two other considerations in interpreting the negative findings between self-esteem and height. First, we may assume that height does not possess as much significance in self-appraisal and in the appraisal by others as is generally believed. Height may not be a valid criterion for all persons, children in general, or children in a particular age group. According to this explanation, merely being tall is insufficient basis for esteem unless it is associated with indications of competence or worthiness. This is not to say that persons may not experience transitory states of enhanced self-esteem or devaluation when they become aware of their height or lack of it, but rather that height is not a salient, persistent criterion for determining one's worth in our culture. Second, we can accept height as an important social basis for esteem but conclude that the appraisal of its relative importance is opened to varied interpretation. This, in effect, would say that there is a general cultural bias in favor of taller persons but that families, peers, subgroups, or individuals may regard it unfavorably, or at least consider other facts as more important. Thus a tall child in a family whose members are generally short may regard himself as abnormal, and the short child who possesses unusual abilities may find his performance weighted more heavily than his height. From these findings on height and from the previous one on physical attractiveness, it seems that these characteristics are either not as important a basis for esteem as is customarily assumed or that other criteria assume greater significance for subgroups and individuals.

### GENERAL CAPACITIES, ABILITY, AND PERFORMANCE

In this section we shall examine the extent to which effectiveness, ability, and school performance are related to self-esteem. These three variables do not appear to be independent of one another, since each is related to the frequency of achieved or potential successes in school and social settings. Intelligence is significantly related to academic performance, which, in turn, appears to be an important criterion in judging the effectiveness of school-age children. With the general orientation toward achievement in American society and the importance of school in the lives of middle-class children, we have good reason to believe that success and failure within that setting will have marked consequences upon self-esteem. The effect will not only consist of the immediate experience of competence in dealing with school materials but also in the additional acclaim of teachers, parents, and peers. The immediate experience

TABLE 7.3 *Mother's estimate of child's general effectiveness relative to his peers*

| Child's effectiveness | Subjective self-esteem | | |
| --- | --- | --- | --- |
| | Low | Medium | High |
| Above average | 24.1% (7) | 23.5% (4) | 63.6% (21) |
| Average | 48.3% (14) | 53.0% (9) | 30.3% (10) |
| Below average | 27.6% (8) | 23.5% (4) | 6.1% (2) |
| Totals | 100.0% (29) | 100.0% (17) | 100.0% (33) |

$\chi^2 = 13.77$        df = 4        p < .01

*Source:* Mother's interview.

is particularly important, since academic achievement is one of the few childhood activities about which frequent and objective indications of relative competence are available. Academic achievement becomes a testing ground for future success and is the object of considerable concern and emotional investment.

In our search for indices of the child's effectiveness we utilized responses obtained from both the child's mother and the child, as well as from objective tests. As we shall see, the reports from these varied sources are in quite close agreement. During the mother's interview we asked her to appraise her son's effectiveness relative to that of his peers. This was elaborated with the definition of effectiveness as competence in dealing with social, academic, and personal matters. From the mothers' responses to this question, we conclude that persons with high self-esteem are significantly more effective than are those with either medium or low self-esteem. As Table 7.3 clearly reveals, 63.6 percent of the mothers of children with high self-esteem believe that their children are above average in effectiveness. The comparable figures (23.5 and 24.1 percent) for the medium and low self-esteem groups indicate that the mothers of these children do not perceive or believe that their children are equally effective. The figures for below-average effectiveness are equally revealing as to how the mothers of our subjects appraise and view their sons. We find that mothers of children with high self-esteem rate their children as below average in only 6.1 percent of the cases. This figure for below average effectiveness is roughly one-fourth of that obtained from the mothers of children with medium (23.5 percent) and low (27.6 percent) self-esteem. These findings may be interpreted in two ways. Accepting the mother's appraisal, we may conclude that the mothers are realistic and objective in their judgments, and that their sons do differ in effectiveness along the lines noted.

TABLE 7.4 *Mother's estimate of child's intelligence*

| Child's intelligence | Subjective self-esteem | | |
| --- | --- | --- | --- |
| | Low | Medium | High |
| Below average and average | 66.7% (20) | 70.6% (12) | 42.4% (14) |
| Above average | 33.3% (10) | 29.4% (5) | 57.6% (19) |
| Totals | 100.0% (30) | 100.0% (17) | 100.0% (33) |
| $x^2 = 11.08$        df $= 2$        p $< .01$ | | | |

*Source:* Mother's interview.

Or, if we assume that the judgments were biased, we may conclude that children with high self-esteem have mothers who are favorably disposed to them and mothers of children with medium and low self-esteem take a relatively unfavorable view toward their son's performance. In either event, by dint of performance or bias, children with high self-esteem are in a more advantageous and enhancing situation.

There is, of course, good reason to believe that intelligence is an important contributor to effectiveness and academic performance, and equally good reason to believe that it is highly valued in its own right by both parents and children. Thus, parental judgment of a child's ability would have considerable meaning for how he was currently regarded, and for the expectations held out for his future success. If we examine the mother's appraisal of her son's intelligence (Table 7.4), obtained in the course of the interview, we note that 57.6 percent of the mothers of children with high self-esteem rate their sons as above average in intelligence, but only about one-third of the mothers of children with medium (29.4 percent) and low (33.3 percent) self-esteem make similarly favorable ratings. We should note that although there were initially three categories for evaluating intelligence—above average, average, and below average, only two are presented in Table 7.4. It was necessary to combine the last two categories, since few mothers believed, perceived, or reported that their children were below average in intellectual capacity. The mothers' generally favorable appraisals of their children, and particularly the high estimations of the child with high self-esteem, appear to be consonant with their children's own appraisal of their abilities. As Table 7.5 reveals, relatively few persons regard themselves as below average in ability, but more than half (53.3 percent) of the high self-esteem group regard themselves as smarter than their peers. The five persons who regard themselves as

TABLE 7.5 *Subject's estimate of his abilities relative to his peers*

| Self-rating in abilities | Subjective self-esteem | | |
| --- | --- | --- | --- |
| | Low | Medium | High |
| Smarter | 22.6% (7) | 47.1% (8) | 53.3% (16) |
| Same as others | 61.3% (19) | 52.9% (9) | 46.7% (14) |
| Not as smart | 16.1% (5) | 00.0% (0) | 00.0% (0) |
| Totals | 100.0% (31) | 100.0% (17) | 100.0% (30) |

$\chi^2 = 12.11$     df = 4     p < .05

*Source:* Subject's questionnaire.

below average are low in self-esteem and there is little likelihood (22.5 percent) that these persons consider themselves to be superior to their peers. The medium group, which was similar to the low self-esteem group in their mother's appraisal, is the only one that shows a favorable shift when appraising their own abilities. In the low self-esteem group 33.3 percent of the mothers rate their sons above average, but only 22.6 percent of the children regard themselves as smarter than their classmates. The figures for the high self-esteem group indicate a similar occurrence: 57.6 percent of the mothers rate their sons average, but only 53.3 percent of the children regard themselves as smarter than their peers. It is only in the medium group—in which 29.4 percent are rated above average by their mothers and 47.1 percent of the children report themselves as smarter—that we have a large favorable increment in the child's judgment of himself. Comparing mother and self-report we obtain minus figures of −10.7 for the low and −4.3 for the high self-esteem groups and a positive figure of +17.7 for the medium self-esteem group. It is apparently this medium group, rather than the low self-esteem group, that is most likely to appraise itself more favorably than do outside observers.

Turning now to objective indices of intelligence, we find in Table 7.6 the mean intelligence test scores of the five self-esteem groups. These scores are based upon the performance of our subjects on the Wechsler Intelligence Scale for Children (WISC). The results indicate that the groups do differ significantly in their average level of intellectual ability and generally parallel the mother's and child's estimates of intelligence, but the Low-High group appears to be an exception to this generalization. Thus, if we examine the

TABLE 7.6 *Mean intelligence test scores (WISC)*
*of groups differing in self-esteem*

| Score | Types of self-esteem | | | | |
|---|---|---|---|---|---|
| | Low-Low | Low-High | Medium-Medium | High-Low | High-High- |
| Mean score | 101.53 | 122.29 | 112.24 | 116.06 | 121.18 |
| SD | 11.90 | 14.13 | 10.72 | 13.84 | 15.62 |

$F = 6.29$ $\quad$ df $= 4, 84$ $\quad$ p $< .01$

*Source:* Clinical study.

scores in the order of *subjective* self-esteem we obtain a regular sequence (in whole numbers) of 101, *122,* 112, 116, 121, broken only by the 122 of the Low-High group. Apparently the self-evaluations of this group are not closely tied to their own appraisals of ability and to the objective indices of intellectual capacity. This suggests either that Low-High individuals do not employ intelligence as a salient base of self-evaluation or that they are generally less responsive to environmental indices of success. In turn, this suggests that the term defensiveness, which we have previously applied to the Low-Highs, subsumes a (partial) insularity from the consensual judgments of one's immediate social environment. These persons march by a different beat than do their peers and are apt to be more demanding rather than self-aggrandizing. The other group labled as defensive (the High-Lows) is more capable than might have been assumed on the basis of the behavioral ratings of confidence and esteem. If we place the scores in order of *behavioral* esteem, we find the sequence to be 101, *116,* 112, 121, 122 with the score of the High-Lows the only one out of sequence. Again we find that the group that we have previously termed as defensive manifests a discrepancy between its capacities and its own judgments of esteem. The subject's behavioral esteem is appraised as lower than his abilities and is markedly discrepant from his own self-judgment. The High-Lows exhibit correspondence between subjective appraisals and abilities, but their behavior is judged as markedly different from these two other correlates of success. Apparently the High-Lows lack or cannot express the behavior that other persons employ in making judgments of confidence and assurance. On this evidence relating esteem and intelligence, it appears that both discrepant groups do not share or express the standard reactions of their social groups; the High-Lows do not express behavior that

TABLE 7.7 *Subject's reported grade point average*

| Grade point average | Subjective self-esteem | | |
| --- | --- | --- | --- |
| | Low | Medium | High |
| High (A, B+) | 29.6% (8) | 77.9% (10) | 51.7% (15) |
| Medium (B, B−, C+) | 29.6% (8) | 7.7% (1) | 31.0% (9) |
| Low (C, C−, D) | 40.7% (11) | 15.4% (2) | 17.3% (5) |
| Totals | 100.0% (27) | 100.0% (13) | 100.0% (29) |

$\chi^2 = 10.01$    df = 4    p < .05

*Source:* Subject's questionnaire.

other persons judge to be indicative of (internal) high self-esteem, and the Low-Highs do not make self-judgments attuned to (external) performance. It appears that the judgment of defensiveness is likely to reflect a lack of shared standards and conventionally expressed behavior as well as or instead of extreme sensitivity to devaluation.

In appraising the relationship between esteem and intelligence we should note that individuals who are low in discrepancy (which appears to be true of most individuals) apparently make realistic appraisals of their intellectual abilities. These persons apparently express their subjective states so that they are readily discerned, and maintain standards shared by their immediate colleagues and peers. Presumably higher levels of intelligence are associated with more frequent successes, which are, in turn, associated with higher self-esteem—provided that these successes are so regarded by the individual and are so expressed in his behavior. If this linkage is correct, then capacity (intelligence) is unlikely to have striking and extended consequences unless it eventuates in performance. In that respect the subject's academic average should be at least as related to his self-esteem as is his intelligence. Although we were unable to obtain an objective report of academic average, there was a question to that effect on the questionnaire administered to each subject. This question asked the subject to indicate his Grade Point Average (GPA). These GPA's were ordered in categories of high (A, B+), medium (B, B−, C+), and low (C, C−, D), and the responses of the groups were compared. Perhaps the most notable finding (Table 7.7) is the great frequency with which persons with low self-esteem report a low average. The percentage of persons with low averages in this group is 40.7 percent, which is more than twice that of medium (15.4 percent) and high (17.3 percent) self-esteem groups. Another striking feature is the inordinately large percentage of persons with medium self-esteem who report a high average. Almost 78 percent of the medium group report their averages as either A or B+, but only 51.7 percent of the high and 29.6 percent of the low self-esteem groups make a similar report. In this regard (that is, GPA), the reports of the medium group are similar to their self-reports on intelligence (Table 7.5). As we noted at that point the medium group is more likely to report favorable experiences than are either those lower or higher in self-esteem: their intellectual level, as rated by them, was higher than that ascribed to them by their mothers or objective tests. Although we have no reason to confirm or disprove their reported GPA, their objective scores on intelligence and the unlikelihood that their performance is superior to that of the more gifted highs make it doubtful that the percentage of high averages could be as great as reported. These findings do raise the possibility that self-aggrandizement and the socially desirable response is at least as (if not more) likely to occur among the medium, "average" group than it is among persons with either high or low self-esteem. (This topic is elaborated in Chapter 12.)

Before concluding this section it should be said that the correlation between subjective self-esteem and intelligence is .28 and that between self-esteem and academic achievement is .30. Although both correlations indicate a statistically significant relationship ($p < .05$), they also indicate that the vast bulk of the contributing determinants cannot be ascribed to the independent variable(s). Thus, we can say that ability and academic performance are significantly associated with feelings of personal worth, but we cannot say that these conditions are the major and overwhelming influences in developing self-esteem. Any relationship in which 90 percent of the variance remains unaccounted for clearly cannot be attributed to the single variable(s) under investigation. It is no more proper to attribute the relationship between self-esteem and popularity to intelligence than it is to posit that maternal role definitions are responsible for the relationship between self-esteem and effective functioning. To assume that self-esteem is largely a function of intelligence appears to be simplistic, on several grounds: (1) from our theoretical analysis, which led us to conclude that a combination of successes, aspirations, values, and defenses are involved in making self-judgments; (2) from our findings indicating that self-esteem is significantly associated with early childhood experiences, parental characteristics, and parental attitudes and treatment; (3) from our proposal that power, significance, and virtue, as well as competence, are bases of esteem. This is particularly so (as in this case) when there are data indicating that these variables exert a minor, albeit significant influence.

## AFFECTIVE STATES

There is good reason to assume that an individual's affective state is significantly related to his self-evaluation. From the vantage of persons who regard themselves poorly, states of positive, happy affect would appear to be highly improbable. Given the negative regard for one's capacities, performance, and attributes implied by low self-esteem, it is difficult to see how an individual could achieve states of happiness and ease while maintaining such an appraisal. Positive states might be achieved for a limited, restricted area, incident, or period, but insofar as the individual maintains contact with reality and remains an integrated unit, he would tend to be negative and depressed. Consistent, self-reinforcing appraisals of inferiority, unworthiness, incompetence, and insignificance are the basis for sadness, depression, and lethargy, not joy or expressiveness.[2] Negative appraisals not only reduce the pleasures of the present but they also subvert or eliminate realistic hopes for the future. The corrosive drizzle of negative appraisal presumably removes the joy of today and the anticipation of tomorrow.

States of happiness, tension, or expressiveness are presumably largely, but by no means exclusively, a consequence of prior experiences and treatment. There is considerable evidence that differences in temperament may have a reliable genetic component.[3] There are a number of human and animal studies that have revealed greater similarity in affective states among individuals with greater genetic similarity than could be explained on the basis of environmental influences. Assuming interaction between heredity and environment, this evidence is not essential, although it does support the possibility of differences in affective states that precede parental treatment and early experience. In raising this point we again wish to underscore the reciprocal interaction between the child's characteristics and capacities and the treatment he receives. There is certainly a possibility that a child who is expressive, tranquil, and smiling will evoke a different response from his parent than one who is irritable or passive. In this regard it is possible, though unlikely, that part of the differences in affective states we shall consider stem from innate sources.

There are three aspects of our subjects' affective life which we shall take up in this section: the total affect expressed by our subjects, the extent of

---

[2] M. Rosenberg. "The association between self-esteem and anxiety." *Psychiat. Res.*, 1:135–152 (1962).

[3] I. I. Gottesman. "Heritability of personality." *Psych. Monogr.*, 77(9), No. 572.

TABLE 7.8 *Total affect as revealed by (projective) sentence completion test*

| Degree of affect | Subjective self-esteem | | |
|---|---|---|---|
| | Low | Medium | High |
| High level of affect | 38.2% (13) | 64.7% (11) | 64.7% (22) |
| Low level of affect | 61.8% (21) | 35.3% (6) | 35.3% (12) |
| Totals | 100.0% (34) | 100.0% (17) | 100.0% (34) |
| $\chi^2 = 5.75$    df $= 2$    p $< .07$ | | | |

*Source:* Clinical study.

anxiety and tension they express, and the amount of happiness they reveal by their words and actions. The measurements of total affect, anxiety, and happiness were obtained by various procedures (such as projective tests, questionnaires, and interviews) intended to reveal overt and covert feeling states.

Turning first to the total affect expressed by our subjects, we may note that this measure indicates the amount of all affect—positive, negative, and neutral—expressed in response to a series of incomplete sentences. This test presumably encourages the subject to project his own sentiments and is thus assumed to reveal more covert feelings. The total affect score indicates the richness and expressiveness of the subjects' affective life. It reveals the extent to which affect is a component of the person's everyday language and thinking. From these scores, presented in Table 7.8, we find that persons with low self-esteem have a more impoverished emotional life than do persons high or medium in self-esteem. There are only 38.2 percent of the low self-esteem group whose responses reveal high levels of affect, but 64.7 percent of the medium and high self-esteem groups attain such levels. The results corroborate earlier impressions relating affect and self-esteem and reveal that persons with positive self-attitudes are richer and more expressive in their emotions.

The test battery administered to our subjects included a children's version of the Taylor Manifest Anxiety Scale,[4,5] which consists of a list of symptoms and experiences that are among the manifest indications of anxiety. In its more covert and central features, anxiety is associated with unfocused feelings of apprehension and uncertainty. The person who experiences this state

[4] J. A. Taylor. "A personality scale of manifest anxiety." *J. Abn. Soc. Psych.*, 48:285–289 (1953).

[5] A. Castaneda, B. McCandless, and D. Palermo. "The children's form of the Manifest Anxiety Scale." *Child Develop.*, 27:327–333 (1956).

TABLE 7.9 *Mean manifest anxiety test scores of groups differing in self-esteem*

| Score | Types of self-esteem | | | | |
| --- | --- | --- | --- | --- | --- |
| | Low-Low | Low-High | Medium-Medium | High-Low | High-High |
| Mean score | 18.4 | 24.00 | 16.5 | 7.1 | 8.7 |
| SD | 7.2 | 11.5 | 6.7 | 3.4 | 4.8 |
| F = 14.93 | df = 2, 83 | p < .001 | | | |

*Source:* Laboratory test.

feels uneasy or frightened but cannot identify the source of his uneasiness. Among the overt consequences of such nameless fears are increased activity of the autonomic nervous system—shortness of breath, pounding heart, perspiration, and the need for elimination—and other symptoms such as insomnia, restlessness, and headaches. Both the central state of anxiety and its consequences are sources of discomfort. In its more intensive forms, anxiety produces a state of terror that interferes with all actions other than those directed toward its diminution. In less acute intensity, anxiety interferes with attention and with the intellectual or emotional life, yet permits the individual to function, although with attendant distress and reduced levels of effectiveness. In still less amounts it serves as a warning of potential and impending difficulties in either the external world or internal reactions.

The experience of anxiety that is measured by the Taylor Scale is marked by rather extreme experiences, which we assume to be indicative of negative affect. Table 7.9 presents the mean manifest anxiety scores of the five self-esteem groups. In this scale, higher scores are indicative of higher levels of anxiety. From the group means, it is clear that subjective self-esteem and anxiety are closely and negatively related. The two groups high in their personal evaluation (High-High and High-Low) possess the lowest mean anxiety scores, 8.7 and 7.1; the two lowest subjective self-esteem groups (Low-High and Low-Low) possess the highest mean scores, 24.0 and 18.4; the group that is medium in self-esteem is also medium in anxiety. The means for the combined subjective self-esteem groups are 7.9 for high, 16.5 for medium, and 21.2 for low self-esteem. The correlation between self-esteem and anxiety is −.67. This indicates that high levels of negative affect, as measured by reports of distress, tension and symptoms, are more likely to be found in persons with low self-esteem. Persons with medium and high self-esteem experience some negative affect but the frequency with which they report distress in experience or symptoms is significantly lower than that for persons low in their own appraisal.

In interpreting this finding, we may briefly note two considerations. First, there is no reason to believe that the sequence between self-esteem and anxiety is unidirectional. Low self-esteem may produce feelings of helplessness and apprehension but these feelings may also result in lowered confidence and self-rejection. Although there are undoubtedly variations in the origins of a cycle from self-esteem to anxiety, the model of a cyclical, self-reinforcing, self-propelling sequence seems appropriate once either state has been established. The relationship between self-esteem and anxiety appears to be a theoretically central topic, which we shall examine in much greater detail in future discussions of our clinical and experimental findings. A second consideration is that the measures of total affect and negative affect presumably tap different levels of consciousness. The total affect score, based on responses to the Sentence Completion Test, is intended to reveal more covert sentiments, but the very title of the manifest anxiety scale indicates that it is geared to surface responses. The similarity of results obtained with indices tapping both levels suggests that conscious and unconscious affect in normal preadolescents is at least as likely to be similar as different. It also suggests that validated measures of affect derived from questionnaire and manifest content scales may provide generally accurate indices of underlying emotions.

The third, and final, aspect of our subjects' affective lives we shall consider is their happiness. Although we have established that persons with high self-esteem are more expressive and less anxious, this does not necessarily mean that they are happier. It is possible that their affective states are mild, neutral, or mixed in nature. The measure of happiness we shall consider was included in the mother interview. One of our questions asked her to indicate the extent of her son's happiness as manifest in his statements and actions. The responses to that question are summarized in Table 7.10. From them we can adduce a linear relationship between self-esteem and happiness. The figures reveal that 66.7 percent of the low self-esteem group are happy; comparable percentages for the medium and high self-esteem groups are 76.5 and 90.1 percent. Thus, judging by their mother's appraisal, most children with high self-esteem express and communicate a pleasant, positive set of emotions, and children with low self-esteem are more likely to be despondent and unhappy. The pattern of findings for the self-esteem groups, across different levels of experience, points to markedly different affective lives for those high and low in self-esteem. Persons with high self-esteem are expressive,

TABLE 7.10 *Mother's appraisal of subject's happiness*

| | Subjective self-esteem | | |
|---|---|---|---|
| Mother's appraisal | Low | Medium | High |
| Relatively happy | 66.7% (20) | 76.5% (13) | 90.9% (30) |
| Relatively unhappy | 33.3% (10) | 23.5% (4) | 9.1% (3) |
| Totals | 100.0% (30) | 100.0% (17) | 100.0% (33) |

$\chi^2 = 5.59$      df $= 2$      p $< .07$

*Source:* Mother's interview.

happy, and relatively free of anxiety; persons with low self-esteem are less expressive, less happy, and relatively anxious.

## PROBLEMS AND PATHOLOGY

We might anticipate that persons who are relatively anxious and distressed, as are persons with low self-esteem, would manifest more psychosomatic symptoms and personal difficulties. There is already some evidence in the Rosenberg study that persons low in self-esteem report that they have more symptoms. The frequency of these self-reported symptoms were validated by observers, leading us to believe that the suffering and symptoms associated with low self-esteem are reliable phenomena. We shall not, at this point, attempt to elucidate the relationship between self-esteem and psychopathology, in general or in relation to specific symptoms and syndromes. That discussion is better left to a more appropriate point than the present discussion of subject characteristics related to self-esteem. In the present context we shall consider three problems: general mental health, incidence of psychosomatic symptoms, and acts of destruction.

Before we do this, however, we should reiterate that all of our subjects were normal and without obvious, gross pathology at the outset of this study. This condition of normality was, in fact, a precondition for acceptance in the study. Thus, the pathology we note here is presently not extreme, although it may become extreme in the future. Our measure of general mental health was obtained in the course of the mother interviews. The mothers were asked to rate the extent to which their children experienced serious or frequent emotional difficulties. From their responses, revealed in Table 7.11, we find that 60.0 percent of the low self-esteem group manifest frequent or serious problems. This is four times greater than the percentage

TABLE 7.11 *Mother's appraisal of child's mental health*

| Mother's appraisal | Subjective self-esteem | | |
| | Low | Medium | High |
| --- | --- | --- | --- |
| Marked, frequent problems | 60.0% (18) | 35.3% (6) | 12.5% (4) |
| Limited, infrequent problems | 40.0% (12) | 64.7% (11) | 87.5% (28) |
| Totals | 100.0% (30) | 100.0% (17) | 100.0% (32) |

$\chi^2 = 15.27$     df $= 2$     p $< .001$

*Source:* Mother's interview.

of the high self-esteem group (12.5 percent) and almost twice the percentage of the medium self-esteem group (35.3 percent). These findings indicate a significant, positive relationship between self-esteem and mental health in the appraisals of the mother.

The mothers' assessment of mental health revealed the general level of their sons' emotional well-being. It did not indicate the specific disturbance or symptoms experienced by those low, medium, or high in self-esteem. Because of the ambiguity of the term mental health, we may presume that the mothers based their appraisals upon particular, concrete bases. Though some of the mothers may have responded in terms of a global negative response set, their judgments were presumably related to the amount of distress and symptoms expressed by their sons. To test this possibility and to validate the mothers' judgments on mental health, we asked our subjects to complete an inventory of psychosomatic symptoms. The inventory consists of sixteen symptoms that are presumed to have a large number of psychological components and that have required medical attention during the past five years. They include such symptoms as stomach ulcers, nail biting, loss of appetite, insomnia, and nervousness. These symptoms are assumed to be a consequence of extreme anxiety, the physiological manifestations of which can result in severe and recurrent physical dysfunction.

Table 7.12 indicates that persons with low self-esteem are more apt to report several symptoms and less apt to report the complete absence of symptoms than are those who are medium or high in their self-appraisal. Comparing the low and high self-esteem groups, we note that 14.7 percent of the low group report the complete absence of symptoms, and that 37.8 percent of the high group report a similar symptom-free testing. At the other extreme, 38.2 percent of the low group report the presence of four to six symptoms,

TABLE 7.12 *Number of psychosomatic symptoms*

| | Subjective self-esteem | | |
|---|---|---|---|
| Number of symptoms | Low | Medium | High |
| No symptoms | 14.7% (5) | 17.6% (3) | 26.5% (9) |
| Few symptoms (1–3) | 47.1% (16) | 76.5% (13) | 55.9% (19) |
| Several symptoms (4–6) | 38.2% (13) | 5.9% (1) | 17.6% (6) |
| Totals | 100.0% (34) | 100.0% (17) | 100.0% (34) |

$\chi^2 = 8.85$     df = 4     p < .08

*Source:* Subject's questionnaire.

but only 17.6 percent of the highs indicate that they have as great a number. The medium self-esteem group generally (76.5 percent) reports the presence of a few symptoms and seldom (17.6 percent) the complete absence of symptoms. Thus we may conclude that the mother's report of her child's mental health is supported by the son's reports of psychological distress. This does not necessarily mean that persons with low self-esteem are neurotics, but rather that they manifest more frequent and notable symptoms. From the theoretical vantage, the relationship between self-esteem and symptom expression appears to be mediated via anxiety. Feelings of weakness and unworthiness result in a sense of apprehension and helplessness when the individual is confronted by strange and demanding conditions. These, in turn, result in heightened autonomic discharges, which produce disturbances in activities under autonomic control (such as the digestive, eliminative, and respiratory), with extended consequences for all bodily functions.

Theoretically, responses to anxiety are of three general kinds: internalization, withdrawal, and externalization. These categories represent customary modes of response to feelings of apprehension and helplessness. These modes of response are not mutually exclusive, although there appear to be preferred, characteristic individual reactions. As we have seen, persons with low self-esteem are more prone to internalize their reactions to anxiety. They manifest more frequent disturbances of physiological systems and greater subjective distress. If we turn to the externalized responses to anxiety, we might assume that persons with low self-esteem might also be notable in this regard. Externalized reactions involve a more direct confrontation or attack upon the sources of anxiety. It thus includes more aggressive as well as more realistic responses to anxiety. There are, in fact, several theorists in the area of delinquent behavior who propose that aggressive, antisocial behavior is a

TABLE 7.13 *Destructiveness of child's behavior*

| Degree of destructiveness | Subjective self-esteem | | |
|---|---|---|---|
| | Low | Medium | High |
| Relatively destructive | 60.0% (18) | 35.3% (6) | 12.1% (4) |
| Relatively undestructive | 40.0% (12) | 64.7% (11) | 87.9% (29) |
| Totals | 100.0% (30) | 100.0% (17) | 100.0% (33) |
| $\chi^2 = 15.84$    df = 2    p < .001 | | | |

*Source:* Mother's interview.

consequence of low self-esteem. To cite but one example, August Aichorn[6] proposes that the delinquent personality is characterized by a soft weak center of uncertainty, which is surrounded by a tougher, masking outer layer. The external presence of toughness represents a disguise against actual weakness and an attempt to gain illicitly what could not be obtained by more direct and appropriate means. Our own findings both confirm and contradict this proposal. The evidence on externalized reactions to anxiety consists of reports of the child's destructiveness in early childhood and present indications of delinquent behavior.

Turning first to the child's destructiveness in early childhood, we may first note that these data were obtained as part of the mother interview. The mother was asked to indicate how destructive her son had been in dealing with personal and household articles during the past five years. These articles included toys, furniture, clothing, and other unspecified items. Table 7.13 shows a regular, negative relationship between childhood destructiveness and self-esteem. Children low in self-esteem were relatively destructive (60.0 percent), the medium less so (35.3 percent), and the high were lowest of all (12.1 percent). This indicates that children with low self-esteem are more prone to vent their hostility against inanimate objects. Destructiveness represents an externalized response but one without confrontation with a person or issue. It is the reaction of an individual who admits his weakness to himself, but is in no position to confront his adversary.

The destruction of one's own goods and those of others is a more guarded reaction than would be physical attack upon another person. Aggression against persons is, in this regard, a more assertive external reaction than is destruction of property. From the reports of the present aggressive be-

[6] A. Aichorn. *Wayward Youth.* New York, Viking Press, 1935.

havior of our subjects, we find that such behavior is not significantly related to self-esteem ($\chi^2 = 1.66$, df = 2, p < .50). These reports were obtained from the mother, as were the reports of destructiveness and over-all antisocial behavior. In addition we should note that the distribution of responses for other forms of delinquency, obtained from the mother and school records, failed to reveal a significant relationship with self-esteem. Although our findings may be partly a function of age, they do indicate that the aggressive actions of persons with low self-esteem are likely to be directed against inanimate objects, in relatively private settings. Acts of a more public nature, or those involving other people, apparently require more assertiveness than these preadolescents of low self-esteem can muster.

We may conclude, from these findings, that persons low in self-esteem are more destructive, more anxious, and more prone to manifest psychosomatic symptoms than are persons medium or high in self-esteem. But they are no more aggressive or delinquent, presumably because such acts require qualities of initiative and assertiveness that are lacking in individuals with low self-esteem.

### SELF-VALUES

In our conceptual analysis of the antecedents of self-esteem we noted that individuals judge their worth in terms of values and ideals that are relevant and important to them. An individual who regards academic achievement as important will view failure in this area as humiliating, with attendant effects upon his self-esteem. If academic performance is considered as irrelevant and inconsequential, then failure in this area has little significance in judging one's worth. The view that individuals vary in the weights they place upon different areas of performance has several implications for the subsequent self-evaluations they make. If individuals are indeed free to vary in their choice of standards, then we could reasonably expect them to select and focus upon those areas in which they believe themselves to excel. This would lead to a high self-esteem for everybody—which is certainly not the situation we find in (sampling) self-judgments. We do find that people are more likely to make favorable than unfavorable self-evaluations, but the distribution of scores (Mean = 70.1, SD = 13.8) reveals that a considerable number conclude that they are not particularly worthy. Another implication of differing criteria for self-judgments is the expectation that areas of (greater) competence will be systematically related to personally important values. Thus we could expect that persons who excelled at sports would report that sports was particularly important to them; those who were confirmed churchgoers would believe that the standards of their religion would be a highly significant basis for judging their worthiness. Presumably such focus upon areas of competence would stem from a desire to judge ourselves as favorably as we possibly can and thereby avoid the depressing and painful experiences associated with negative self-appraisals. This is, at least, what a rational analysis of the topic, based upon a hedonistic view of human motivation, would suggest. Judging, however, by the distribution of self-esteem scores, it appears that this rational analysis does not reveal the actual criteria for self-judgment. We are therefore led to a more empirical approach to the questions of how much latitude an individual has in selecting self-values, the relation between these values and his competencies, and how value saliences are related to self-judgments.

Our answers to these questions on the formation and use of self-values is based upon responses to one section of the questionnaire administered to the subjects. In that section the subjects were asked to indicate which, if any, of a list of forty-three values were important to them and how important they were. This list ranged far and wide over the domain of values, including such diverse items as the tough, the religious, the imaginative, the intelligent, the hard-working, and the logical. In each instance the subject first indicated whether he was greatly, moderately, or "un" concerned about the value and then indicated the extent to which he believed himself to excel in that value. He might indicate that he cared a great deal about whether he was intelligent and then estimate that he was very intelligent, or alternately indicate that he cared a great deal about being clear-thinking but did not believe that such a characterization could be applied to him. Analysis of the responses revealed that there were virtually no differences in value preferences among the groups that differed in subjective, behavioral, or discrepant esteem. In only one of the forty-three values do we find a difference sufficiently large to meet the conventional 5 percent level of acceptability. In such important areas of preadolescent life as academic performance, athletics, friendliness, attractiveness, intelligence, and independence, we find that groups differing in their level of esteem hold these and other values equally important. This would imply that persons high, medium, and low in the various expressions of esteem tend to employ much the same criteria for judging their worth. They are equally likely to attach importance to being likable, honest, and intelligent, and equally unlikely to be concerned about being mature, kind, and standing up for their rights. In itself this finding would be interesting but not very surprising—these children do, after all, come from similar white, middle-class backgrounds—were it not for two findings we have already reported. The first of these indicated that the parents of subjects with low self-esteem espoused values of social accommodation, and those of subjects with higher self-esteem favored (academic) achievement (Table 6.3). The failure to find similar differences in the value preferences of their sons suggests that parental values are not closely related to the values espoused by preadolescents. The second source of surprise at our negative finding arises from the consideration that subjects who differ in self-esteem do indeed differ in their general effectiveness (Table 7.3), scholastic achievement (Table 7.7), and intellectual ability (Table 7.6). In more immediate and specific terms it indicates that persons who are less intelligent and receive lower grades place as great a value upon capacity and competence as do the persons who are markedly superior in these areas. This indication—that groups differing in competence and performance do not differ in their value preferences— suggests that the assumption that values are selected on hedonistic grounds requires critical examination.

At the heart of the issue of self-value preferences is the question of whether individuals are indeed free to focus upon their areas of greatest competence. Can the person who is failing in school, or not earning a living, focus upon his athletic prowess or driving ability and conclude that he is a worthy person? From our results we are led to conclude that self-value preferences are relatively circumscribed and defined by one's social group. For though it is entirely conceivable that an individual might place great importance upon a goal that is relatively unimportant by his group's standards, such an occurrence is far more likely to be the exception rather than the rule. It is far more likely that he will learn what is regarded as desirable by his group and judge himself by the standards other persons employ in appraising his behavior. The values acquired through exposure, imitation, and social support are more likely to be employed in self-judgments than are the values that might be independently developed to maintain a faltering self-esteem. Rejection of communal standards is likely to evoke censure and rebuke, forms of treatment to which persons with low self-esteem are unusually sensitive (Tables 3.7 and 3.8) and which are likely to drive them back to the shelter and shadows of accepted group norms. Even though we may believe that individuals care a great deal about characteristics, capacities, and competencies that are of little concern to the members of their group, it is nonetheless unlikely that they use these independently derived standards as a *major* basis for judging their own worthiness. As long as they are members of the group and are able and desirous of sharing its support, they recognize that there are communal standards of success and recognition. These are the major standards against which performance and character are judged, with all others relegated to a secondary and peripheral position. In sum, self-values are environmentally derived and supported so that there is relatively little latitude for focusing upon (socially) deviant values as a major basis of self-esteem. William James was undoubtedly correct in his conclusion that "our self feeling depends entirely on what we back ourselves to do": what he did not appreciate was the social definitions and limits within which such "backing" occurs.

Knowing that persons generally employ social norms as self-values leads us to conclude that these values cannot be readily selected, shifted, and transformed to attain favorable self-judgments. It is, however, possible that an individual can accept a social norm on which he fares badly and come to a favorable resolution by an aggrandized estimate of his performance. An example of such aggrandizement would be the person who is doing poorly in his studies, places a high value upon academic performance, and then judges his performance as more than satisfactory. There is, in effect, latitude in interpreting the adequacy of one's performance even where the standards are shared and public. It is in this regard—that is, in estimates of meeting standards, rather than in value selection—that favorably inflated self-judgments are likely to be achieved. Our data indicate that unfavorable self-appraisals are associated with conditions under which the activity is valued and the individual estimates that his performance is relatively inferior. Thus a person who believes that honesty is very important, but who does not believe that he is honest, is virtually compelled to conclude that he is unworthy. Negative self-estimates on values that were less important or unimportant are much less likely to be associated with low self-esteem. By and large, the trend of our findings was remarkably consistent and similar to the results previously reported by Rosenberg.[7] They indicate that it is the combination of salient self-value and estimates of satisfying that value that is associated with the various levels of subjective self-esteem.

A final result of some theoretical interest is the strong value orientation of the medium self-esteem group. These persons are far more likely to report that values are important to them than are those low or high in self-esteem. Persons with medium self-esteem appear to be more concerned about virtually all values, regardless of their nature, than are other persons in the population. This is revealed by the over-all results of our analysis of self-values. On thirty-

---

[7] M. Rosenberg. *Society and the Adolescent Self-Image.* Princeton, Princeton University Press, 1965, pp. 243–254.

six of the forty-three values sampled, the percentage of persons in the medium self-esteem group who report the value to be important exceeds that of either the high or low self-esteem groups. This applies equally to such diverse values as honesty, ambition, logic and reason, academic excellence, dancing, considerateness, sociability, athletics, religion, and good taste. Despite this consistent value orientation, there are only two values—refinement and dancing—in which the difference between the medium self-esteem group and the other groups achieves statistical significance. Given the number of values considered, this frequency (2 of 43) might well represent chance occurrences. However, the greater frequency with which persons with medium self-esteem cite values as important (83.7 percent of the values considered) does call attention to the strong value orientation of this group. It suggests that concern with values is likely to be greater among persons whose worth is not as clearly and definitely anchored as it is among those who mark the ends of the continuum. To be in the middle is a more ambiguous position (Chapter 13) and may induce a greater need to structure one's personal world. Persons with higher and more certain self-esteem apparently accept their personal judgments as guides or are not as concerned about or threatened by the value declarations made in their social milieu. Persons with low self-esteem would appear to accept social definitions of what is important but are not necessarily enthusiastic about standards that virtually commit them to judgments of failure. Sketchy as our evidence is, it does suggest that the greatest concern for values is in persons who have moderate levels of self-esteem and who may well employ those values to stabilize their ambiguous and uncertain positions.

ASPIRATIONS

Our theoretical model proposes that self-judgments of worthiness are based upon a comparison of performance and capacities with personal standards in valued areas of behavior. If the level of performance meets or exceeds standards in these areas, the individual presumably concludes that he is worthy; if it falls markedly below them the individual is likely to conclude that he is a failure and to judge himself harshly. This suggests that knowledge of "objective" success—academic excellence, social and material success, other successes—is not a sufficient basis for determining self-judgment. If we are to appreciate how and why two persons who have experienced equal objective success can come to dramatically opposite conclusions about their worthiness, we must also know their hopes, pretensions, ideals, and aspirations. In specific operational terms, we seek to determine whether persons differing in

TABLE 7.14 *Mean level of aspiration on beanbag toss for groups differing in self-esteem*

| Score | Types of self-esteem | | | | |
|---|---|---|---|---|---|
| | Low-Low | Low-High | Medium-Medium | High-Low | High-High |
| Mean | 5.67 | 6.28 | 6.06 | 5.94 | 6.11 |
| SD | 1.29 | 1.08 | 0.84 | 0.94 | 0.90 |
| F = .77 | df = 2, 84 | n.s. | | | |

*Source:* Laboratory study.

self-esteem applying different standards to judge their performances. Our theoretical exposition suggests that self-judgments may be related either to absolute level of criteria—that is, persons with high self-esteem make lesser demands upon themselves—or to the relative discrepancy between standards and performance—that is, persons with high self-esteem live up to their standards regardless of the level at which they are set. In the first instance the individual comes to a favorable conclusion by maintaining demands that are readily met; in the second he maintains a balance between prior experiences and future possibilities.

In this section we shall consider four indices of aspiration, which were obtained from (1) a beanbag toss, (2) occupational preference, (3) Ideal-Self scores, and (4) Self-Ideal-Self discrepancy.

The first index was obtained from one of our laboratory studies, and we shall briefly describe the situation that confronted our subjects. They were individually brought to a large room in which a series of ten targets were arranged at increasing distances from a common base line. Each of the targets was colored differently to facilitate identification and to indicate relative difficulty of attainment. The subjects were asked to select a target and toss a beanbag into the rectangular opening. After a series of ten practice trials, which also determined his relative competence at this task, the base line was adjusted and the series of twenty beanbag tosses began. Table 7.14 indicates the mean level of targets selected by the members of the five self-esteem groups. As these means reveal, there is no regular relationship between any dimension of esteem and the level of target generally selected, nor is there any single group that is significantly higher or lower than others (F = .77, df = 2, 84, p < 50). Thus the groups with high subjective self-esteem have mean levels of 6.11 and 5.94, which are quite similar to the

TABLE 7.15 *Occupation that child would like to enter*

| | Subjective self-esteem | | |
|---|---|---|---|
| Occupational preference | Low | Medium | High |
| Professional, higher management | 26.1% (6) | 25.0% (3) | 38.5% (10) |
| Lesser professions, technical, office, clerical, sales | 34.8% (8) | 50.0% (6) | 38.5% (10) |
| Skilled and semiskilled crafts | 39.1% (9) | 25.0% (3) | 23.0% (6) |
| Totals | 100.0% (23) | 100.0% (12) | 100.0% (26) |

$\chi^2 = 2.42$      df $= 4$      p $< .70$

*Source:* Subject's questionnaire.

averages of 6.28 and 5.67 of those with the most negative self-attitudes.

This indication that self-esteem is unrelated to absolute level of aspiration is also borne out by our data on the occupational preferences of our subjects (Table 7.15). Thus, we find that persons who make positive self-appraisals are only slightly, and not significantly, more likely to select higher-level occupations than are persons with medium and low self-esteem. Though individuals with low self-esteem do tend to select crafts positions more frequently (39.1 percent) than do those with medium (25.0 percent) and high (23.0 percent) self-esteem, neither that result nor the entire pattern of results differs markedly from chance occurrence ($\chi^2 = 2.42$, df $= 4$, p $< .70$). Our initial conclusion, based on these two indices of aspiration level, is that the absolute level the individual sets for himself is unrelated to his self-appraisal or behavioral poise. This means that the person who does not think highly of himself is as likely to set lofty goals as is the person who concludes that he is a worthy individual.

The negative findings for absolute level of aspiration appear consistent and related to the negative findings for social values. Together they seem to indicate that persons in a given social group will express public support for the norms advocated by that group. They will support the norms of achievement, honesty, and so on, and they will select a level of competence that is generally regarded as acceptable to their peers. Judging by Tables 7.14 and 7.15, that level is slightly above the mean for the targets and occupations presented to them. These findings suggest that the level of aspiration obtained in response to our queries was not closely related to the personally significant

TABLE 7.16 *Mean Ideal-Self scores for groups differing in self-esteem*

| | Types of self-esteem | | | | |
|---|---|---|---|---|---|
| Score | Low-Low | Low-High | Medium-Medium | High-Low | High-High |
| Mean | 72.24 | 68.12 | 76.71 | 84.35 | 88.18 |
| SD | 15.80 | 16.58 | 9.43 | 11.98 | 10.38 |
| $F = 6.38$ | $df = 2, 84$ | $p < .01$ | | | |

*Source:* Laboratory tests.

criteria of our subjects. That is to say, it may have meant little whether or not they succeeded or failed in tossing beanbags or selected occupations that they believed would be socially acceptable. In effect, the decisions indicated in both instances may have had little, if any, pragmatic significance and could accordingly be treated as abstract, almost fantasy, choices. Persons could select targets and occupations that they might otherwise, and more realistically, have regarded as beyond their scope and not closely tied to their interests. The more cogent and psychologically significant question for our study is whether persons who differ in self-esteem also differ in the personal standards they set for themselves and in the standards they set for occupations they fully expect to enter. Our results suggest that an affirmative answer to this question is clearly in order.

Our first indication of support comes from the Ideal-Self scores reported by our subjects, our third index of aspiration. These scores were obtained from Q-sorts of the items in the Self-Esteem Inventory in response to the instructions "Sort these into two piles of 'Like Me' and 'Unlike Me' according to how you believe the kind of person you would like to be would make such a division." The piles were then examined and scored to obtain total Ideal-Self scores in the same manner as the self-esteem scores had themselves been established. The mean Ideal-Self scores, presented in Table 7.16, show that persons with higher subjective self-esteem have higher self-ideals than do those with lower appraisals of their worthiness. There is a regular, positive relationship ($r = .59$) between the self-esteem scores and the ideal-self scores expressed by each subject, with a significant difference between the three levels of esteem ($F = 6.38$, $df = 2, 84$, $p < .01$). This indicates that persons with high self-esteem set *higher* rather than lower levels for themselves in those (self) areas that are salient and psychologically significant. The kind of person they would like to be is more successful and regards himself more

TABLE 7.17 *Mean differences (Ideal-Self — self-esteem + 50)
for groups differing in self-esteem*

| | Types of self-esteem | | | | |
|---|---|---|---|---|---|
| Score | Low-<br>Low | Low-<br>High | Medium-<br>Medium | High-<br>Low | High-<br>High |
| Mean | 65.1 (15.1) | 57.5 (7.5) | 52.8 (2.8) | 48.7 (−1.3) | 50.9 (0.9) |
| SD | 16.76 | 18.27 | 11.31 | 14.63 | 13.69 |
| $F = 2.94$ | $df = 4, 80$ | $p < .05$ | | | |

*Source:* Laboratory tests.

favorably than is the kind of person conceived by those lower in esteem. Thus persons with high self-esteem seem to expect more of themselves than do others and presumably gain their own esteem by meeting those expectations rather than lowering their self-demands.

This, of course, brings us to the question of the relationship between aspiration and performance—whether persons with high self-esteem come closer to meeting their personal standards than do persons who feel they are unworthy. Our first answer to this question is revealed in the difference scores between Ideal-Self and Self presented in Table 7.17. (A constant of 50 has been added to each score to avoid the use of negative numbers; the raw difference scores are given in parentheses in the table.) The means in this table reveal that persons with high subjective self-esteem have smaller differences (0.9 and −1.3) between their present self-appraisals and their ideals than do individuals with medium (2.8) or low (7.5 and 15.1) self-esteem.[8] If we combine the scores at various levels of subjective esteem, we find difference scores of −0.2 for high esteem, 2.8 for medium esteem, and 11.3 for low esteem groups. The differences for the five groups, and three levels of subjective esteem are statistically significant ($p < .01$). The results indicate that the gap between aspiration and fulfillment is less for persons with high self-esteem than it is for persons who conclude they are unworthy. The smaller difference for high esteem persons exists despite the significantly higher aspirations they set for themselves (Table 7.16). Thus it is the com-

[8] E. Silber and J. S. Tippett. *Self Esteem: Clinical Assessment and Measurement Validation.* Psychological Reports Monograph Supplement 4–V16: 1017–1071 (1965). These authors employ the discrepancy between ideal self and self appraisals as an index of self-esteem.

bination of higher aspirations and greater fulfillment of these aspirations that we find associated with favorable self attitudes. Persons with lower esteem not only set lesser standards, they also fall shorter of achieving them.

It is possible to interpret the small ideal-self discrepancy of high self-esteem subjects in a variety of ways. We could attribute it to the "ceiling effect," which prevents an individual from achieving a score greater than 100 on the Self-Esteem Inventory. An individual who receives a score of 96 is limited to a 4-point upward difference when he wishes to portray his ideal, but the individual who has a score of 56 has a much greater range in which to reveal his standard. This limitation of range for those with high self-esteem scores, rather than greater fulfillment of ideals, could thus underlie their smaller Ideal-Self—Self discrepancies. This is certainly a possibility and raises measurement problems that are beyond the scope of our discussion. There is, however, an alternative interpretation of these same hypotheses and findings. Persons who rate themselves as highly as 96 out of 100 do indeed have little room to express higher ideals—this applies as much to the real world as it does to the mathematical world of measurement. Such persons find it difficult to express negative statements about themselves in the various areas we sampled (peers, school, family, and self) and, not surprisingly, have even greater difficulty in indicating how they could be improved. In effect, we propose that the "ceiling" is just as likely to be a function of perceived deficiencies as a measurement artifact.

Finally, we may ask the bases of the higher (self) aspirations of the individual with high self-esteem. These bases presumably derive from more frequent academic successes, respectful treatment, and greater competence, all of which lead him to believe he will generally succeed and will be capable of dealing with difficult and adverse circumstances. The ratio of success and failures he has experienced is so weighted with successes that he is, so to speak, conditioned to expect further and greater success. We propose, in short, that experiences of success lead to expectations of success and that aspirations mirror these expectations. Support for this position comes from a previous study,[9] which revealed that persons with low self-esteem are as desirous of success as are others but that they are far less likely to expect that success will actually occur. These persons do not believe they have the capacities that make for successful achievement and social acceptance, and they anticipate that their goals will remain unfulfilled, their ambitions frus-

[9] M. Rosenberg. "The association between self-esteem and anxiety." Psychiat. Res. 1:135–152 (1962).

trated. This pessimism presumably lowers aspirations, and the lack of confidence will, in the nature of a self-fulfilling prophecy, increase the likelihood of aborted, half-hearted efforts. To amplify William James once again, we may conclude that experienced success $= \dfrac{\text{success}}{\text{expectations}}$, rather than $\dfrac{\text{success}}{\text{pretensions}}$.

*Chapter eight*

# EARLY HISTORY
# AND EXPERIENCES

I n the preceding three chapters we have considered the relationship between self-esteem and various characteristics of the social background, parental influence and the subject himself. We shall now consider the influence of several kinds of early experiences upon the development of self-esteem. The experiences to be discussed can be divided into three broad categories: (1) the influence of family size and ordinal position of child, (2) the circumstances surrounding birth and early handling, and (3) early relationships with siblings and peers. The topics subsumed by these categories relate to major or central hypotheses of earlier and recent investigations of personality formation.

The first topic, on family size and ordinal position, represents an attempt to determine whether children who are born into smaller families or are firstborn or only children are higher in self-esteem. This variable was of particular interest to Alfred Adler, who regarded the individual's place in the family constellation as a major determinant of his attitudes and expectations. The second topic enables us to test several hypotheses derived from psychoanalytic theory, dealing with the importance of severe early traumata and the specific practice employed in early feeding. The third topic deals with the relationship between sibling and peer relationships and self-esteem. The hypotheses that cordial, congenial relationships with sibs and peers would have an enhancing effect appears reasonable, but without prior experimental support. Extending this topic on early social influences still further, we shall examine the relationship between peer acceptance and parental relations with one's peers and the child's self-esteem.

As we have indicated, the variables to be considered in this chapter represent a set of early childhood experiences that are generally regarded as significant in personality formation. They are not aspects of the broader social background, although their occurrence might be related to that background, nor are they attributes of either parents or child. They are part of the early history of each child reared in this culture and they presumably play an important part in the formation of his personality. Exactly *how* important is far from clear and it is our present goal to clarify that very question. This group of variables could provide us with an indication of the nature, extent, and regularity of early social stimulation. Family, sibs, and peers are the social milieu of the young child and compose the environment that establishes personal norms and motivations. It is in these settings of parental treatment and sibling relationships that the growing child first learns what he may expect from the world outside himself. In this regard, early social environment may well be as important in its general stimulating effects as it is in the particular experiences it provides. This is certainly a way of viewing early experiences other than that customary in personality theory, but it is one that is consistent with recent studies on sensory enrichment and deprivation. Following this line of reasoning we shall discuss the early experiences of our subjects from the vantage of their general effects as well as specific and more limited consequences.

### FAMILY SIZE AND ORDINAL POSITION

We might well assume that persons born into families of different size or in different ordinal positions would differ in self-esteem. This could be anticipated largely on the basis of differential attention from parents and experiences with siblings. Children who are born into families in which there are few offspring would presumably receive greater attention and more intense emotional investment from their parents than would children from large families. Parents have only a limited amount of time available to them and, to the extent that their attention is associated with the child's self-esteem, they can provide less basis for esteem for each of a large family than they can for an only child or a small number of children. In addition, we might anticipate that the parents' involvement with each child might decrease as their number increased. Whereas the arrival of a first or second child might be considered an unusual and significant event, the arrival of subsequent children might well evoke less response. This might be particularly true if there were several children of the same sex already in the family or if financial resources were limited. Following this logic, we should think that children in smaller families will be higher in their self-esteem than those in families with a larger number of children.

The results, however, run counter to expectations, and indicate that children in smaller families are no higher in self-esteem than are those in larger families ($\chi^2 = 1.22$, df = 2, p < .70). This would suggest that if family size does have an influence upon self-esteem, it is not as a condition in isolation but as one of several interacting conditions. Among these we might propose that such conditions as sibling position or age differences between children might well have consequences for the individual child's self-esteem. In the present instance, we may conclude that family size per se is unrelated to self-esteem. This negative finding is concordant with the weak relationship, previously noted, between social class and self-esteem. Presumably individuals in the larger families of the lower economic classes suffer little if any devaluating effects because of the larger numbers in which they find themselves. Poverty and overpopulation may have deleterious consequences upon other personality traits, but insofar as they are measured by our instruments and sample, they have little, if any, effect upon self-esteem.

The ordinal position of the individual among his siblings would appear to be an important influence in his early social experiences. A child who is born early in the sequence of a series will encounter a family environment in which there is little if any competition for attention, affection, and status. Later children find an environment in which the earlier arrivals are bigger, stronger, and more knowledgeable. The later child starts with a potential disadvantage of an established competition, although he may compensate for this in other ways and be treated equally by his parents. It is therefore not surprising to find that the experiences associated with birth order have been associated with a number of personality characteristics.[1,2,3] Children born earlier in the sequence have been found to affiliate with others more frequently; they are also more likely to achieve scientific eminence. Children

[1] E. Chen and S. Cobb. "Family structure in relation to health and disease." *J. Chronic Diseases,* 12, 5(1950):544–567.

[2] H. L. Koch. "Some emotional attitudes of the young child in relation to the characteristics of his sibling." *Child Develop.,* 27:393–426 (1956).

[3] S. Schacter. *The Psychology of Affiliation.* Stanford, Calif., Stanford University Press, 1959.

TABLE 8.1 *Distribution of siblings in family*

| Distribution | Subjective self-esteem | | |
| --- | --- | --- | --- |
| | Low | Medium | High |
| Only child | 3.7% (1) | 00.0 (0) | 12.1% (4) |
| No older sibs | 26.0% (7) | 29.4% (5) | 45.5% (15) |
| Younger and older sibs | 37.0% (10) | 41.2% (7) | 30.3% (10) |
| No younger sibs | 33.3% (9) | 29.4% (5) | 12.1% (4) |
| Totals | 100.0% (27) | 100.0% (17) | 100.0% (33) |

*Source:* Mother's interview.

who are born later in the series are more apt to be asocial, poorer in performance, and schizophrenic.[4] Therefore children born earlier in the series should be higher in self-esteem than are those in middle or later positions. If we examine the relationship between sibling position and self-esteem (Table 8.1), we can determine the extent to which this hypothesis is sustained.

From the table we note that the sibling position of persons low or medium in self-esteem differs from the position of our high self-esteem subjects. Over 70 percent of the low (70.3 percent) and medium (70.6 percent) self-esteem groups are either youngest or middle children but only 42.4 percent of the high self-esteem group are in similar sibling positions. Individuals with high self-esteem tend to be either firstborn or only children; 57.6 percent of them are in these positions. This percentage is almost double that of the medium (29.4 percent) and low (29.7 percent) self-esteem groups. This distribution tends to confirm our hypothesis that children who are in positions that receive more attention (firstborn and only children) are likely to be higher in their self-esteem. A statistical test comparing the distribution of first and only (and other children) in the high self-esteem group with the combined distribution of the low and medium groups revealed that the differences in distribution were unlikely to be a chance occurrence. The $\chi^2$ value was 4.51, which, with one degree of freedom, is a difference that is likely to occur less than five times in a hundred.

It is worth noting that Rosenberg's study confirms and extends our finding on the relationship between self-esteem and ordinal position. His results indicate that high self-esteem is more common among only children, but that other ordinal positions are unrelated to feelings of worth. Whether one

---

[4] C. Schooler. "Birth order and schizophrenia." *Arch. Gen. Psychiat.*, 4:91–97 (1961).

is a first, second, or third child is of less importance than whether one has any siblings at all. Inasmuch as this result applies to only male children and not to females in the same position, it would appear that it is emotional investment rather than relative attention that is largely responsible for the differences in self-esteem of persons in different ordinal positions. The finding that Jewish boys who are only children or who are born after several girls are particularly high in self-esteem lends greater credence to such an interpretation. Apparently the tradition that the male is heir to family aspirations and maintains the family name results in greater attentiveness, concern, and deference to only-child males. Such treatment presumably gives these children a sense of significance that is not attained by the only-child females who are reared under similar physical circumstances.

### FEEDING PRACTICES

The feeding of infants and children has long been regarded as fraught with psychological as well as nutritional consequences. Psychoanalytic theory in particular has maintained that specific methods and schedules of feeding have significant consequences for the child's sense of security and well-being. According to this theory, breast-feeding indicates the mother's acceptance and responsiveness to her child, and this acceptance is communicated to the child, who gains greater assurance and physical well-being from the "natural," "warmer" experiences of breast-feeding than he would from more artificial methods. These benefits presumably derive from the mother's willingness and ability to satisfy the child's demand for food as he requires it rather than insist upon a fixed schedule. Flexible, self-demand schedules, regardless of the method of feeding, are seen as providing the child with the assurance that his needs will be met as they arise, by an environment that is geared to his demands. Behavioristic theories of childrearing took the view that it was nutrition rather than the container that was essential in infant feeding and that fixed schedules provided relief for the mother and regularity for the child. The passage of time has brought evidence[5] that the specific type of feeding or other childrearing practices employed by the parents are seldom or only indirectly related to subsequent personality characteristics. The question has, however, remained one of general and professional interest, and we shall therefore consider the relationship between self-esteem and the type and schedule of infant feeding employed.

---

[5] H. Orlansky. "Infant care and personality." *Psych. Bull.*, **46**:1–48 (1949).

TABLE 8.2 *Type of feeding employed in infancy*

| | Subjective self-esteem | | |
|---|---|---|---|
| Type of feeding | Low | Medium | High |
| Breast-fed 4 months or more | 33.3% (10) | 11.8% (2) | 30.3% (10) |
| Bottle-fed from birth | 40.0% (12) | 58.8% (10) | 66.7% (22) |
| Bottle-fed—early shift from breast | 26.7% (8) | 29.4% (5) | 3.0% (1) |
| Totals | 100.0% (30) | 100.0% (17) | 100.0% (33) |

$\chi^2 = 10.85$     df = 4     p < .05

*Source:* Mother's interview.

Proponents of the psychoanalytic position conclude[6] that breast-feeding increases the child's sense of security and well-being. Such feelings presumably derive from the greater sense of acceptance that comes with breast-feeding, which cannot be achieved by more artificial methods. To test whether persons who are high in self-esteem were more likely to have been breast- or bottle-fed, we asked their mothers to specify the type of feeding procedures they had employed. Their responses, summarized in Table 8.2, are divided into three categories: children breast-fed four months or more; children bottle-fed from birth; and children who were bottle-fed after early attempts at breast-feeding. Comparison of the responses of mothers whose children differ in self-esteem indicates that the type of feeding employed in infancy is unrelated to present levels of self-esteem. The percentage of breast-fed subjects in the high self-esteem group is 30.3 percent, which is not significantly different from the percentage of 33.3 percent in the low self-esteem group. There is a tendency for mothers of children with high self-esteem to employ *bottle-feeding* more frequently (66.7 percent) than the mothers of children with low self-esteem (40.0 percent). However, this result, and the most striking feature of Table 8.2, is in the mothers who began breast-feeding and subsequently shifted to the bottle. These mothers account for 26.7 percent of the low self-esteem group and 29.4 percent of the medium self-esteem group, but account for only 3.0 percent of the high self-esteem group. These results suggest that it is not necessarily breast- or bottle-feeding that eventuates in a sense of assurance but the mother's physical and psychological resolution of the

[6] S. Brody. *Patterns of Mothering: Maternal Influences during Infancy.* New York, International Universities Press, 1956.

TABLE 8.3 *Schedule of feeding employed in infancy*

| | Discrepant self-esteem | |
| --- | --- | --- |
| Time of feeding | High discrepancy groups (High-Low, Low-High) | Low discrepancy groups (High-High, Medium-Medium, Low-Low) |
| Flexible, self-demand | 74.2% (23) | 51.0% (25) |
| Scheduled | 25.8% (8) | 49.0% (24) |
| Totals | 100.0% (31) | 100.0% (49) |

$\chi^2 = 4.28$     df $= 1$     p $< .05$

*Source:* Mother's interview.

issue toward one method or the other. The mothers of children with high self-esteem are either more certain of their decision or less apt to fail in breast-feeding once they initiate it. It is worth noting too that the mothers who shifted from breast- to bottle-feeding were prone to express guilt and uneasiness about the shift and to defend the necessity of such a move. Since the hypothesis that breast-feeding is more likely to result in high self-esteem has been disproved, it appears that the specific feeding practice is less important for the child's esteem than is the consistent, continued use of the same (initial) procedure.

The second aspect of feeding practices to be considered is the use of flexible, "self-demand" schedules as compared to those which involve fixed routines and schedules. Since self-demand schedules place the mother at the child's disposal, they are likely to provide rapid and reliable sources of gratification and result in a greater sense of control over the environment. This sense of control is not conscious or explicit in the infant, and exists more in his fantasy and imagination than in the control he exerts over the real world. Some ego psychologists have proposed that these early fantasies and convictions are a significant contributor to the infant's sense of omnipotence. Such feelings of power and control as are subsumed by the term omnipotence would presumably indicate that the individual believed himself to be a source of power and an object of importance. To determine whether self-demand feeding was related to the experience of high self-esteem, we compared the schedules employed by the mothers of our self-esteem groups. The results indicated that infant feeding schedules were unrelated to the subjective experience or behavioral expression of self-esteem but they were significantly related to the discrepancy between them. Thus, we see in Table 8.3 that those persons with large discrepancies—the High-Low and Low-High groups —are likely to have been fed on self-demand far more often (74.2 percent) than are persons with small discrepancies (51.0 percent). This would indicate that self-demand is apt to be associated with subjective evaluations that are markedly discrepant from overt behavioral manifestations of esteem. Since these subjective evaluations are as likely to be low (Low-High) as high (High-Low), there is no basis for assuming that self-demand schedules eventuate in feelings of omnipotence. The child brought up under such a regimen apparently does not encounter a sufficiently well-defined environment to permit him to arrive at an integrated appraisal of his competencies and acceptance. Therefore the concept of defensiveness we have previously applied to these discrepancy groups is as likely to arise from uncertainty of response as from sensitivity to rebuke and fear of exposure. Such an interpretation would be consistent with the present finding and with previous indications that discrepant self-esteem is related to conditions of social instability and poorly defined parental characteristics. The over-all results of our examination of the relation between self-esteem and feeding practices are to negate the view that breast-feeding and flexible schedules are best for the child. Clear, decisive resolution of feeding practices, using either method and either schedule, are most likely to produce positive and stabilizing effects.

## CHILDHOOD TRAUMA AND PROBLEMS

There are certain sorts of events in the course of childhood that are presumed to have a profound and deleterious influence upon subsequent development. Such occurrences as serious illnesses or accidents may affect the child himself, or they may touch those close to him and alter his perceptions and reactions to the world. There are numerous instances in the clinical literature[7] where individuals have suffered severe blows in childhood and have retained the residues and scars of those events for several years and sometimes for the remainder of their lives. Experimental studies of traumatic avoidance conditioning[8] with nonhuman species have indicated that such traumatic experiences retain their influence for long periods of time and are difficult to extinguish even then. Thus, though events as drastic as those subsumed under the term "trauma" may be presumed to be rare, they are capable of exerting prolonged harmful influences. In theory, at least, it is possible to

---

[7] A. Freud and D. Burlingame. *Infants without Families*. New York, International Universities Press, 1944.

[8] R. L. Solomon and L. C. Wynne. "Traumatic avoidance learning: The principles of anxiety conservation and partial irreversibility." *Psych. Rev.*, 61:353–385 (1954).

TABLE 8.4 *Incidence of serious illness, accidents, and events during childhood*

| Traumatic occurrences | Subjective self-esteem | | |
|---|---|---|---|
| | Low | Medium | High |
| No notable events, episodes, illness | 53.3% (16) | 70.6% (12) | 63.6% (21) |
| One or more notable events, episodes, illness | 46.7% (14) | 29.4% (5) | 36.4% (12) |
| Totals | 100.0% (30) | 100.0% (17) | 100.0% (33) |

$\chi^2 = 1.50$     df = 2     p < .50

*Source:* Subject's interview.

propose that persons who have experienced severe trauma might be less venturesome in their efforts and more guarded in their convictions of mastery. In the present section we shall consider the relationship between the frequency of such traumata and self-esteem.

Our data on the traumatic events experienced by our subjects were obtained from the subjects and from their mothers. They included events that occurred from the time of the mother's pregnancy and delivery until the time of interview. Turning first to the birth of our subjects, an event which some theorists invest with traumatic import, we find no (significant) difference between the self-esteem groups ($\chi^2 = 2.85$, df = 2, p < .30). This would indicate that, so far as the subjects and their mothers recall and report, difficulties surrounding birth are unrelated to present feelings of esteem.

The second source of potential trauma we examined was the extent to which the subject had received extensive care from adults other than his parents. This included instances of total separation because of illness, travel, and so on, and instances in which both parents were working and could not attend to their children. There were few cases of total separation and those that did occur showed no relationship with self-esteem. There were also no differences in the relationship between those cases that required extensive nonparental care and self-esteem ($\chi^2 = .73$, df = 2, p < .50).

Our third and final concern was the incidence of serious illnesses, accidents, and other events during our subject's childhood, including all episodes that were recalled and deemed unusually severe or unusual by the subjects. The frequency of such events for the groups differing in self-esteem is presented in Table 8.4. Statistical analysis reveals that the distribution does not differ significantly from chance occurrence ($\chi^2 = 1.50$, df = 2, p < .50). Thus,

TABLE 8.5 *Frequency of problems during course of child's development*

| Frequency of problems | Subjective self-esteem | | |
| --- | --- | --- | --- |
| | Low | Medium | High |
| Relatively rare or infrequent | 33.3% (10) | 47.1% (8) | 66.7% (22) |
| Relatively frequent | 66.7% (20) | 52.9% (9) | 33.3% (11) |
| Totals | 100.0% (30) | 100.0% (17) | 100.0% (33) |

$\chi^2 = 7.06$     df $= 2$     p $< .05$

*Source:* Mother's interview.

judging by our findings on these three types of trauma, such events are unrelated to self-esteem. It appears that continued persistent mistreatment or lack of successes are required to produce long-term, negative self-evaluations. Single, critical episodes can rarely achieve that end without additional support.

Although these results indicate that self-esteem is unrelated to the occurrence of severe or dramatically damaging experiences, they do not establish that childhood was equally placid and smooth for persons at all levels of self-esteem. It is possible that less severe or dramatic occurrences were more frequent in some groups than others. Such events, by their repetitive occurrence, might well have a more depressing effect than would be achieved by more isolated, dramatic episodes. The frequency of problems encountered by the child during the course of his development was obtained during the course of the mother interview. Problems were distinguished from trauma by their lesser severity, their more casual character, and their less abrupt occurrence. They included such difficulties as bedwetting, thumbsucking, extended or repetitive illnesses, and academic stresses and failures. As Table 8.5 reveals, the frequency of such problems is significantly related to self-esteem. The mothers' reports indicate that two-thirds of children with low self-esteem experienced frequent problems, but only one-third of the children with high self-esteem and one-half of the children with medium self-esteem were plagued by equally frequent difficulties. The differences are statistically significant in this instance ($\chi^2 = 7.06$, df $= 2$, p $< .05$), indicating that recurrent problems are more likely to have an effect upon self-esteem than are severe or dramatic episodes or events. Though the results are clear, they give no indication of sequence—whether low self-esteem is likely to result in more frequent problems or whether the problems result in lowered self-

TABLE 8.6 *Extent to which subject spent time alone or with others during childhood*

| Degree of gregariousness | Subjective self-esteem | | |
|---|---|---|---|
| | Low | Medium | High |
| Generally alone | 17.7% (6) | 00.0% (0) | 00.0% (0) |
| Generally with others | 82.3% (28) | 100.0% (17) | 100.0% (34) |
| Totals | 100.0% (34) | 100.0% (17) | 100.0% (34) |

*Source:* Subject's interview.

appraisal. Nor do these results indicate whether the mothers of children with low self-esteem are more likely to define events as problems than are the mothers of other children. All we can conclude is that difficulties more frequently arise in the backgrounds of children with low self-esteem than in the backgrounds of others, but they are no more likely to experience severe or traumatic episodes.

### EARLY SOCIAL RELATIONSHIPS

The social relationships of the child generally extend outward from the nurturing mother to the father, siblings, and neighborhood peers. These persons form the social context for the vast majority of experiences encountered during childhood. The extended family, parental acquaintances, and strangers may occasionally play an important role, but it is parents, siblings, and peers who are the major defining influences. In this section we shall consider some features of the early social environments in which our subjects were reared. We shall focus upon the subject's relationships with peers and siblings and consider the child's relationships with his parents in the next four chapters (Chapters 9, 10, 11, and 12).

The first feature of the subject's early social environment we shall consider is the amount of time he spent alone, as compared to the time he spent with other persons. Although this is not necessarily a measure of popularity or social skills, it does provide an index of the early social stimulation to which our subjects were exposed. Such an index would apply specifically to interpersonal stimulation rather than to intellectual or cultural stimulation, which could be attained by nonsocial means. The subjects reported the amount of time they generally spent alone and spent with others during their childhood; the results are summarized in Table 8.6. More than one in six of the subjects with low self-esteem report that they were generally alone during childhood, but none of the persons in either the high or medium self-esteem groups report such experiences of isolation. Although the distribution of scores does not meet the assumptions required for statistical analysis, the results have enough theoretical import and manifest enough difference to warrant a brief discussion. There are three potential bases for the social isolation of the child with low self-esteem: they are not valued and sought by others, they prefer isolation, and their environments provide limited opportunities for social interaction. From the data we and other investigators have obtained it appears that all three of these possibilities hold for those low in self-esteem, with the end result apparently a form of social impoverishment. Thus we find that subjects with low self-esteem report that they feel awkward and uncomfortable when in the presence of others,[9] that they are less likely to be selected as friends by their peers,[10] and (as we shall see in Chapter 9) they are less likely to receive attention and concern from their parents. Other social conditions that may contribute to this social isolation are more frequent moves made by the families of children with low self-esteem and the likelihood of prolonged separation or the death of one of their parents. Neither of these differences is statistically significant but both are suggestive ($p < .20$), in the same direction and in accord with theoretical expectations. These occurrences might interfere with the continuation of established relationships and contribute to an isolation already induced by personal preferences and the reactions of others.

The most immediate social environment of the child is that which prevails with his parents and siblings. The child's siblings provide him with the most readily available sources of comradeship and stimulation as well as his immediate and threatening competition. Parents may contribute to the development of competitive attitudes in their children or they may resist and countermand them. Whatever their source, it seems reasonable to assume that constant comparison and competition would prove distressing and devaluating for most, and probably for all, children in the family. All children would have to be continually on guard, and even those who were favored by parents would suffer the ill will of their less favored brothers and sisters.

It is interesting to note that sibling rivalry has long been a source of interest and concern, but its counterpart—sibling support and friendship—has been

---

[9] M. Rosenberg. *Society and the Adolescent Self-Image.* Princeton, Princeton University Press, 1965, Chapter Nine, "Interpersonal Attitudes and Behavior," pp. 168–187.
[10] S. Coopersmith. "A method of determining types of self-esteem." *J. Abn. Soc. Psych.,* **59:**87–94 (1959).

TABLE 8.7 *Extent to which siblings "stuck together"*
*during childhood (only children not included)*

| | Subjective self-esteem | | |
|---|---|---|---|
| Sibling cohesiveness | Low | Medium | High |
| Relatively close | 69.0% (20) | 50.0% (8) | 85.2% (23) |
| Relatively distant | 31.0% (9) | 50.0% (8) | 14.8% (4) |
| Totals | 100.0% (29) | 100.0% (16) | 100.0% (27) |

$x^2 = 6.10$      df $= 2$      p $<$ .05

*Source:* Subject's interview.

less closely examined. In the present instance we sought to determine whether close and congenial sibling relationships, and the attendant feelings of acceptance, would be associated with higher self-esteem. To ascertain whether this was indeed the case, we asked our subjects to indicate the extent to which they and their siblings "stuck together" during childhood. These responses were placed along a four-point scale that ranged from very close to very distant. The responses of only children, inappropriate in this context, were excluded from the analysis. The distribution of responses for the self-esteem groups is presented in Table 8.7. Examination of the table reveals that only 14 percent of the high self-esteem group report that they and their siblings have been relatively distant, whereas more than twice that number of the low self-esteem group (31.0 percent) and three times as many members of the medium self-esteem group report such feelings of distance. The most striking feature of the distribution is the large percentage of individuals with high self-esteem who report that they and their siblings generally "stick together." This suggests that high self-esteem is more likely to develop where there is mutual support among siblings than where they are distant or antagonistic.

A brief interpretation may clarify the bases of sibling cohesiveness. Among the possible sources of cohesiveness on which we have evidence are age and sex distribution. Our own findings fail to indicate any significant relationships between sibling cohesiveness and the distribution of ages and sex, or the interaction of these two variables. This suggests that the source of such cohesiveness is more likely to be found in the children's characteristics, the parental methods of treating their entire complement of children, or, most likely, the interaction of these two conditions. Our data on the subjects themselves suggest that individuals with high self-esteem are socially skilled

TABLE 8.8 *Subject's relationship with peers during childhood*

| | Subjective self-esteem | | |
|---|---|---|---|
| Relationship with peers | Low | Medium | High |
| Excellent or good | 53.3% (16) | 94.1% (16) | 76.7% (23) |
| Moderate or poor | 46.7% (14) | 5.9% (1) | 23.3% (7) |
| Totals | 100.0% (30) | 100.0% (17) | 100.0% (30) |

$\chi^2 = 9.51$    df = 2    p < .05

*Source:* Subject's interview.

persons who get along well with other children. Convinced of their own worth, they are less inclined to make an issue of superiority or to bully others; low in anxiety, they can be more relaxed and assured in dealing with situations that threaten or distort their social relationships; successful in outside (nonfamilial) activities, these children have less need to displace aggressive feelings toward their siblings and parents. The over-all impression of these children is that they are likely to be congenial and accepting individuals who can be members or leaders, and who are effective in their social relationships. The manner by which parents might increase sibling cohesiveness is one on which we have no direct information. Our knowledge of the parents indicates that they are generally assured, stable, and self-reliant individuals who are likely to deal with issues and problems directly and realistically. They probably deal with the relationships between their children in the same effective manner with which they deal with other issues that confront them. To anticipate slightly, we may indicate that they define conditions clearly, enforce them vigorously, and express concern, attention, and love.

Extending our examination beyond the family, we now turn to the child's relationships with his peers. Information on this point would indicate whether the quality of relationships established with parents and sibs would generalize to nonfamilial age-mates. The evaluation of the subject's relationship with peers was made by the subject himself. The distribution of responses for each self-esteem group is presented in Table 8.8. It shows that persons with low self-esteem are far more likely to report poor or moderate relations with their peers (46.7 percent) than are those who are medium (5.9 percent) or high (23.3 percent) in self-esteem. From these self-reports it appears that persons with low self-esteem have poorer social relationships with their peers as well as their sibs. The implications of Tables 8.6, 8.7, and 8.8 are that persons with low self-esteem have less congenial and stimulating social experiences than do persons who are loftier in esteem. Thus, above and apart from their relationships with their parents (which we shall shortly consider), we find that persons with low self-esteem have suffered estrangement from their sibs and peers.

In summary of this chapter, we may note several features of early experience that are associated with self-esteem. Self-esteem is higher among first and only children than it is among children who occupy other ordinal positions. Children high in self-esteem are less likely to have experienced frequent, non-serious problems during the early years of their childhood. However, they are just as likely to have experienced serious traumata. Family size is unrelated to self-esteem, as is the type of feeding the mother employs with her infant. What is important is the certainty of the mother's resolution of which method she should employ. Mothers who shift from breast to bottle early are more likely to have children with low self-esteem. The early social relationships of children who differ in self-esteem differ in several ways. Children with high self-esteem are less likely than others to have been "loners" in their childhood and more likely to have been close to their siblings. They also report that they have good social relationships with nonfamilial peers. The results indicate that persons with high self-esteem have more frequent, positive, and congenial experiences during their childhood years.

# Chapter nine

# Parent-child relationships I: ACCEPTANCE

The present chapter, and the three that follow, will deal with the relationship between parental attitudes and practices and the self-esteem of their children. These chapters will deal with the interaction between parent and child as it occurred in the past and as it occurs in the current home situation. This section on parent-child interaction will fill out our design of considering children and parents separately, and then jointly, as mutually affecting, interacting forces. Though assuming interaction, we shall here emphasize the attitudes and practices of the parents. Children are undoubtedly able to influence parental actions, but the bulk of the influence is necessarily and inevitably in the opposite direction. Children—young children especially—are so vulnerable and dependent upon their parents that they survive and thrive largely by accommodating themselves to parental standards. This focus upon parental action will not be exclusive, however, since we shall indicate the child's reactions to parental treatment and his perceptions of the practices they employ. Our intent in these four chapters is to provide a detailed picture of the practices that prevail in the households of our subjects. Inasmuch as they come from normal, typical middle-class backgrounds, the practices we shall discuss are presumably those which prevail in a large segment of American society. The parental attitudes and behavior we shall consider are those that appear most relevant to the formation of self-esteem as this process is conceptualized in our theoretical analyses (Chapter 2). Specific behaviors are presented under four categories, which reflect their theoretical cohesiveness and the results of factor analyses of parental behavior.

The first dimension we shall consider is acceptance, the second permissiveness, the third democratic practices, and the fourth independence. Each of these will be examined and discussed in a separate chapter, with the focus in each case upon the relationship between those practices and the formation of self-esteem. The present chapter will consider the relationship between parental acceptance and the child's self-esteem and consider how such acceptance is expressed.

### PARENTAL ACCEPTANCE

At the core of parental sentiments toward their child are their attitudes of love and approval for the child as he is. Other persons will value him for his appearance, abilities, performance, or other qualities, but parents can express love and approval to a child who is limited in his attributes and functioning. They can feel love and express acceptance to the disfigured and retarded child as well as to the child who is bright and handsome. It is undoubtedly easier to be loving to a gifted, charming, and attractive child, but such approval and support may be given to any child. In the abstract, the child need neither earn nor gain their love and approval; he has achieved it by being their child. His value to them is not achieved but ascribed; their regard for him will not be lost by the judgments of peer, school, or community. Parental love and approval, the expressions of value and regard, may be expressed in a variety of ways but, in the ideal, it remains an insistent and consistent expression of parental attitudes and behavior.

Previous studies have revealed some of the more important ways in which acceptance can be expressed: devotion to the child's interests, sensitivity to his needs and desires, and expressions of affection and approval. In other contexts, these expressions of affection and close rapport have been subsumed under such terms as warmth and child-centeredness. Parents who are warm and accepting express their appreciation of their child by both mundane and lofty acts. They are concerned with his whereabouts and welfare, solicitous about his health, and supportive when he experiences distress or failure. Though they may express disapproval about particular deeds the child may have performed or omitted, their acceptance of the child himself is unconditional.

The characteristic actions of rejecting parents stand in sharp distinction to the warmth and approval expressed by those more accepting in nature. These parents are hostile, cold, and disapproving of their child and regard him as an intrusive, valueless, or even negative object. They express their rejection by neglecting their child and by a callous indifference to his requests, needs, or aspirations. He is depreciated and treated as a burden who must be borne—an affliction and legal responsibility rather than a valued and desirable trust. These attitudes of disapproval, lack of affection, and hostility may be expressed as either passive or active forms of rejection. In the passive form the parent adopts a casual, indifferent attitude in which the child is ignored, the nonchalance presumably reflecting passive unconcern for the child. The more active form of rejection results in more overt and vigorous manifestations of hostility, such as open declarations of dislike, harsh and unwarranted punishment, and deprivation of physical necessities and social attention. Both passive and active forms of rejection express disinterest, disapproval, and distaste for the child.

Our major premise in this chapter is that parental acceptance has an enhancing effect upon self-esteem in particular, and psychosocial development in general. Parental rejection, at the other extreme, presumably results in an impoverished environment and a diminished sense of personal worthiness.

Before turning to our findings, we should clarify three issues on our manner of defining and conceptualizing the dimension of acceptance. First, this discussion of parental acceptance deals only with those parental attitudes and practices directed specifically toward the child. It does not include such indices as acceptance of parental roles or regard for the child's wishes in making family decisions. These facets of parental behavior are discussed elsewhere in this book (Chapters 6 and 11). In making this distinction we are proposing that parental role definitions may be independent of the good will, love, and approval that is expressed directly to children. Thus, whereas our previous findings indicated that the mothers of children with high self-esteem tend to take a more assertive view of the maternal role and reject some of its negative features, we are now proposing that these mothers may well be more favorably disposed toward the children themselves. The important issue at hand is whether acceptance of one's children is independent of particular definitions of feminine or maternal roles or whether there is a necessary connection between the two. In this study we assume that a woman who enjoys her work outside the family is as likely to accept and love her children as a woman who devotes herself exclusively to homemaking.

The second and related issue concerns the extent of acceptance required to enhance a child's self-regard. As generally employed, the terms of acceptance and rejection refer to unmixed and unlimited states of love, support, and approval. Because of this usage it is often assumed, by both professionals and laymen, that the most beneficial effects for the child are derived from parental attitudes and practices that are most extremely positive. This assumption is a defensible one, but it is nonetheless an assumption rather than a demonstrated or confirmed finding. For example, the work of Levy[1] suggests that extreme, unrelieved expressions of acceptance may be associated with underlying and well-defended feelings of rejection. The over-all results of that study suggest that parents who genuinely accept their children are not hesitant about rebuffing or disciplining their child when such action appears warranted. A subsequent study[2] of mother attitudes prior to pregnancy and their subsequent reaction to the child indicates that mothers who are rejecting often show their rejection by a solicitous overprotective concern for their child. A more moderate acceptance, marked by appropriate reactions to the child's behavior and a delineation of limits as to what he may expect and demand may have more favorable consequences for self-esteem than unqualified, unlimited approval. This is a point we shall elaborate later in this chapter and in the theoretical interpretation to be presented in Chapter 13. It is, however, important for our subsequent discussion to propose that favorable, but not extreme, attitudes of acceptance—expressed in ways appropriate to the child's age and the cultural norms—may be more enhancing than are less favorable or unbounded expressions of acceptance.

The third issue is the ambiguity of the concept of acceptance, with resultant difficulties of achieving common definitions and measurement. The concept of acceptance has been interpreted in so many different ways and attributed to so many varied behaviors that it has virtually lost specific meaning and operational significance. Although it is not our present purpose to dwell upon the varied meanings of that term, it is important that the term we employ and measure have clear and specific referents. We have already indicated that unconditional love and approval of the child is at the core of parental and sex role definitions, and of any limits upon child behavior that parents may establish. We further propose that the child's view of whether or not his parents are accepting is at least as important as the parents' view on the particular practices employed. On this last point

---

[1] D. M. Levy. *Maternal Overprotection.* New York, Columbia University Press, 1943.
[2] M. R. Zemlick and R. I. Watson. "Maternal attitudes of acceptance and rejection during and after pregnancy." *Amer. J. Orthopsychiat.*, 23:570–584 (1953).

TABLE 9.1 *Rating of mother's affection for her child*

| Rating of mother | Subjective self-esteem | | |
|---|---|---|---|
| | Low | Medium | High |
| Little or moderate affection | 43.3% (13) | 17.6% (3) | 21.2% (7) |
| Considerable or strong affection | 56.7% (17) | 82.4% (14) | 78.8% (26) |
| Totals | 100.0% (30) | 100.0% (17) | 100.0% (33) |

$\chi^2 = 5.05$    df $= 2$    p $< .08$

*Source:* Interviewer's report.

we may note that attempts[3,4] to relate specific antecedent parental practices with specific consequent personality variables have been generally unsuccessful. It appears that the specific practice employed by the parents is not as crucial as their generally prevailing attitudes toward their child. Those attitudes may be expressed in a variety of behaviors and with different degrees of intensity so that no single practice is in itself a sufficient or accurate index of acceptance. Under the circumstances, we have emphasized general attitudes of acceptance expressed by the parents rather than those more specific attitudes and practices described in the interview and questionnaire. The latter were limited in number and generally employed as indices of broader attitudinal predispositions.

Our discussion of parental acceptance is based on the assumptions just noted. It is divided into three parts, each focusing upon different manifestations of this general category of behavior. The first deals with general attitudes of acceptance as expressed by the mother; the second examines the child's feelings toward his parents; and the third considers several particular manifestations of parental acceptance.

## MATERNAL ACCEPTANCE AND AFFECTION

We obtained two general indices of maternal acceptance and affection. These were an interviewer's rating of maternal affection and an index of the closeness of the mother-child relationship. Both were derived from the impressions

---

[3] H. Orlansky. "Infant care and personality." *Psych. Bull.,* **46:**1–48 (1949).
[4] W. H. Sewell, P. H. Mussen, and C. W. Harris. "Relationship among child training practices." *Amer. Sociol. Rev.,* **20:**137–148 (1955).

TABLE 9.2 *Mother-child rapport*

| Degree of rapport | Subjective self-esteem | | |
|---|---|---|---|
| | Low | Medium | High |
| Distant or moderate | 50.0% (15) | 11.8% (2) | 12.2% (4) |
| Close | 50.0% (15) | 88.2% (15) | 87.8% (29) |
| Totals | 100.0% (30) | 100.0% (17) | 100.0% (33) |

$\chi^2 = 13.99$      $df = 2$      $p < .001$

*Source:* Score of scale based on mother's responses in interview.

and information obtained during the course of the mother interview. The rating was based upon the interviewer's impressions of the mother's affection for her child, which were summarized in a rating along a seven-point scale of affection. The interviewers were instructed to use all indications of affection in their appraisal and to evaluate these expressions according to their judgment of the genuineness of the feelings expressed. The distribution of these appraisals for groups differing in subjective self-esteem is presented in Table 9.1. These results indicate that mothers of children with low self-esteem are likely (43.3 percent) to express only limited affection for their children; the mothers of children with medium and high self-esteem generally express considerably greater affection (82.4 percent and 78.8 percent, respectively). The differences between the various levels of esteem approach statistical significance ($p < .08$) and suggest that persons with low self-esteem receive less affection than those with more favorable self-regard. This finding would support the belief that the absence of reflected favorable approval and support have demeaning consequences.

Our second index of parental acceptance deals with the closeness that exists between mother and child. The actual score employed was derived from the mother's responses to a series of questions dealing with rapport, joint activities, and respectful consideration. Coders examined the responses and summarized them in a rating on a five-point scale. The negative end of the scale illustrates the nature of the questions considered. This point of the scale is described as "(mother considers) child difficult, inferior, unusually bad, girls may be preferred, activities tend to be parent-centered, little time (spent) together, intrusive and disrespectful attitude." The other end of the scale was marked by a closer and more favorable relationship. Two coders independently reviewed the items in the scale and assigned a scale score. The correlation between their scores, prior to a conference to resolve their differences, was .82. Table 9.2 shows the percentage of mothers of the subjective self-esteem groups who maintain close or distant relationships with their children.

From Table 9.2 it is clear that the mothers of children with low self-esteem are far more likely to maintain distant relationships than are the mothers of medium and high self-esteem children. Thus we find that half of the mothers in the low self-esteem group (50 percent) are rated as having a distant or moderate relationship, but less than one-fourth that percentage of the medium (11.8 percent) and high (12.2 percent) are similarly evaluated. Whether by reflected appraisal or the consequences of the practices actually employed, to be treated with concern, affection, and attention appears to have enhancing consequences. And unless that treatment were apparent in relatively overt manifestation of closeness, it could not be so readily rated by persons unfamiliar with mother and child.

### CHILD'S PERCEPTIONS OF PARENTAL ACCEPTANCE

Maternal expressions of affection and closeness are not necessarily viewed as such by their children. Children do not necessarily or always view parental actions as stemming from the same favorable motives as do their parents, nor do they necessarily view them as the supportive, loving, and approving figures the parents may wish to believe. This is not only a case of differing perceptions or wishful thinking, but may be an inevitable consequence of the developmental process. Parents are required to play the dual roles of satisfier and frustrater, provider and limiter, comrade and authority. In the course of development, they will inevitably be compelled to discipline and restrict the activities of their children. The manner and extent to which they assert authority will influence their child's perceptions of them but the (real or apparent) necessity and inevitability of such actions may permit even harsh and disapproving parents to believe that they are acting solely for their children's benefit. This belief need not be shared by the child, who may regard the self-congratulating parent as a rejecting and insensitive despot. If parents are to be viewed as accepting and approving while they, at the same time, limit and frustrate their children, it is essential that they be consistently and deeply well disposed. If, in the face of restrictions and demands, the children continue to perceive their parents as accepting, we may conclude that they are genuinely convinced that parental actions stem from concern and love rather than hostility. Under the varied demands and frustrations of child-

TABLE 9.3 *Extent to which subject agrees with views of other members of the family*

| Agreement with family | Subjective self-esteem | | |
|---|---|---|---|
| | Low | Medium | High |
| Generally agrees | 56.7% (17) | 58.8% (10) | 100.0% (27) |
| Tends to disagree | 43.3% (13) | 41.2% (7) | 00.0% (0) |
| Totals | 100.0% (30) | 100.0% (17) | 100.0% (27) |

$\chi^2 = 15.77$     df $= 2$     p $< .001$

*Source:* Subject's questionnaire.

rearing, favorable perception of parents indicates the child's acceptance of his parents—a response presumably evoked by their long-term favorable actions toward him.

The indications of child acceptance we shall consider express the child's reactions to the parental treatment he has received. Inasmuch as it is difficult for a child to express direct criticism of his parents (and unwise of us to encourage such criticisms), we employed indirect expressions of acceptance to gauge his attitude. The first response we shall consider is the extent to which the subject agrees with the opinions of other members of his family. Such agreement would indicate the general consensual agreement within the family and, more particularly, the extent to which the child agrees with and shares the opinions of his parents and sibs. Such agreement presumably indicates great cohesiveness, support, and exchange between family members and could thus be taken as an indirect expression of family solidarity. Where the subject reports that his views are generally in agreement with those of other family members, we may assume that he feels more accepting and accepted than if he reports a lack of harmony. This line of reasoning is sustained by the results revealed in Table 9.3. As that table shows, all members of the high self-esteem group generally agree with the other members of their families. This compares with less than 60 percent of the medium (58.8 percent) and low (56.7 percent) self-esteem groups who express similar levels of support. Persons with high self-esteem apparently feel more at one with their families and are more favorably disposed toward their views.

Another gauge of the child's perception of parental acceptance is the amount of concern they express for his welfare. This can be revealed in concern for his health, performance, whereabouts, acquaintances, or a host of other fea-

TABLE 9.4 *Extent to which mother is acquainted with subject's friends*

| Degree of acquaintance | Subjective self-esteem | | |
|---|---|---|---|
| | Low | Medium | High |
| Knows some or none | 35.5% (11) | 5.9% (1) | 00.0% (0) |
| Knows all or most | 64.5% (20) | 94.1% (16) | 100.0% (30) |
| Totals | 100.0% (31) | 100.0% (17) | 100.0% (30) |

$x^2 = 16.25$     df = 2     p < .001

*Source:* Subject's questionnaire.

tures of his life. Among the more anxious concerns of parents of preadolescent boys is his selection of friends. This concern reflects the belief that "evil" companions can have a deleterious influence upon social, moral, and intellectual development. It also reflects the mother's general interest in her child and the extent to which she maintains a vigilant eye on his affairs. Children may object to frequent questioning and appraisal of their friends and regard such efforts as troublesome intrusions upon their private affairs, but previous studies[5] indicate that such "negative" attention has more favorable consequences than a general lack of interest. To examine the child's perceptions of parental concern, we asked our subject to indicate the extent to which their mothers were acquainted with their friends. Table 9.4 gives the frequency for each of the three subjective self-esteem groups. Judging by the reports of their children, the mothers of children with high and medium self-esteem are far more likely to know most of their children's friends than are the mothers of children with low self-esteem. None of the mothers of the high self-esteem group know less than half their sons' friends; 5.9 percent of the medium group and 35.5 percent of the low self-esteem group are equally unfamiliar with their child's acquaintances. That over one-third of the children with low self-esteem do not see their mothers as concerned and interested in their friends suggests that these children perceive their parents as uninvolved or unconcerned in their affairs. The fact that this lack of acquaintance is so much greater in families of children with low self-esteem suggests that parental ignorance of peers is taken as a sign of disinterest rather than great trust. This finding confirms our earlier impression that the parents of children with low self-esteem are likely to be rejecting and indicates an avenue by which that rejection is expressed.

[5] M. Rosenberg. *Society and the Adolescent Self-Image.* Princeton, Princeton University Press, 1965.

TABLE 9.5 *Nature of relationship with mothers as revealed in Thematic Apperception Test*

| Type of responses | Subjective self-esteem | | |
| --- | --- | --- | --- |
| | Low | Medium | High |
| Repeated negative referrals | 41.2% (14) | 41.2% (7) | 17.6% (6) |
| Positive, neutral referrals | 58.8% (20) | 58.8% (10) | 82.4% (28) |
| Totals | 100.0% (34) | 100.0% (17) | 100.0% (34) |
| $x^2 = 5.22$      df $= 2$ | p $<$ .08 | | |

*Source:* Clinical test.

Our final index of the child's perception of his parents is derived from the Thematic Apperception Test (TAT). As indicated in Chapter 4, this projective test was part of the clinical battery administered to all our subjects. The test, originated by Henry Murray and his collaborators,[6] consists of a series of pictures, which are used to elicit stories from the subject. The stories presumably reveal the respondent's underlying motivations and chief concerns. We obtained six stories from each subject and scored them by a method worked out according to the need system developed by Murray and a special experiential analysis developed for this study. Since the details of this scoring system are not germane to the present report, we shall omit them here, simply noting that the experimental analysis of projective material involves scoring each story for each of twenty-six different scales. All are five-point unidimensional scales. The scales we shall consider in the present context are those dealing with "Nature of relationship with mother." The high end of both scales is characterized by extremely negative, frustrating, or destructive influences exerted by the parental figures in the story. Repeated references of such a negative nature in a projective test presumably indicates that the subject believes that parent to be a nonsupportive, negative influence, although the subject is not necessarily aware of this belief. In our analysis of the TAT scores we noted the number of individuals in each self-esteem group who made repeated, extremely negative references about their mother and father. Operationally this meant that the individual received a score of four or five on at least two of the six stories. Table 9.5 indicates the number of

[6] H. A. Murray. *Explorations in Personality.* New York, Oxford University Press, 1938.

individuals in each of the subjective self-esteem groups who made repeated negative references about their mother.

Persons with high self-esteem are less likely (17.6 percent) to perceive their parents as negative or destructive influences than are persons with medium (41.2 percent) of low (41.2 percent) self-esteem. Judging by these findings, more children with high self-esteem have favorable opinions of their mothers and view them in a more favorable light in their unconscious projections as well as in their more overt statements. Where children with lower self-esteem express more frustration and rejection, those with high self-esteem see less rejection and a greater amount of approval and facilitation. The results indicate that children with lower self-esteem unconsciously view their mothers as more hostile and antagonistic than do those with loftier self-evaluations. The projections that the stories disclose presumably reflect prior experiences and the currently prevailing interpretation of the mother. This finding is consistent with other indications of the children's perceptions of their parents and confirms the impression that children with low self-esteem view their parents as less supportive and concerned about their welfare. Analysis of the projective data on the child's relationship with his father failed to reveal any differences between the self-esteem groups (p < .40). They indicate that the fathers of subjects at all levels of self-esteem are unlikely (less than 20 percent) to be portrayed in a negative or destructive manner.

### SPECIFIC MANIFESTATIONS OF PARENTAL ACCEPTANCE

The discussion to this point has revealed that the mothers of children with low self-esteem are less affectionate and accepting and that their children perceive them in just this way. This presumably indicates that parental actions and attitudes are interpreted in much the same way by an outside observer, i.e., the interviewer, as they are by the child. The whole tenor of the results so far supports the general hypothesis that parental rejection results in feelings of personal insignificance. Thus, if we were asked to state a means of enhancing self-esteem, we could say that acceptance in general—and more particularly concern, affection, and close rapport—appears to have enhancing effects. The way to ensure a child's assurance is to care and to express that care so that it becomes an inherent part of the relationship. That acceptance is, in itself, insufficient to enhance self-esteem is something that will become clearer in the remaining chapters. That acceptance is an important and possibly necessary determinant of the child's self-esteem appears to be amply borne out by the findings already presented.

The ways in which a parent can express acceptance would appear to be unlimited. However, this appears to be truer for specific manifestations of acceptance than for the general, everyday expressions of concern and devotion. Parents can, for example, show their concern in such diverse ways as a hug, a talk, a toy, or a ride but each of these must convey some sense of interest if they are to have an enhancing effect. If such a sentiment is not conveyed, then the act is relatively devoid of psychological significance and its influence is correspondingly diminished. We have already noted that the intent and context of the act as well as the act itself are appreciated by the child. Thus, children with high self-esteem who are punished as often as children with lower self-esteem view their treatment as justified; those with less self-esteem believe they are being mistreated. Apparently rejecting parents convey their disapproval so that it is readily perceived, despite its varied and multifaceted expression. This would suggest that there are some common features of the language of acceptance that are readily appreciated by children, who employ them to gauge the underlying dispositions of their parents. In this section we shall consider several such features that tend to discriminate the various self-esteem groups. They consist of maternal attitudes and actions revealed by the mothers' responses to a questionnaire on childrearing practices.

The four items we shall discuss were included in the PARI questionnaire already mentioned. The mothers were presented with an inventory of eighty statements and asked to indicate whether they agreed or disagreed with each statement. The first statement concerns the relationship between the mother's interest in her children and their happiness. The mother's response indicates whether she believes that children would be happier and better behaved if parents were more interested in their affairs. Presumably persons who agree with this statement are more likely to show such interest, although there is no assurance that they will express it in their behavior. Agreement, however, does indicate a favorable predisposition toward such an attitude, which is not present in those who disagree. Agreement is greatest (100.0 percent) among the high self-esteem groups, and lowest among the low self-esteem groups (79.4 percent). That is, more mothers of children with high self-esteem believe that interest in their children is important and salutary than do the mothers of children with either low or medium self-esteem. The expression of such interest in their children's everyday affairs apparently is viewed as an indication of acceptance and would thus have enhancing effects. We may also note that though the majority of mothers in each group agree that parental interest has beneficial effects, the mothers of children with low and medium self-esteem are more likely to disagree with this opinion.

TABLE 9.6 *"Children would be happier and better behaved if parents would show an interest in their affairs"*

| Reply | Subjective self-esteem | | |
|---|---|---|---|
| | Low | Medium | High |
| Disagree | 20.6% (7) | 18.7% (3) | 00.0% (0) |
| Agree | 79.4% (27) | 81.3% (13) | 100.0% (31) |
| Totals | 100.0% (34) | 100.0% (16) | 100.0% (31) |
| $\chi^2 = 7.11$    df $= 2$    p $< .05$ | | | |

*Source:* Mother's questionnaire.

Another ready expression of maternal acceptance is her *availability* in times of distress and discomfort. By providing assistance and support when such events occur, the mother is able to bolster her child and assist him in dealing with his anxieties and fears, be they realistic or imagined. In doing so, she becomes a bastion from which the child can gain strength and reassurance, someone who will give advice and perspective. By being available during times of distress, she shows that her prior acceptance of the child is not contingent upon complete success and tranquillity. Availability to her children under such circumstances reflects maternal concern for her child's welfare and sensitivity to his distress. The questionnaire item dealing with such availability requires that the mother agree or disagree with the statement, "Children should not annoy their parents with their unimportant problems." Table 9.7 reveals that mothers of children with low self-esteem agree with the statement significantly more often (73.5 percent) than do the mothers of children with medium (31.3 percent) or high (45.2 percent) self-esteem. The mothers of children with low self-esteem do not wish to be disturbed by their children's problems and prefer that their children handle their difficulties without involving them. Perhaps the key phrase in the questionnaire statement is "unimportant problems." There is no way for a mother to know which problems are important and which are unimportant without discussion with her child. To ask that the child bring only his important problems is to evince an attitude that she not be disturbed unless the problem is of major proportions. Such a limitation is hardly indicative of support that can be depended upon in periods of adversity.

One reason often given against being always available to children is their propensity to seek attention from parents and other adults. According to this position, children will talk to any sympathetic listener and are prone to pro-

TABLE 9.7 *"Children should not annoy their parents with their unimportant problems"*

| Reply | Subjective self-esteem | | |
|---|---|---|---|
| | Low | Medium | High |
| Disagree | 26.5% (9) | 68.7% (11) | 54.8% (17) |
| Agree | 73.5% (25) | 31.3% (5) | 45.2% (14) |
| Totals | 100.0% (34) | 100.0% (16) | 100.0% (31) |

$x^2 = 9.54$     $df = 2$     $p < .01$

*Source:* Mother's questionnaire.

duce conversation, stories, and problems to keep their audience. Whatever the truth of this is, it is equally apparent that it can be employed to rationalize parental disinterest in their children. A mother who rejects her child and feels hostile toward him may justify her actions by claiming that his demands for attention and affection are insatiable. She may conclude that limiting her attention is required to maintain her effectiveness as a homemaker, and to gain some privacy for herself, and that it will be unlikely to have unfavorable consequences for her child. Although all women who hold such a view are by no means rejecting, the mother's attitude toward *attention-seeking* may be indicative of her general concern for her child. The manner in which she deals with the child's overtures, the frequency with which she satisfies them, and the context in which such actions occur clearly contribute to the significance of her behavior. The child's efforts to gain his mother's attention cannot be dismissed in a superficial fashion without suggesting that the mother is unconcerned about him.

Another item with which the mothers were asked to agree or disagree was the statement, "The trouble with giving attention to children's problems is that they usually just make up a lot of stories to keep you interested." The responses, summarized in Table 9.8 show that mothers of children with low self-esteem are much more likely to believe the statement (70.6 percent) than are the mothers of children with medium (37.5 percent) or high (35.5 percent) self-esteem. This finding corroborates the impression that the mothers of children with low self-esteem tend to be rejecting and suggests that their rejection is expressed by less attention to their children's needs. It also suggests that these mothers are more apt to rationalize their own indifference by statements impugning the child's motives and sincerity.

The final statement we shall consider deals with the parents' attitudes

TABLE 9.8 *"The trouble with giving attention to children's problems is they usually just make up a lot of stories to keep you interested"*

| Reply | Subjective self-esteem | | |
| --- | --- | --- | --- |
| | Low | Medium | High |
| Disagree | 29.4% (10) | 62.5% (10) | 64.5% (20) |
| Agree | 70.6% (24) | 37.5% (6) | 35.5% (11) |
| Totals | 100.0% (34) | 100.0% (16) | 100.0% (31) |

$\chi^2 = 9.37$     df = 2     p < .01

*Source:* Mother's questionnaire.

toward joint activities: "When you do things together, children feel close to you and can talk easier." The mother's response can be taken as an indirect indication of her belief that joint activities have favorable consequences for the child and can improve the parent-child relationship. As Table 9.9 shows, the mothers of children with low self-esteem are more apt (20.6 percent) to disagree with the statement than are the mothers of children with medium (00.0 percent) and high (3.2 percent) self-esteem. The mothers of those in the low self-esteem group (roughly 1 in 5) believe that joint activities do not give the child a sense of acceptance, but the great majority of all mothers tested did believe this (73 in 81). This suggests either that these women have a different relationship with their children than do other mothers or that their responses to this question reflect a defense against the lack of joint activities in their own families. It seems safe to conclude that negation of joint activities is associated with a disapproving, hostile attitude toward the child. This finding indicates a general attitude toward joint activities, but our interview data reveal that the actual amount of time spent in joint activities does not differ for the three self-esteem groups ($\chi^2 = .48$, df = 2, p < .80). Presumably it is the quality of experience in joint activities, rather than their quantity, that has a facilitating effect. Togetherness is enhancing if there is a feeling of acceptance and camaraderie, not merely physical assembly.

Before concluding, let us briefly summarize our findings on acceptance. The findings are all consistent, regardless of the instrument or source of information. They reveal that the mothers of children with high self-esteem are more loving and have closer relationships with their children than do the mothers of children with less self-esteem. The mothers of children with medium self-esteem tend to respond in a fashion that is generally similar to

TABLE 9.8 *"When you do things together, children feel close to you and can talk easier"*

| Reply | Subjective self-esteem | | |
| | Low | Medium | High |
| --- | --- | --- | --- |
| Disagree | 20.6% (7) | 00.0% (0) | 3.2% (1) |
| Agree | 79.4% (27) | 100.0% (16) | 96.8% (30) |
| Totals | 100.0% (34) | 100.0% (16) | 100.0% (31) |

$x^2 = 7.68$    $df = 2$    $p < .05$

*Source:* Mother's questionnaire.

those of children with high self-esteem, with both groups markedly different from the mothers of those low in self-esteem. The greater acceptance of the child with high and medium self-esteem is manifested by interest, concern about companions, availability, and congenial joint activities. The child apparently perceives and appreciates the attention and approval expressed by his mother and tends to view her as favoring and supportive. He also appears to interpret her interest and concern as an indication of his significance; basking in these signs of his personal importance, he comes to regard himself favorably. This is success in its most personal expression—the concern, attention, and time of significant others.

Some potential, indirect implications of parental acceptance and rejection should also be noted. These implications appear to be more readily apparent in the case of rejecting parents who fail to provide stimulating and facilitating environmental conditions than in the accepting families that do provide them. In the rejecting families we find conditions of isolation and deprivation like those that have proved to have debilitating effects in human and infrahuman infants.[7,8] The parents in these families are more likely to withdraw from their children, and by their inattentive and neglectful treatment to produce a milieu that is physically, emotionally, and intellectually impoverished. They are less likely to fondle or physically caress their infants, a form of stimulation that has been found to have beneficial effects in infrahuman primates. Viewed in the broader perspective of general psychological research, the rejecting family manifests many of the features of an environment that

[7] W. Goldfarb. "Psychological privation in infancy and subsequent adjustment." *Amer. J. Orthopsychiat.*, **15**:247–255 (1945).
[8] H. F. Harlow. "Effects of early experiences on personal, social, sexual and maternal behavior." Paper read to the Society for Research in Child Development, Berkeley, Calif., April 11, 1963.

provides little sensory stimulation. Thus, many of the frequently noted effects of rejection—flat affect, withdrawal, docility, and self-distrust—may be partially a function of the stimulation level within the household rather than issuing from the direct acts of hostility or lack of affection. Thus a recent summary[9] of the cognitive consequences of early sensory deprivation concludes that an impoverished environment "produces an adult organism with reduced ability to discriminate, with stunted strategies for coping with roundabout solutions, with less taste for exploratory behavior, and with a notably reduced tendency to draw inferences that serve to cement the disparate events of its environment." It is worth noting that personality theorists, psychotherapists, and social psychologists have attributed many of these same deficiencies to lack of self-esteem.

---

[9] J. S. Bruner. "The cognitive consequences of early sensory deprivation." *Psychosom. Med.*, **21**:89–95 (1959).

# Chapter ten

# Parent-child relationships II:
# PERMISSIVENESS
# AND PUNISHMENT

The evidence presented so far indicates that acceptance is associated with high self-esteem—but acceptance, like love, may not be enough. For though we have proposed that concern, approval, and affection are necessary to produce favorable self-evaluations, it does not appear that these expressions of acceptance are in themselves sufficient to produce such an effect. Acceptance is expressed in a context of other attitudes and behaviors, and there is every reason to assume that these will affect the self-appraisal finally achieved. There is abundant evidence[1,2] that other dimensions of parental behavior whose effects may exist independently of acceptance should also be considered. Parents who are equally accepting of their children may differ in the amount of control they exercise, the independence they encourage, and their willingness to share planning and decision-making. The belief that parents who are accepting are necessarily permissive, democratic, and nonpunitive appears to be an obscuring overgeneralization, and one that has

---

[1] A. L. Baldwin, J. Kalhorn, and F. H. Breese. "Patterns of parent behavior." *Psych. Monogr.,* **58**:268 (1945).

[2] E. S. Schaefer and R. Q. Bell. "Patterns of attitudes towards child rearing and the family." *J. Abn. Soc. Psych.,* **54**:391–395 (1959).

repeatedly been demonstrated to be false. Empirically refuted, by factor analytic studies,[3] this belief nonetheless persists as an interpretative set influencing consideration of the origins of poor adjustment, prejudice, and delinquency.[4] Studies on these behavioral difficulties generally conclude that they derive from the combined, corrosive effects of rejection, domination, and either over- or underindulgence. That they may arise from extreme single conditions or a more limited set of conditions is certainly a possibility worth considering. In the present study we shall examine each of the conditions that might affect the development of self-esteem separately, and then integrate the separate findings to determine their pattern, independence, and relative contribution. In this chapter we shall consider the effects of permissive and punitive treatment upon the development of self-esteem. Although these aspects of parental behavior are often associated with acceptance, we shall differentiate them from that dimension in our analysis and discussion.

## PERMISSIVENESS

The concept of permissiveness received its most forceful advocacy by early adherents of psychoanalytic theory. They argued that children would develop into better adjusted and more secure adults if they were reared under open, flexible schedules that were geared to their needs. They proposed that the use of such schedules would result in more immediate gratification and relief and hence provided the child with a sense of trust in himself and confidence in others. Parents who employed such flexible, self-demand procedures, and who thus accepted the onerous obligations of ready and obedient response, were presumed to be more devoted to their children. The commitment, devotion, and presumably greater sensitivity of these permissive parents were assumed to indicate greater acceptance of their children, and were likely to eventuate in healthy—that is, nonneurotic—personality development. The advocates of permissive rearing pointed to the adverse effects of repressive treatment and concluded that nonrestrictive, self-demand procedures would permit greater self-expression and self-trust. This uncritical extension of psychoanalytic theory was based on the implicit assumption that greater impulse expression and gratification was associated with more favorable development, greater happiness, and better adaptation. Structuring of the

---

[3] W. C. Becker, D. C. Peterson, L. A. Hellmer, D. J. Shoemaker, and H. C. Quay. "Factors in parental behavior in children." *J. Consult. Psych.*, **23**:107–118 (1959).

[4] M. J. Rosenthal, M. Finkelstein, E. Ni, and R. E. Robertson. "A study of mother-child relationships in the emotional disorders of children." *Genet. Psych. Monogr.*, **60**:65–116 (1959).

environment by regular schedules and definite restrictions and demands was assumed to be repressive in effect and to manifest too little concern and acceptance of the child. Parents who employed such procedures were presumably seeking to exclude their own sources of anxiety and were thus more likely to be unaware of their motives and to be extreme in their actions. This view led to the general proposition that less permissive parents were likely to employ harsher forms of punishment and to employ them more frequently than did those who favored impulse expression. In this context parental permissiveness or restrictiveness was taken as an indication of parental mental health, acceptance of the child, and concern for his present and future well-being.

Though this position is no longer expressed with the same vehemence or extremity as it was in the period between 1930–1950, its decline is associated with changes in styles of childrearing rather than with clarification or disproof. The term permissiveness remains a vague one, generally associated with the absence of demands and restrictions, and indicative of greater parental acceptance, love, and democratic practices. Such interpretations, however, are connotative rather than denotative meanings of a term that has remained vague despite extended usage, and permissiveness as a procedure remains of uncertain consequences. In the present context we shall employ the term "permissive" as characterizing the demands and firmness of management procedures employed by parents in regulating and satisfying the requirements of their children. This usage refers solely to the structuring of the child's world of rules and demands and carries no connotations of acceptance or democratic practices—in effect, a philosophy of management that may be carried out with varying sentiments of good will and affection. The consequences of that philosophy for the child's self-esteem is a question to which we shall now seek empirical solution.

Our study provided information on three aspects of parental permissiveness: the strictness of training, the demands that children meet (parental) standards, and the consistency with which rules were enforced and violations punished. This information was obtained from each mother and child, utilizing both interview and questionnaire procedures. Before turning to the specific findings, we should note that all our results indicate that the parents of children with high self-esteem are significantly *less* permissive than are the parents of children with less self-esteem. We shall discuss this surprising finding after the results have been presented.

The first aspect of permissiveness, the strictness of parental training, indicates the extent to which parents require that their children act in close conformity to the procedures the parents have established. Such strictness

TABLE 10.1 *"Children are actually happier under strict training"*

| Reply | Subjective self-esteem | | |
|---|---|---|---|
| | Low | Medium | High |
| Agree | 5.9% (2) | 6.3% (1) | 38.7% (12) |
| Disagree | 94.1% (32) | 93.7% (15) | 61.3% (19) |
| Totals | 100.0% (34) | 100.0% (16) | 100.0% (31) |

$\chi^a = 13.57$      df = 2      p < .01

*Source:* Mother's questionnaire.

would be contrary to the open, flexible system of demands and gratification espoused by advocates of permissiveness. In our own definition, strictness represents a clearly defined, structured, and enforced set of demands. We determined the mother's attitude toward strictness by her response to the questionnaire item, "Children are actually happier under strict training." The mothers' responses of agreement or disagreement are summarized in Table 10.1, which reveals that mothers of children with high self-esteem are much more likely to agree with this statement than are the mothers of other children. The actual percentages indicate that more than six times as many mothers in the high self-esteem group believe that strictness has beneficial consequences (38.7 percent) as mothers in the medium (6.3 percent) and low (5.9 percent) esteem groups. Thus it appears that permissiveness is *negatively* related to feelings of personal worth or, to state it in reverse, greater strictness is associated with greater self-esteem. In this same vein we note that more mothers of children with high self-esteem regard discipline as very important (84.8 percent) than do the mothers of children with medium (64.7 percent) and low (66.7 percent) self-esteem. This information came from the mother's interview, and furnished a corroboration of the mothers' consistency of responses to questionnaire and interview. Other indications were the larger percentage of mothers in the high self-esteem groups who agreed with the statements, "Children who are held to firm rules grow up to be the best adults" and "No child should ever set his will against his parents."

A second way of gauging permissiveness, and another aspect of its occurrence, is the number of parental demands imposed upon the child. Under extreme permissiveness, the environment provides gratifications for the child, whose needs are expected to be freely expressed. The needs presumably arise from the child rather than the expectations and requirements of the parent. Parental demands presumably represent restrictions upon the child's freedom

TABLE 10.2 *Relative importance to parents: child enjoying himself or meeting high standards*

| Important parental values | Subjective self-esteem | | |
| --- | --- | --- | --- |
| | Low | Medium | High |
| Enjoying himself | 60.0% (9) | 28.6% (2) | 20.0% (3) |
| Meeting high standards | 40.0% (6) | 71.4% (5) | 80.0% (12) |
| Totals | 100.0% (15) | 100.0% (7) | 100.0% (15) |
| $\chi^2 = 5.40$    df $= 2$    p $< .08$ | | | |

*Source:* Subject's questionnaire.

and limit the extent to which he might seek alternative or lower levels of gratification. By imposing greater demands, parents imply that a given level of performance must be achieved before they will judge their child as competent. Lesser demands or the complete absence of demands presumably imply that whatever level the child did achieve, so long as it was not markedly below par, would be acceptable. Our appraisal of the level of demands made upon persons who differed in self-esteem was based upon the responses of our subjects. They were asked whether their parents regarded the meeting of high standards or personal enjoyment as more important guides of conduct. The figures in Table 10.2 indicate the number of children in each group who reported that their parents favored high standards as against personal enjoyment. If these reports are taken as indices of parental value preference, we would conclude from Table 10.2 that the parents of children with low self-esteem place less importance on high standards (40.0 percent) than do the parents of children with medium and high self-esteem (71.4 percent and 80.0 percent, respectively). Or, in reverse terms, the parents of children with low self-esteem are more than twice as likely to endorse immediate gratification (60.0 percent) as are the parents of children with medium (28.6 percent) or high (20.0 percent) self-esteem. That lesser demands are associated with lower self-esteem, like the previous finding on strictness, runs counter to assertions regarding the presumed affects of permissive treatment.

The third and final aspect of permissiveness we shall consider is the consistency with which regulations are enforced. That is, whereas the prior two findings indicated the firmness and extent of demands, the present variable deals with the question of whether these demands are backed up by supervision and control. Our information on parental enforcement was obtained during the course of the mother interview. The mothers were asked

TABLE 10.3 *Care and consistency with which rules are enforced*

| Degree of enforcement | Subjective self-esteem | | |
| --- | --- | --- | --- |
| | Low | Medium | High |
| Relatively careful and consistent enforcement | 60.0% (18) | 58.8% (10) | 87.9% (29) |
| Moderate or little enforcement of rules | 40.0% (12) | 41.2% (7) | 12.1% (4) |
| Totals | 100.0% (30) | 100.0% (17) | 100.0% (33) |

$\chi^2 = 7.59$   df $= 2$   p $< .05$

*Source:* Mother's interview.

to indicate the care and consistency with which they supervise the rules they had established, and their responses are summarized in Table 10.3. From these responses it is clear that the mothers of children with high self-esteem are more zealous in their enforcement of familial rules than are the parents of children with medium and low self-esteem. Comparison of the groups reveals that almost nine out of ten (87.9 percent) of the mothers of children with high self-esteem carefully and consistently enforce established rules, and only approximately six out of ten (60.0 and 58.8 percent) of the low and medium group mothers are as attentive. Thus the mothers of children with high self-esteem are apt to be more zealous both in enforcing the regulations they establish and in being stricter and more demanding in their requirements. In effect, the level of demands and the degree of enforcement are both greater for children with high self-esteem.

The negative relationship between permissiveness and self-esteem revealed in Tables 10.1, 10.2, and 10.3 runs counter to theoretical expectations and popular belief. Inasmuch as it appears to be a reliable finding, confirmed by both parent and child, its interpretation is all the more intriguing and significant. Our discussion will focus upon two questions that appear to underlie the surprising results obtained: "Why should strict and demanding regulatory procedures be associated with high self-esteem?" and "How firm or demanding are the nonpermissive conditions associated with high self-esteem?" The first question is the real nub of the discussion because it requires an analysis of the particular effects of firm and open management procedures. The second represents an attempt to determine the operational meaning of the terms "strict and demanding" and the extent to which the mothers of children with high self-esteem can be placed at the polar opposite of "permissiveness."

It is evident that the mothers of the high self-esteem group are stricter and set higher demands, but should these conditions have an enhancing effect upon the children? Although the findings are clear and consistent, our interpretation will, of necessity, be more tentative and exploratory. The results not only go counter to the usual assertions on the effects of permissiveness; they also extend beyond previously presented theoretical formulations relating to the antecedents of self-esteem (Chapter 2). In that context we concluded that the sources of self-esteem could be subsumed under the general concepts of defenses, successes, values, and aspirations— without, however, specifying how these applied to the actual practices of childrearing. A more specific consideration of the practices associated with permissive and restrictive practices suggests that the relevant concepts are defenses and successes, particularly since the concept of success is associated with parental concern and affection. Turning first to the concept of defenses, we may propose that firmer management will tend to result in more effective inner controls and greater confidence in one's definition of a situation. Parents who establish rules and enforce them are presenting their children with a definition of reality that they believe to be objective and functional. They are establishing a set of beliefs that there are certain ways of acting toward parents, siblings, tasks, and other elements of the environment that are preferable to other ways. By their verbal statements and their actions these parents lead their children to believe that there is a shared world and that there are preferred solutions for the tasks which they encounter. There are preferred methods of expressing respect and appreciation; preferred resolutions on how and when aggression should be expressed; and preferred answers on the meaning and sources of failure and how it can be avoided. On each of these and other issues, parental resolutions provide the child with answers that diminish doubt and anxiety. To the child these answers are not merely one resolution among many but, coming as they do from the major authoritative force in his life, they assume the weight of Biblical injunction to the fundamentalist believer. These are the methods, the correct ways, the answers, and the goals by which love, peace, and success can be achieved and all doubts put to rest. The firm, demanding parent who is establishing rules and enforcing them is providing definitions to his children and indicating how to interpret the world so as to maximize success and minimize anxiety. When these definitions and solutions are internalized and applied to problematic situations, they are customarily referred to as controls and defenses.

A second basis of the relationship between nonpermissive regulation and self-esteem lies in the greater self-definition that results from consistently enforced rules. Such rules compel the individual to acknowledge forces outside of himself, and to recognize the needs and powers of other persons. The resulting distinction between internal experiences and external events brings with it an awareness of the social environment and the difference between wish and reality. The extremely permissive environment in which no demands are made and no rules are enforced provides little basis for distinguishing between personal and social events, and presents only a limited definition of what is valued or functional. In its extreme manifestation such an environment presents a picture of life that is distant from that encountered in other areas of living as well as blind to the intervention and direction practiced by even the most beneficent of parents. Parents who proclaim that they advance no rules and exercise no authority are likely to confuse the child about the existence, significance, and benefits of (even legitimate) authority or to cause him to be suspicious of parental statements and motives. In any event such conditions make for poorer, less distinct differentiation between self and nonself, and provide a less accurate and realistic picture of the importance of rules, no matter how disguised they may be. Over an extended series of events, children who can distinguish self and nonself, who are sufficiently reality-oriented to appreciate the needs and demands of others, and who are aware that some rules are always operating are likely to achieve greater and more enduring successes.

The third basis by which strict and demanding procedures may enhance esteem is that they symbolize parental attention. We have already presented evidence that attention of even a negative nature has a more enhancing effect than lack of concern. Hence it seems that the very posing and enforcement of rules necessarily leads to greater interaction between parent and child. This interaction need not be expressed as concern or affection, it need only occur to present an enhancing effect. It is also worth noting that the favorable effects of permissiveness, whatever they are, are more likely to occur during infancy and early childhood than during subsequent development. During these early periods, the major foci are bodily processes, which cannot be hastened or drastically altered without great pressures or the possibilities of aberrant development. Beyond these early stages guidance toward familial and cultural norms is a valid and important function, which at the same time provides enhancing attention to the child. In sum, this increased attention, the more frequent (social and academic) successes provided by a more accurate reality orientation, and the more established controls and resolutions provided by parental norms would appear to underlie the higher self-esteem of children reared under firmer regulatory procedures.

Having suggested how nonpermissive procedures may enhance self-esteem, we now consider the *extent* of demands made by the parents of children with high self-esteem. For, though we have indicated that the parents of these children establish and enforce more regulations than do the parents of children with low self-esteem, our data provide relative rather than absolute indices of permissiveness. To give a broader perspective on the total range of this dimension we shall examine the results of other studies of permissiveness and attempt to gauge that portion from which our sample was drawn. There are studies[5,6] that indicate that either extreme method of management, be it complete permissiveness or rigid and inflexible control, have equally poor consequences for the child. Children reared under either extreme regimen are more likely to suffer from difficulties in adjustment and in behavior problems. Less extreme methods of management have equally favorable effects upon personality development. What is important for our purposes is that truly extreme regulatory procedures are associated with *higher* levels of *maladjustment,* but the children in our high self-esteem group have *fewer* symptoms and behavior disorders. This suggests that the procedures employed by the parents of these children are not extreme but only appear to be so when compared to those of the other parents we studied. In this same vein we may note another study,[7] which reveals that children who come from restrictive homes have greater difficulty in relating to their peers and academic settings. But again, the children with high self-esteem whom we are studying have more congenial and successful relationships with their siblings, peers, and schoolmates. From all this it appears that the regulatory procedures employed by the parents of children with high self-esteem are firm, clear, and demanding but cannot be termed rigid, inflexible, or unduly restrictive. Although we cannot delineate the specific operational meaning of less extreme management procedures, we can conclude that they establish firm, structured rules and demands that are consistently enforced by reasonable persons.

---

[5] E. H. Klatskin, E. B. Jackson, and L. C. Wilkin. "The influence of degree of flexibility in maternal child care practices on early child behavior." *Amer. J. Orthopsychiat.,* **26:**79–93 (1956).

[6] E. H. Klatskin. "Shifts in child care practices in three social classes under an infant care program of flexible methodology." *Amer. J. Orthopsychiat.,* **22:**52–61 (1952).

[7] M. J. Radke. *The Relation of Parental Authority to Children's Behavior and Attitudes.* Minneapolis, University of Minnesota Press, 1946.

CONTROL

Parents adopt not only a general attitude toward regulation but also some specific ideas on the "shalls" and "shall nots" of child behavior. These are expressed as rules which the parent employs to influence the direction of character formation and to train the child to act along desired lines in the future. We shall here consider the control procedures employed by the mothers of our subjects, and ascertain how these are related to self-esteem. We shall discuss the type of controls employed, the agent who administers them, the frequency and severity with which they are employed, and whether they are effective. Though there is clearly a basis for believing that the controls employed vary according to the age, sex, and particular behavior involved, there is also reason to believe that parents behave in a relatively consistent manner at any given time.[8,9] Inasmuch as we are interested in the controls parents have generally employed in their recent treatment of our subjects and not in the specific controls exercised for sex, aggression, and other types of behavior, we shall limit our present discussion to general, consistently applied procedures.

First, do the parents employ positive or negative techniques to influence their children's behavior? Positive techniques consist of rewarding, praising, and supporting the child in desired activities; negative techniques are reflected in physical punishment, isolation, and withdrawal of love. The most general measure of these techniques is the mother's expressed attitude toward the use of either positive or negative procedures. Our gauge of this attitude was obtained from the mother's response to the statement, "It is more effective to punish a child for not doing well than to reward him for succeeding." Mothers who agree with this statement presumably favor negative procedures, and mothers who disagree with it presumably incline toward positive procedures. From the responses, summarized in Table 10.4, we conclude that the mothers of children with high self-esteem are more likely to favor a positive approach than are the mothers of children with lower self-esteem. Only 19.4 percent of mothers of the high self-esteem group believe that punishment is more effective than reward; 32.5 percent of the medium and 47.1 percent of the low self-esteem group express such a conviction. This linear relationship

---

[8] A. L. Baldwin, J. Kalhorn, and F. H. Breese. "Patterns of parent behavior." *Psych. Monogr.*, **58**:268 (1945).

[9] See Footnote 7.

TABLE 10.4 *"It is more effective to punish a child for not doing well than to reward him for succeeding"*

| Reply | Subjective self-esteem | | |
| --- | --- | --- | --- |
| | Low | Medium | High |
| Agree | 47.1% (16) | 32.5% (6) | 19.4% (6) |
| Disagree | 52.9% (18) | 67.5% (10) | 80.6% (25) |
| Totals | 100.0% (34) | 100.0% (16) | 100.0% (31) |

$\chi^2 = 5.58$     $df = 2$     $p < .07$

*Source:* Mother's questionnaire.

between parental attitudes toward the use of positive techniques and their children's self-esteem suggests that the parents of children with high self-esteem exercise control in a more rewarding fashion. Confirmation for this conclusion comes from previous studies of childrearing, which indicate that the use of positive techniques is associated with greater social adequacy and more desirable personality traits, and that negative techniques are associated with poorer and less desirable performance and characteristics. These studies also reveal that parents who employ positive techniques are generally more accepting and interested in developing the capacities of their children.

Turning now to the specific controls generally employed by the mothers, we first note that they fell into three categories. Two of these—corporal punishment and withdrawal of love—are essentially negative techniques, but the third is more neutral and moderate in its actions—restraint, denial, and separation. Inasmuch as the mothers indicate they employ these procedures when established rules are violated, it is not surprising that positive techniques, such as reward, are not proposed. The percentage of mothers in each self-esteem group who employ corporal punishment, withdrawal of love, and management techniques when rules are violated is presented in Table 10.5. It shows that the mothers of children with high self-esteem are most likely to employ management procedures and least likely to employ the more negative procedures of corporal punishment and withdrawal of affection. The differences between the groups are most notable for management procedures, which are employed by almost one-half of the high self-esteem group (48.5 percent) as compared to roughly one-third of the medium (35.3 percent) and only one-eighth (13.3 percent) of the low self-esteem group. That is, the parents of children with high self-esteem are more likely to employ

TABLE 10.5 *Type of control generally employed by mother when rules violated*

| Type of control | Subjective self-esteem | | |
| --- | --- | --- | --- |
| | Low | Medium | High |
| Corporal punishment | 63.3% (19) | 47.1% (8) | 42.4% (14) |
| Withdrawal of love | 23.4% (7) | 17.6% (3) | 9.1% (3) |
| Management: restraint, denial, isolation | 13.3% (4) | 35.3% (6) | 48.5% (16) |
| Totals | 100.0% (30) | 100.0% (17) | 100.0% (33) |

$\chi^2 = 9.43$     df $= 4$     p $< .06$

*Source:* Mother's interview.

procedures that deal with difficulties as they occur but that do not abuse or degrade the child. Prior studies[10] indicate that the management procedures employed by parents of children with high self-esteem facilitate the development of independent and effective behavior, and that the negative techniques employed by other parents are more likely to result in aggressive, dependent behaviors and a poorly developed conscience.

The results up to this point indicate that the mothers of children with low self-esteem believe that punishment is more effective than reward and are also more inclined to employ harsher methods of control. By their general attitudes and specific techniques these women appear to profess the advantages of force as a means of achieving their goals. Although this could be taken as a presumptive sign that they find negative techniques effective, we included a more explicit question to that effect in our mother interview. The mothers were asked to appraise the effectiveness of their punitive procedures in eliminating undesired responses and encouraging behaviors that they desired. Their appraisals are summarized in Table 10.6, which shows that the control procedures employed by parents of children with high self-esteem are most likely to be judged effective (93.9 percent), those of the medium self-esteem group are less effective (75.6 percent), and those of the low self-esteem group are least likely to achieve the desired goal (56.7 percent). Even the parents who employ harsher means of punishment find these to be ineffective, and from our vantage point we can appreciate their destructive influences upon the child. The parents who support the use of rewards and employ management

---

[10] R. R. Sears, E. Maccoby, and H. Levin. *Patterns of Child Rearing*. Evanston, Ill., Row-Peterson, 1957.

TABLE 10.6 *Effectiveness of punishment*

| | Subjective self-esteem | | |
|---|---|---|---|
| Degree of effectiveness | Low | Medium | High |
| Generally effective | 56.7% (17) | 76.5% (13) | 93.9% (31) |
| Generally ineffective | 43.3% (13) | 23.5% (4) | 6.1% (2) |
| Totals | 100.0% (30) | 100.0% (17) | 100.0% (33) |

$\chi^2 = 13.06$     df $= 2$     p $< .01$

*Source:* Mother's interview.

methods of control are also most likely to report their procedures to be effective. Thus, we find that the procedures that have the most beneficial consequences (in terms of esteem) are also those that are most effective in reducing undesired behavior.

Perhaps the most notable general conclusion on the use of negative procedures is that they are "ineffectual over the long term . . . for eliminating the kind of behavior toward which they are directed." [11] It is not only that these procedures tend to produce behavior that is socially undesirable and interfere with maximum usage of the child's potentialities, but even more pointedly they simply do not achieve their goal. Even though parents may be able to eliminate specific acts in any given situation by the use of punishment, the effects of such procedures over an extended time are much more sharply limited. The net result appears to be that negative techniques are likely to increase the likelihood that the (undesired) behavior will recur and are liable to produce pernicious side effects. Though these results are consistent with our expectations and the results of previous studies, the results obtained for the frequency of punishment are more surprising. They reveal that there is no difference (p < .60) in the frequency with which all methods of control (both positive and negative) are employed by the parents in the various groups. These results suggest that the type and severity of punishment that is employed is more important for self-esteem than is the frequency with which it is administered. Another possibility, which we shall now consider, is that the punishment directed against children with high self-esteem occurs under different circumstances and is interpreted differently than is the case for those low in self-esteem.

In examining this possibility, let us first consider how the child interprets

[11] M. J. Radke. *The Relation of Parental Authority to Children's Behavior and Attitudes.* Minneapolis, University of Minnesota Press, 1946.

TABLE 10.7 *Son's opinion on whether punishment administered by parents is deserved*

| Son's opinion | Subjective self-esteem | | |
| --- | --- | --- | --- |
| | Low | Medium | High |
| Punishment generally deserved | 44.8% (13) | 31.3% (5) | 75.9% (22) |
| Punishment generally undeserved | 55.2% (16) | 68.7% (11) | 24.1% (7) |
| Totals | 100.0% (29) | 100.0% (16) | 100.0% (29) |
| $\chi^2 = 9.90$     df $= 2$ | p $< .01$ | | |

*Source:* Subject's interview.

the punishment that his parents administer. There is a world of difference in the child's reactions to himself and to his parents if he believes that their punishment follows an actual misdeed and is warranted or if he believes that they are acting unjustly. To determine the child's perceptions of whether punishment was generally warranted, we included a question to that effect in the sons' questionnaire. The responses are summarized in Table 10.7, which shows that children with high self-esteem are less than half as likely (24.1 percent) to believe that the punishment administered by their parents was undeserved than are children with medium (68.7 percent) or low (55.2 percent) self-esteem. The belief that parents are fair in their actions and that they do not exercise their power and strength in an unwarranted and abusive manner has important implications for the child.[12] It assures him that he will be treated with due consideration and respect, that his parents are fair and reasonable, and that they maintain as well as profess values of justice. The resultant sense of personal significance should contribute to heightened feelings of self-esteem and lead him to expect respectful treatment from other persons.

Another condition that may affect the interpretation of punishment is the parent who customarily administers it. A son may respond differently when he is punished by his father, whom he regards as the stronger and more authoritative figure in the family, than when his mother is the disciplinarian. Despite the increasing powers and responsibilities of the American female, there is evidence that the male as husband and father is generally

[12] See Footnote 11.

TABLE 10.8 *Parent more likely to administer punishment*

| Parent likely to punish | Subjective self-esteem | | |
|---|---|---|---|
| | Low | Medium | High |
| Mother | 26.7% (8) | 14.3% (2) | 17.3% (5) |
| Father | 43.3% (13) | 57.1% (8) | 51.7% (15) |
| Both equally | 30.0% (9) | 28.6% (4) | 31.0% (9) |
| Totals | 100.0% (30) | 100.0% (14) | 100.0% (29) |

$\chi^2 = 9.32$     df $= 2$     p $< .07$

*Source:* Son's interview.

perceived by American children as the family authority. More intensive study of these perceptions[13,14] reveals that fathers are generally perceived as the agent of punishment, the economic provider, and the dominant family figure. Mothers tend to be perceived by their children as friendlier, more emotional, and less punitive. These differences in perception of parents are greater for younger children than they are for the preadolescent group we are studying. Children over ten, both male and female, tend to view their same-sex parent as more punitive. This is presumably a function of more specific handling by parents as the sex identity of the child becomes more pronounced. It is based on the theory that the male child should be treated as a male as well as a child and that discipline by the same-sex parent fosters character and identification. Inasmuch as the father is perceived as a general authority, disciplinary action against his daughters as well as his sons would appear to be acceptable if not necessarily advisable. However, given the cultural values and general perceptions of the children just reported, punitive actions by the mother against her preadolescent sons could well have unfavorable consequences. When we further analyze the punitive agents in the families of our subjects, we find indications of such unfavorable consequences. The subjects were asked to indicate which of their parents was more likely to administer punishment to them. The alternatives from which they could select were either father or mother or both equally. Table 10.8 shows the

[13] L. P. Gardner. "An analysis of children's attitudes towards father." *J. Genet. Psych.*, 70:3–28 (1947).
[14] J. Kagan and J. Lemkin. "The child's differential perception of parental attributes." *J. Abn. Soc. Psych.*, 61:440–447 (1960).

percentage of persons in each group who indicate one or the other parent as the principal agent of punishment.

The responses of our subjects reveal that the mothers of children with low self-esteem are more likely to be the punitive agent (26.7 percent) than are the mothers of children with medium and high self-esteem (14.3 and 17.3 percent). In terms of the same-sex parent, fathers are more likely to be the disciplinarian to boys medium and high in self-esteem (57.1 and 51.7 percent) than they are to boys with low self-esteem (43.3 percent). From these results it would appear that punitive action by the mothers of preadolescent boys or lack of paternal action has a devaluating effect upon the boys' self-esteem. Whether this effect is attributable to a general familial pattern, such as a dominant mother or conflict between parents, or is a specific function of punishment by the mother is not clear. We could, however, hypothesize that maternal punishment of a sexually maturing male could adversely affect sexual identification and produce uncertainty of nascent capacities.

Before concluding, it would appear worthwhile to summarize and integrate the separate findings for the high and low self-esteem groups. The conditions that exist within the families of children with high self-esteem are notable for the demands the parents make and the firmness and care with which they enforce those demands. Reward is the preferred mode of affecting behavior but where punishment is required it is geared to managing undesired responses rather than to harsh treatment or loss of love. The fathers of these boys are, more often than not, the ones to administer punishment, although they often share that responsibility with the mother. The total amount of punishment administered in these families is no less than in others, but it is different in its expression and is perceived as justifiable by our high self-esteem subjects.

A summary of the familial conditions that exist in the background of children with low self-esteem would focus upon lack of parental guidance and relatively harsh and disrespectful treatment. These parents either do not know or do not care to establish and enforce guidelines for their children. They are apt to employ punishment rather than reward, and the procedures they do employ lay stress on force and loss of love. The mothers are more likely to administer punishment to these boys, which may have negative connotations and significance for children in this age group. There is an inconsistent and somewhat emotional component in the regulatory behaviors of these parents. They are less concerned, on one hand, and inclined to employ more drastic procedures, on the other. They propose that punishment is a preferred method of control, yet state that they find it generally ineffective. Their children apparently smart under such a regimen and believe that the control behaviors of their parents are often unwarranted.

The relationships between self-esteem and control are surprising in two respects: first, that firmer and more demanding regulations are associated with higher esteem and, second, that frequency of punishment is unrelated to esteem even though the type of punishment is related. We have suggested that children interpret these limits and demands as expressions of concern, and these external regulations also contribute to the formation of the child's inner controls. Punishment apparently is interpreted in the context of other expressions of attentive and respectful treatment and does not assume any added positive or negative significance. Other studies[15,16] have suggested that it is the perception of his parents, and not necessarily the specific attitudes and actions that they express, which the child employs in interpreting parental actions. Children who view their parents favorably perceive their actions as positive, regardless of the particular procedures or regimen they employ. They may report their parents to be overbearing and dominating and yet reveal they are favorably disposed toward them. Children who take a negative view of their parents display the converse interpretive bias: they see all actions in a negative light. Thus, the same degree of punitiveness may be viewed differently, depending upon the perceiver's interpretation of the agent and his motives.

The combined findings on permissiveness and punishment provide an interesting insight into the significance of parental restrictions. Parents who are more restrictive are *less* likely to employ harsher forms of punishment; those who are less restrictive are more likely to employ corporal punishment and love-depriving techniques to achieve their ends. This suggests that parents who employ restrictions are thereby indicating their concern for the child, and the interest thus expressed is given a favorable interpretation by their children. These children may rail and complain against the restrictions, but they apparently consider them expressions of parental concern and interest. In this sense, the mother who is willing to establish and enforce rules is indicating that she is concerned about the child's well-being as well as the rules themselves. The mother who allows her child to roam free is also more likely to punish him severely, thereby indicating that she is more indifferent about the child's welfare than she is interested in his freedom. Such parents

---

[15] A. G. Brown. "Sex-role preference in young children." *Psych. Monogr.,* **70:** No. 421.

[16] W. Itkin. "Relationships between attitudes towards parents and parents' attitudes towards children." *J. Genet. Psych.,* **86:**339–352 (1955).

apparently ignore their children except when trouble arises, at which point they descend upon them in a harsh and vindictive manner. The association of nonrestrictive procedures, harsh punishment, and low self-esteem suggests that limited restrictions are indicative of lack of parental interest and are interpreted in that way by children.

# Chapter eleven

# Parent-child relationships III:
# DEMOCRATIC PRACTICES

Every social group, no matter what its size, must establish patterns of authority and delegate power, status, and responsibility to its members. This is as true for the family group as it is for more formal and public bodies. The patterns reflect the group's interpretation of the rights and privileges of its members, and show how the group specifies its leaders and indicates the extent and limits of their powers. The procedures established by either formal or informal codes indicate the extent to which group members should be recognized and consulted as well as the general limits of permissible deviation. They set out the means by which intragroup differences should be resolved and respect accorded to minority opinions. In achieving resolution, the willingness to discuss, clarify, and compromise is in many ways as important as the end product that is achieved, for it is in the exercise of power and authority that recognition and respect for others is expressed. Steamroller tactics, arbitrary procedures, and exclusion from consultation leave the minority with a sense of powerlessness, which presumably subverts their sense of esteem.

The allocation of power and the manner in which such power is employed express a person's significance in the group. Individuals who possess greater authority, and whose needs and ideas are considered, are more significant in that setting than are those who are ignored and cannot affect decisions. We would expect that those persons who are delegated power and who are treated in a respectful manner would regard themselves as more significant than persons who are unrecognized and powerless. If self-perception is a reflection of the appraisal of others (as Mead maintains) and is associated with the ability to affect events in the real world (as James and Adler maintain), then authority and respect should be associated with personal feelings of esteem. In the present chapter we shall examine how different patterns of authority—democracy and domination—are related to self-esteem.

It would perhaps be wisest to begin our discussion by indicating three important distinctions between the family and other groups. All three bear upon the relationships of power and authority within the family and all have consequences for interpreting the procedures that are employed. The first distinction is that the family necessarily and invariably presents us with an *unequal distribution of power*. Parents possess greater material resources, knowledge, experience, and skills and strength than do their children. This is particularly true during early childhood, but it remains true until the child is well into his adolescent years and generally beyond that time. During this period the parents have control over familial resources and their dictates are backed by physical strength as well as cultural and social supports advocating obedience and respect. The child is faced by a situation in which his physical and social survival and well-being are dependent upon large and powerful others. He has no power to begin with and any power he receives is by virtue of parental love, good will, and ideology rather than his ability to enforce compliance.

This brings us to the second difference between the family and most other groups. In the vast majority of cases the newborn infant, last to arrive in the group, is *admired and desired* by his parents. Because of parental affection and parental desire for reciprocal affection, the child has a powerful means for gaining concessions and recognition. Love and the desire to be loved is the basis upon which parents grant power, and they feel they have gained rather than lost. Love is also employed as a means of gaining concessions and privileges in nonfamilial relationships, but it is not so common and intense a part of such relationships, nor is the difference in power so great. The love of parent for child is socially espoused and supported, and the absence of love or more hostile feelings is treated as immoral or abnormal.

The third distinguishing mark of the parent-child relationship is its *longevity and resistance to dissolution*. Human children remain infantile and dependent for a longer period than the young of other species. By virtue of initial physical necessities and subsequent cultural restraints, they remain with one or both of their parents until economic independence is achieved. Differences between parents may result in the dissolution of their union, but the child will generally remain with one of them for a minimum of fifteen years. The relationship between parent and child is perhaps the one we can most be certain will endure over lengthy periods.

This pattern of characteristics—great difference in power, love given and required, and a relationship of dependency that extends over lengthy periods —distinguishes the family from other groups. The pattern has consequences for the distribution and use of power, and the meaning assigned to such terms as democracy, autocracy, and domination, when they are applied to childrearing. The basic conditions as they generally occur are clear; an infant is born to parents who desire him and who will have to provide for him for an extended period of his life. Lacking innate guidance mechanisms and slow to mature physically, the infant is dependent upon his parents for survival and well-being. Lacking knowledge of the physical, social, and cultural environment, with limited intellectual and cognitive experience, the child must receive protection and guidance if he is to grow to independence and maturity. The parents, who possess the resources, skills, knowledge, and capacities to facilitate their child's development, are generally well-disposed toward him. Social institutions, values, and mores support this affection, and urge the parents to care for and love their child, at the same time urging the child to show respect, appreciation, and affection toward his parents. The combination of unequal capacities and a dependency that is necessarily prolonged leads to a vesting of power and authority in parental hands. This concentration is initially absolute, but it may be altered by parental love for the child and the desire to be loved in return.

The conditions we have described are not conducive to those practices and privileges subsumed under the term democracy. The dictionary[1] variously defines that term as "a form of government in which the supreme power is vested in the people and exercised by them (or their elected agents) under a free electoral system" and "a state of society characterized by formal equality of rights and privileges." Neither of these usages applies to the conditions that necessarily exist in families with young children, and both are only approximated in families with children of a more advanced age. Inasmuch as young children cannot be given formal equality to decide issues of which they are unaware or less knowledgeable, power cannot be equally distributed in the family without raising the possibility that more knowledgeable members

---

[1] *The American College Dictionary.* New York, Random House, 1959.

will be overruled. Parents inevitably establish some restrictions on what is subject to discussion and change. They do not give the child voice as to whether he can wander in streets of heavy traffic, eat whatever comes to hand, or play in water beyond his depth. Parents have the strength and power to enforce their demands and they establish the limits and framework within which their children function. They also determine the latitude of discussion within that framework, and the manner and extent to which differences will be compromised. As becomes evident from this discussion, full equality of rights and participation in decision-making does not and cannot exist for young children. For them the parents assume the position of nurturing, benevolent authorities who define rights and privileges, establish the constraints on freedom, and gradually prepare their child for future independence. To that extent, the more specific and realistic issue is whether children are treated with respect and whether their rights and privileges increase as their competence increases.

Therefore the children in a family operate within the policies and limits established by their parents. These limits will extend and policies change, as the child matures, to the extent that the parents respect their child and hold him to be significant. Parental respect[2] is manifested by efforts to clarify and justify policies, willingness to allow free expression of opinions, and freedom to participate in planning and decision-making. Though these efforts are geared to the age of the child, the common feature is recognition of and respect for the child's significance and individuality. If a mother gives her child the right to express an independent opinion, it indicates that she does not regard him as an extension of herself but as a separate and significant individual. The dominating mother is prone to see the child as an extension of herself without the right to independent views, as altogether subordinate and insignificant. Another expression of democratic practices is the use of general principles, rather than isolated separate rules, as guidelines. Authority and policies of greater generality are more likely to provide objective guidelines than are particularized and delineated rules. Still another expression is the extent of freedom permitted within the established limits. Parents who view discussions within these bounds as explorations rather than the basis of coercion and subordination are recognizing the rights of their child. If discussions necessarily conclude with suggestions that the child must accept and which can neither be examined nor rejected, the child is living in a tightly delimited and controlled world. The essential

---

[2] A. L. Baldwin, J. Kalhorn, and F. Breese. "Patterns of parent behavior." *Psych. Monogr.*, **58**:268 (1945).

features of democratic practices are clearly established policies, established to permit the greatest possible latitude in individual behavior, within which discussion, disagreement, and deviation are permitted without punishment or coercion. Within these bounds, policies must be justified, and members must be given voice and choice on issues that bear upon their welfare and privileges. Freedom within established limits, and the right to participate in the ongoing dialogue within those limits and without penalty, are the benchmarks of the democratic family.

The consequences of democratic and dominating practices upon personality development have received considerable attention. Among personality theorists, Erich Fromm[3] has been most concerned with the effects of dominating and authoritarian procedures. Fromm believes that authoritarian procedures instill a desire to live within safe and secure limits and curtail the desire for freedom and love. Persons learn that if they submit to authority and conform to its demands, they will be accepted and incorporated as members of the group. This acceptance will alleviate the anxiety that follows isolation and deviation but it will not fulfill the needs for personal expression and intimacy. Freud[4] had previously proposed that attitudes toward parental authority generalized to other sources of authority, who were also treated with a mixture of awe, respect, uncertainty, and underlying hostility. As an example of such generalization, he proposed that an individual's attitude and belief in a supernatural God was transferred from earlier attitudes toward parental figures. More empirical studies[5] reveal that the pattern of authority has effects upon motivation, originality, assertiveness, and foresight. Children reared in homes that employ democratic procedures are generally self-confident, competitive, and assertive to the point that they are regarded as bossy and aggressive outside their families. This assertiveness does not appear to interfere with their social success, since they are popular and possess high status with their peers. Children from democratic homes were also found to be more spontaneous and original and inclined to pursue their activities with greater tenacity. They were involved in their work, and actively and persistently pursued it to completion. These children apparently had grown accustomed to respectful handling, recognition, and freedom within bounds, and were assertive, expressive, and exploratory within those bounds.

As might be anticipated, dominating practices tend to produce submissive,

---

[3] E. Fromm. *Escape from Freedom.* New York, Rinehart, 1941.

[4] S. Freud. *Moses and Monotheism.* London, Hogarth Press, 1955.

[5] M. J. Radke. *The Relation of Parental Authority to Children's Behaviors and Attitudes.* Minneapolis, University of Minnesota Press, 1946.

dependent, apathetic children.[6,7] Such children have learned to be obedient and to comply with the demands made upon them. They accept the regulations and goals established and do not venture contrary or exploratory opinions and actions. Inasmuch as these children are passive nonparticipants in discussion and decision-making, they tend to become uninterested and quarrelsome when the sources of authority are not present. Their reactions to peers veer from the extremes of shyness and withdrawal[8] to active belligerence and lack of consideration.[9] This suggests that these children abandon all hope of self-respect in an attempt to survive and salvage what esteem they can. Thus, we see that dominating practices tend to result in lowered self-esteem, whereas democratic practices tend to be enhancing. We shall examine the relationship between these practices in the two remaining sections of this chapter. The first will consider the nature and extent of limits imposed upon the child, and the second will examine procedures and practices employed within those limits. The emphasis is upon the attitudes and practices that are currently employed, rather than those that were employed during earlier periods of the child's life.

### LIMITS: THE BOUNDARIES OF PERMISSIBLE BEHAVIOR

The limits established by parents may vary in several ways, two of which will be considered here: the number and extent of rules established and the decisiveness of parental decision. Turning to the first of these, we note that the range of limits extends from virtual absence of rules to an extensive list of proscribed actions. In the one case the child is permitted to proceed with a minimum of parental limitations; in the other he must take cognizance of a large number of unalterable restraints. These limits are defined by the parent and merge into the regulations we have previously discussed in Chapter 10. In that context we indicated that relatively strict training and a high level of demands were indicative of parental attention and concern for the child, provided that these demands were not unreasonable. We further indicated that these regulations had the effect of defining and objectifying the environ-

---

[6] K. H. Read. "Parents' expressed attitudes and children's behavior." *J. Consult. Psych.*, 9:95–100 (1945).

[7] K. A. Miles. "Relationship between certain factors in the home background and the quality of leadership shown by children." Reported by J. E. Andersen. "Parents' attitudes on child behavior: a report of three studies." *Child Develop.*, 17:91–97 (1946).

[8] D. R. Peterson, W. C. Becker, D. J. Shoemaker, I. Hellmer, and L. A. Hellmer. "Child behavior problems and parental attitudes." *Child Develop.*, 32:151–162 (1962).

[9] See Footnote 2.

ment. They provided evidence that there were others outside of oneself whose opinions and sensitivities were to be considered before pursuing one's own course of action. The evidence and reasoning presented in that context also has relevance for our present discussion of limits. First, the parents of children with high self-esteem are more likely to establish and enforce strict rules than are the parents of children with lesser esteem (Tables 10.1 and 10.3); although the rules established by these parents are restraining, they are not extremely so, nor are they harsh or punitive. From our discussions of parental characteristics (Chapter 6) and acceptance (Chapter 9), we learn that the parents of children with high self-esteem are stable, self-reliant, likable persons who accept and appreciate their children. Though they make high demands, their own characteristics and their concern for their children suggest that they would not be authoritarian in their practices. From our knowledge of the parents and of their acceptance of their children, we may propose that the limits established for children with high self-esteem are well-defined and enforced, but not harsh or unduly restrictive. These limits presumably define the bounds of what is permissible but apparently they do so without destroying the child's belief in his own worth.

In this section we shall examine the number of regulations established by parents and the diversity of areas in which they apply. This aspect of control refers to the boundaries that define and delimit the child's permissible behavior, whereas our previous discussion (Chapter 10) dealt with the context and enforcement of parental regulations. We shall use a scale derived from the mother's responses to a series of questions dealing with the regulation and control of her child's behavior. The scale scores of high, moderate, and low control indicate both the number and extensiveness of parental regulations. Thus a high score would indicate that the parents established a large number of regulations and that these regulations covered a wide range of behavior. The scores from the mothers' responses are summarized in Table 11.1. It is clear that the mothers of children with high and medium self-esteem are more likely to establish a larger number and more comprehensive rules than are the mothers of low self-esteem children; only 16.7 percent of the low self-esteem group exercise moderate or high control, but more than 40 percent of the medium (41.2 percent) and high (45.5 percent) self-esteem groups exercise these higher levels of control. Thus we find that more extensive limits are associated with high rather than low self-esteem. This finding is consistent with those previously presented, which indicate that greater regulation is associated with higher levels of esteem.

Parents not only differ in the rules they establish but also in the firmness

TABLE 11.1 *Extent of parental control*

| Degree of control | Subjective self-esteem | | |
|---|---|---|---|
| | Low | Medium | High |
| High to moderate | 16.7% (5) | 41.2% (7) | 45.5% (15) |
| Limited | 83.3% (25) | 58.8% (10) | 54.5% (18) |
| Totals | 100.0% (30) | 100.0% (17) | 100.0% (33) |
| $\chi^2 = 6.36 \qquad df = 2$ | $p < .05$ | | |

*Source:* Mother's interview.

with which they establish them. They express rules with differing degrees of seriousness, severity, and decisiveness, thereby indicating the importance in which they are held. Parents undoubtedly do not attribute equal importance to all rules, but some parents may be generally more decisive than others. Such decisiveness may reflect either greater concern with rules or a more general personality characteristic of the parent. In the present instance we sought to determine the seriousness with which they viewed the rules they had established. This was determined on the basis of the mother's response to a question concerning the importance of the rules established for their children and their willingness to change them. The responses of the mothers of our subjects are summarized in Table 11.2.

As the table shows, parents of children with high self-esteem are more than twice as likely (84.8 percent) to be firm and decisive as are the parents of children with low self-esteem (40.0 percent). These findings are consistent with our previous results on parental attitudes toward rules, and suggest that the parents of the various self-esteem groups differ in their general posture toward regulation. Parents of children with high self-esteem establish extensive and relatively strict rules that are not readily subject to change or removal. The parents of children with low self-esteem take a more casual attitude toward regulation. They have fewer and less demanding rules, which are readily modified and not strictly enforced. The parents of children with medium self-esteem generally take an intermediary position in the extent, firmness, strictness, and enforcement of regulations. In most instances, their practices come closer to those employed by the high rather than the low self-esteem group.

Interpretation of these findings necessarily revolves around the issue of why rules and procedures that are restraining should have a more enhancing effect than less controlling regulations. The underlying logic of our inter-

TABLE 11.2 *Firmness of parental decisions*

| Degree of firmness | Subjective self-esteem | | |
|---|---|---|---|
| | Low | Medium | High |
| Relatively firm and decisive | 40.0% (12) | 70.1% (12) | 84.8% (28) |
| Relatively hesitating and vacillating | 60.0% (18) | 29.9% (5) | 15.2% (5) |
| Totals | 100.0% (30) | 100.0% (17) | 100.0% (33) |
| $\chi^2 = 14.19$     df = 2 | p < .001 | | |

*Source:* Mother's interview.

pretation is similar to that employed to explain the higher self-esteem found in less permissive families.

It may be best to begin our interpretation with the reminder that our entire sample consists of normal children who come from middle class backgrounds. Even though this limitation permits considerable generalization, it does exclude children who may have experienced extremely harsh or depriving conditions, or whose families are members of the unrepresented social classes. Inasmuch as more restrictive and dominating conditions are more likely to be found in both these backgrounds,[10,11] it may well be that our sample presents us with a truncated range. If this were the case, the extreme of restrictiveness, which we found associated with high self-esteem, would in point of fact represent a more moderate position. This possibility appears to be more satisfying from both an empirical and a theoretical basis. Our evidence suggests that parents of children with high self-esteem are decisive, personable, stable, and self-reliant individuals. These parents are most concerned and accepting of their children and least likely to be severe in their punishment. They may insist on "running a tight ship" but they appear markedly different from parents who are authoritarian in practice and character structure.[12] On a more theoretical level, we encounter grave difficulties and little support in associating high self-esteem with extreme

[10] W. McCord, J. McCord, and I. K. Zola. *Origins of Crime.* New York, Columbia University Press, 1959.

[11] M. Zuckerman and M. Olfean. "Some relationships between maternal attitude factors and authoritarianism, personality needs, psychopathology, and self-acceptance." *Child Develop.,* 30:27–36 (1949).

[12] T. W. Adorno, E. Frenkel-Brunswik, D. J. Levinson, and R. N. Sanford. *The Authoritarian Personality.* New York, Harper, 1950.

restrictiveness. There is contrary evidence,[13] indicating that extreme restrictiveness has deleterious effects, and there is no logical or psychological basis for assuming that sharply curtailed freedom is enhancing. On both scores, we are best advised to assume that the limits established in the families of children with high self-esteem are above average but not extreme in the population at large.

The interpretation of our findings, based on this assumption of the value of restriction, focuses on the benefits the child gains from definite limits. If these limits are reasonable and there exists a positive relation between parent and child, we propose that children with high self-esteem would internalize a set of definite values and attainable standards, which would provide a clear and relatively unequivocal basis for judging success and failure and allow these children to gauge their worth accordingly. The conditions surrounding limit-setting for children with high self-esteem are likely to result in unambiguous and accepted values. The child would also believe that the standards espoused by his parents are important as well as definite. By living in conformity with these limits the child would come to a favorable self-appraisal and gain the approval of his parents, too. In time these limits, and the approval conferred by living within their bounds, would become an unconscious and recurrent source of enhancement. The use of fewer and more ambiguous limits would have effects opposite to those just enumerated. The child could not judge himself favorably or unfavorably, but would remain in a state of doubt as to his "true" worth. Without limits to gauge attainment, and (in the case of children) without the resource to form standards of their own, it is difficult, if not impossible, to gauge personal competence and success.

### THE GROUND RULES WITHIN

We have investigated the limits placed upon child behavior. We now turn to an examination of some specific procedures and practices employed within these boundaries. The first topic we shall consider is parental tolerance for independent and contrary opinion. Our evaluation of parental attitudes regarding this was based upon the mother's separate responses to questionnaire and interview inquiries. One of the questionnaire items stated, "The child should not question the thinking of his parents." Mothers who agree with this statement are presumably less tolerant of contrary opinion than

---

[13] W. H. Lyle and E. E. Levitt. "Punitiveness, authoritarianism and parental discipline of grade school children." *J. Abn. Soc. Psych.*, **51**:42–46 (1955).

TABLE 11.3 *"The child should not question the thinking of the parents"*

| Reply | Subjective self-esteem | | |
| --- | --- | --- | --- |
| | Low | Medium | High |
| Agree | 50.0% (17) | 25.0% (4) | 19.4% (6) |
| Disagree | 50.0% (17) | 75.0% (12) | 80.6% (25) |
| Totals | 100.0% (34) | 100.0% (16) | 100.0% (31) |
| $\chi^2 = 7.48$    df = 2    p < .05 | | | |

*Source:* Mother's questionnaire.

are those who disagree with it. The responses, summarized in Table 11.3, reveals that the mothers of children with high and medium self-esteem are more tolerant of contrary opinion than are the mothers of children with low self-esteem. Half of the mothers of the low self-esteem group (50.0 percent) agree with the statement, but only 25.0 percent of the medium and 19.4 percent of the high self-esteem group express such agreement. From these responses we gain our first inkling that the parents of children with low self-esteem espouse autocratic, authoritarian practices.

Another facet of parental attitudes toward authority is their acceptance of the child's right to independent opinions. These opinions need not be conflicting with or contrary to those held by the parent—merely different. Parental attitude toward such independent opinions was determined by the mother's response to the statement, "A child has a right to his own point of view and ought to be allowed to express it." The tolerance for independent opinions reflected in this question is different and milder than the acceptance of direct opposition considered in Table 11.2. In the present instance, agreement with the statement indicates respect for the child's right to *a* point of view, not necessarily one which is at variance with that of his parents. The mothers' responses, summarized in Table 11.4, reveal that the parents of children with low self-esteem are much more likely to deny the child's right of independent opinion (32.4 percent) than are the parents of children with high (9.7 percent) or medium (00.0 percent) self-esteem. This finding and the previous one indicate that parents of children with medium and high self-esteem are relatively tolerant of independent and contrary opinions and are willing to permit their children to express their personal convictions. This tolerance and respect within limits stands in marked contrast to the stricter and more demanding limits within which these attitudes and procedures are enforced.

TABLE 11.4 *"A child has a right to his own point of view and ought to be allowed to express it"*

| Reply | Subjective self-esteem | | |
|---|---|---|---|
| | Low | Medium | High |
| Agree | 67.6% (23) | 100.0% (16) | 90.3% (28) |
| Disagree | 32.4% (11) | 00.0% (0) | 9.7% (3) |
| Totals | 100.0% (34) | 100.0% (16) | 100.0% (31) |
| $\chi^2 = 10.00$ | df = 2 | p < .01 | |

*Source:* Mother's questionnaire.

Another expression of respect is the parents' willingness to compromise on those issues on which differences do exist. By their willingness to make concessions, the parents are expressing their respect for the rights and privileges of their children and are not insisting that their views prevail inviolate. Compromise is, after all, a procedure in which both parties express their views and then attempt to resolve their differences by partially yielding their initial claims. This procedure involves discussion, common examination, and mutual concessions, all of which betoken the independence of both parties. To ascertain parental attitudes on compromise, we included the following statement in the mothers' questionnaire: "There is no reason parents should have their own way all the time, any more than that children should have their way all the time." Those who agree with this statement are presumably in favor of compromise and moderation, and those who disagree are apparently in favor of total, uncompromising parental authority. The responses of the mothers, summarized in Table 11.5, show that the mothers of children with low self-esteem are less likely to compromise than are the mothers of children with medium and high self-esteem. Over one-half the mothers of children with low self-esteem (55.9 percent) believe that parents should always have their way, but only one-quarter of the medium (25.0 percent) and high (25.8 percent) self-esteem parents favor such a position. The parents of children with the higher self-esteem apparently proceed on the assumption that needs, issues, and circumstances should affect the resolution of any given issue and that the views of both parents and children should be considered, and they reject the idea that parental opinions have the force of law and should always prevail. Their willingness to limit authority and settle differences by partially yielding indicates a recognition and respect for their children as independent and noteworthy forces.

TABLE 11.5 *"There is no reason parents should have their own way all the time, any more than that children should have their own way all the time"*

| Reply | Subjective self-esteem | | |
| --- | --- | --- | --- |
| | Low | Medium | High |
| Agree | 44.1% (15) | 75.0% (12) | 74.2% (23) |
| Disagree | 55.9% (19) | 25.0% (4) | 25.8% (8) |
| Totals | 100.0% (34) | 100.0% (16) | 100.0% (31) |

$\chi^2 = 7.70$     df $= 2$     p $< .05$

*Source:* Mother's questionnaire.

A more direct expression of parental respect is their willingness to give the child a voice in planning and decision-making. This is a form of recognition which, if overtly expressed, indicates acceptance of the child as a significant individual who is entitled to participate in decisions that affect him. Informal enfranchisement of this sort points to an appreciation of the child as an autonomous individual who should be permitted to represent himself. By permitting their child to voice his views and participate in shaping policies, these parents tend to integrate him into the family and foster cooperation among family members. Discussions in which members can express their views and seek common bases of agreement will tend to result in higher levels of satisfaction and productivity.[14,15] Thus the procedure that appears to be enhancing to individual family members also appears to increase their cohesiveness to the group. One item in our questionnaire was intended to reveal the parents' attitude toward the child's participation in planning. The mothers were asked to indicate whether they agreed or disagreed with the statement, "Children should have a say in the making of family plans." From the results (Table 11.6) it is clear that the parents of children with low self-esteem are less likely to believe that children should have a voice in planning than are the parents of children with higher self-esteem. Almost three-fifths (58.8 percent) of parents in the low self-esteem group believe that children should not have a say in planning; only one-third (33.3 percent) of the medium and less than one-fourth (22.6 percent) of the high group wish to exclude them. Such exclusion and refusal to consult with the child make it impossible for him to make his views known, so that in effect it is

[14] K. Lewin, R. Lippitt, and R. White. "Patterns of aggressive behavior in experimentally created social climates." *J. Soc. Psych.*, 10:271–299 (1939).
[15] H. H. Andersen. "Domination and integration in the social behavior of young children in an experimental play situation." *Genet. Psych. Monogr.*, 19:341–408 (1937).

TABLE 11.6 *"Children should have a say in the making of family plans"*

| Reply | Subjective self-esteem | | |
| --- | --- | --- | --- |
| | Low | Medium | High |
| Agree | 41.2% (14) | 66.7% (12) | 77.4% (24) |
| Disagree | 58.8% (20) | 33.3% (6) | 22.6% (7) |
| Totals | 100.0% (34) | 100.0% (18) | 100.0% (31) |

$\chi^2 = 9.29$  df $= 2$  p $< .01$

*Source:* Mother's questionnaire.

the parents who dictate family policies and plans. This procedure betokens little respect for the child and it is not surprising to find it associated with low self-esteem.

A specific example of the child's right of expression would perhaps be indicative of more general parental attitudes on authority. It is possible that the parents might agree to something in principle that they would be reluctant to grant in the specific instance. To gauge parent attitudes toward the particular, we asked the mothers during the interview how the child's bedtime was decided and how differences on this point were resolved. Children are notorious for wanting to stay up to a later hour than their parents deem advisable, and the method for resolving differences on this generally sensitive point should provide a good indication of parental commitment to the child's rights. The responses were coded into two categories: those in which the child's view took precedence and those in which the parent's opinion determined the outcome. The distribution of responses is presented in Table 11.7, from which we can conclude that the parents of children with high self-esteem are far more responsive to the opinions of their children than are the parents of children with lower self-esteem. Only 16.7 percent of mothers in the low esteem group allow the child's views to prevail, but 29.4 percent of the medium and 45.5 percent of the high esteem group are willing to accept his decision. This willingness to respect the child's opinions on a recurrent and central issue is a notable sign of sensitivity and respect for the child's rights. In interpreting this finding we should, at the same time, take cognizance of the more demanding and extensive limits established by the parents of children with high self-esteem. It is possible that these parents establish more explicit bedtime procedures and permit their children to exercise their own discretion within the limits thereby established. This

TABLE 11.7 *The person who decides child's bedtime*

| Person deciding | Subjective self-esteem | | |
|---|---|---|---|
| | Low | Medium | High |
| Child decides | 16.7% (5) | 29.4% (5) | 45.5% (15) |
| Parents decide | 83.3% (25) | 70.6% (12) | 54.5% (18) |
| Totals | 100.0% (30) | 100.0% (17) | 100.0% (33) |

$\chi^2 = 6.10$    df = 2    p < .05

*Source:* Mother's interview.

would not only enable the child to exercise his own judgment but would at the same time reduce the possibility of conflict with his parent.

It is, however, inevitable that differences between parent and child will arise. They may occur in areas of ambiguity in which alternative interpretations are possible or in new situations that have not been considered, or they may arise as a result of the child's developing capacities. Wherever they do occur they pose a problem that can either be ignored or, more generally, resolved by parental action. The parent may adopt a coercive posture and intimidate the child into compliance or may employ reasoning, advice, and noncoercive suggestions to make the point. The procedure applied will clearly vary according to the situation but there are apt to be consistencies in the procedures employed by any given parent. To determine the procedures generally employed by the parents of our subjects, we asked them to indicate the principal methods they used to gain compliance. Their responses were coded into two categories: those that stressed discussion, reasoning, and advice, and those that stressed coercion, force, and control. The results, summarized in Table 11.8, indicate that the parents of children with high self-esteem are more likely to use discussion and reasoning than are the parents of children with low or medium self-esteem. Parents of children with low and medium self-esteem employ force twice as often (60.0 percent and 47.1 percent) as do the parents of children with high self-esteem. In this regard, as well as in those previously indicated, the parents of children with high self-esteem manifest greater respect and recognition for their children.

Before concluding this chapter, we shall summarize the different patterns of authority we have found in the families of children with high, medium, and low self-esteem. The results point to a negative relationship between the

TABLE 11.8 *Procedure generally employed to obtain child's cooperation or compliance*

|  | Subjective self-esteem | | |
|---|---|---|---|
| Procedure | Low | Medium | High |
| Stress discussion and reasoning | 40.0% (12) | 52.9% (9) | 78.8% (26) |
| Stress force, autocratic means | 60.0% (18) | 47.1% (8) | 21.2% (7) |
| Totals | 100.0% (30) | 100.0% (17) | 100.0% (33) |
| $\chi^2 = 10.06$    df $= 2$    p $< .01$ | | | |

*Source:* Mother's interview.

limits established for the child and the freedom he is granted within those limits. Thus we find that the families of children with high self-esteem not only establish the closest and most extensive set of rules, but are also the most zealous in enforcing them. This establishes the authority of the parent, defines the environment, and provides standards by which the child can judge his competence and progress. Parental treatment within these limits is noncoercive and recognizes the rights and opinions of the child. His views are sought, his opinions are respected, and concessions are granted to him if differences exist. The latitude that prevails within the general limits permits the child to enter into discussions as a significant participant and to gain the benefits of self-assertion.

The pattern for the low esteem group included in this study consists of few and poorly defined limits and harsh and autocratic methods of control. The parents of this group either do not express their authority to their children or express it so vaguely that it lacks clarity and force. This may reflect uncertainty about their own standards or immaturity, or a neglectful attitude toward their children. Whatever the case, they do not provide the external standards from which inner controls are formed. This does not necessarily have a devaluating effect, but it does result in doubts about whether performance is up to standards. Such doubts may be as corrosive in their own way as critical appraisals and may be associated with hesitant and unassertive behavior. Within the limits, weak as they are, these parents are controlling, dictatorial, rejecting, uncompromising. They determine policies without consulting the child, refuse to tolerate deviant opinion, and resolve differences by dictum and by force. This pattern has been found to be less effective and to produce pernicious side effects.[16] These parents appear to demand absolute compliance without providing the guiding limits that would indicate what sorts of behavior they value and desire. The lack of standards and the accompanying disrespectful treatment that prevail in these families cause their children to feel uncertain of whether and when they have succeeded and to feel insignificant and powerless. There are indications that these parents are themselves low in self-esteem, that they themselves lack confidence to establish a family framework, and that they rely upon harsh treatment to exercise control over their children and achieve resolution of differences.

---

[16] W. C. Baker. "Consequences of different kinds of parental disciplines." In M. L. Hoffman and L. W. Hoffman (Eds.). *Review of Child Development Research,* New York, Russell Sage Foundation, 1964, Vol. 1, pp. 169–208.

# Chapter twelve

# Parent-child relationships IV:

# TRAINING FOR INDEPENDENCE

Each individual is of necessity partially dependent upon other persons throughout his life. No man can stand completely apart from his fellows in his adulthood any more than he can in his infancy. Each of us depends upon others for stimulation, companionship, and the satisfaction of needs. If the human condition is inevitable aloneness, as some contend, it is at the same time an aloneness that occurs in concert. Born helpless, reliant upon others for our survival, and living in a world of vast and cumulative symbolic wisdom, we are a species whose members must depend upon one another. The more specific and direct issues that confront man are not his dependence or isolation, each of which is true in its own way, but the *extent* of independence to be achieved, and the individual equation between dependence and independence. These issues are resolved differently by persons in different societies, and our own[1] is among those that make the greatest demands for independence. It is, at the same time, a society that manifests considerable concern and ambivalence as to the balance of dependent and independent behavior any individual should express. These issues of value and balance are raised at the outset, since they underlie and will affect the definitions and interpretations we shall present. As we shall see, the relation

---

[1] J. W. M. Whiting and I. L. Child. *Child Training and Personality: A Cross-cultural Study.* New Haven, Conn., Yale University Press, 1953.

between training in independence and self-esteem is more complex than may appear on the surface, and will require a careful and considered appraisal.

The definition of independence we employ is "freedom from the influence or control of others." This freedom may be expressed in virtually any behavior or aspect of performance. It may be expressed in the individual's insistence upon feeding or dressing himself, providing for his own housing or educational needs, or insisting upon his sole right of political decision.

However expressed, all efforts are necessarily relative, since all persons are to some extent subject to the influence of others. This is particularly true for children, who must depend upon the good will, knowledge, and support of others for their survival and development.

In the present study, we are specifically interested in the individual's *reliance upon others for judgments of esteem*. Such a reliance would be established to the extent that the individual's judgment of his worth was subject to the opinions, influence, and authority of other persons. The independent person is relatively detached from outside social forces of appraisal, and relies heavily upon himself in making judgments and appraisals. He will undoubtedly receive information from outside sources but he can reject and disregard them readily and without distress. The dependent person is much more at the mercy of the judgments of those in his effective interpersonal environment. There are some sources, possibly as few as one, which he cannot dismiss and which have the capacity to raise, lower, threaten, or stabilize his self-appraisal. This dependence, like any other, varies in degree and will be present to some extent in all individuals. Presumably it will be greater for children than for older persons, who have developed a broader base for gauging their competence and acceptance. Such dependence need not necessarily be related to any given level of esteem since the effective source(s) of appraisal may be enhancing, neutral, or devaluating. The dependence may, however, occur more frequently at some levels of esteem than at others and this is the issue that will concern us here.

Our usage of the term "independence" differs in certain respects from those customarily employed. The definition does not focus upon the level of independence achieved in specific areas of performance but to the sources employed in making judgments and (self) evaluations. Thus, we are not concerned with whether a youngster is an accomplished athlete but whether he employs other persons' judgments of his performance as a basis for evaluating his own worth. Another example may further clarify the focal concern of our discussion. Suppose that a child completes a painting or a model, is satisfied and proud of it, and then shows it to his friends. They may make praising, disparaging, or neutral statements, or they may offer their opinions of the ability of the artist as well as on the quality of the painting. Whatever they express, our concern is with the influence these various statements exert upon the child's definitions of his worthiness, rather than with the painting itself. The child may appreciate the opinions and criticisms of his peers and parents and recognize their validity and sincerity, without these opinions sharply changing his prior self-evaluation. Although the level of self-esteem may show small and temporary changes in virtually all individuals who are being appraised, we are concerned with the weight given to the personal, inner frame of reference relative to the opinions expressed by external evaluations.

Our usage of the term independence also differs from those customarily employed in its omission of the favorable and unfavorable connotations of that term. The more favorable connotations of independence are initiative, persistence, and exploratory behavior,[2] and its negative implications include assertiveness,[3] loneliness, and social isolation.[4] For our purposes the major and central feature of independence is psychological differentiation from others. This implies detachment and the lack of influence of others but it does not imply lack of awareness, interest, or concern for other individuals. We can thus say that an individual is relatively free from influence without implying that he does or does not show initiative, social concern, or aggressiveness. The consequences of differentiation will vary according to other personality characteristics and situational factors, and are not necessary concomitants of independence. Whether a positive, neutral, or negative value is assigned to independence will depend upon the observer's own system of values and the particular issue under consideration.

At first glance we would anticipate that persons high in self-esteem would be more independent than those low in their own estimation. This would certainly be the case if our definition of independence was limited to the more favorable connotations of the term. Assertiveness, initiative, nonconformity, and popularity are certainly behaviors that have been associated with high self-esteem as well as independence.[5] In similar fashion, the behaviors associated with dependence—seeking help, proximity, and attention—are

---

[2] K. K. Beller. "Dependence and independence in young children." *J. Genet. Psych.*, **87**:25–35 (1955).

[3] G. Heathers. "Emotional dependence and independence in a physical threat situation." *Child Develop.*, **24**:169–179 (1953).

[4] H. A. Witkin, R. B. Dyk, H. F. Paterson, D. R. Goodenough, and S. A. Karp. *Psychological Differentiation.* New York, Wiley, 1962.

[5] M. Rosenberg. "Self-esteem and concern with public affairs." *Pub. Opin. Quart.*, **26**:201–211 (1962).

generally associated with low self-esteem. There are, however, certain lines of evidence that make it difficult to posit a positive relationship between independence and personal feelings of worth. Our own findings on democratic practices and permissiveness raise questions on whether that relationship is indeed positive. From the results on democratic practices cited in Chapter 11, it appears that persons with high self-esteem operate within a firm and demanding set of rules, which effectively compel contact and compliance. Persons with low self-esteem have more expanded limits but the procedures and patterns of authority that exist in their families leave them continually subject to external jurisdiction and authority. Thus the evidence on democratic practices can be used to support the greater dependence (that is, nondifferentiation) of persons with either high or low self-esteem. This same inference could be drawn from our findings on permissiveness, given in Chapter 10. There we found that the parents of children with high self-esteem establish and maintain extensive and well-defined rules, and that the parents of children with low self-esteem are less directive and demanding. Parents in the low self-esteem group are, however, more given to harsh forms of punishment, which are administered under uncertain circumstances. It is not clear whether the greater latitude given to the low self-esteem group represents a parental desire to grant independence or a parental lack of concern and rejection. Our interpretattion favors the latter alternative, but both alternatives would leave the child at considerable psychological distance from the parent.

The results on the effects of acceptance and rejection pose other issues and complications. From parental and child reports we can assume that children with high self-esteem are closer to their parents than are the more rejected individuals with low self-esteem. The children report themselves to be closer to their parents; the parents on their part report more accepting attitudes and practices. These statements of initial acceptance point to the presence of a close and warm relationship, which can be taken as a presumptive indication that persons with high self-esteem are less separated from their parents than are individuals with low self-esteem who are ignored, rebuffed, and denied support.

Whichever theory of dependency formation we adopt, it can be argued that the greater independence of individuals with high or low self-esteem could result either from the emotional deprivation resulting from rejection or from the greater self-appreciation that comes with acceptance. Therefore we can make no a priori proposals on the relationship between self-esteem and independence or upon the set of conditions likely to produce a child who is not dependent upon his parents for his definition of worth. The discussion also suggests that much of the behavior associated with independence appears to follow from other characteristics that become apparent when and if separateness is achieved. Persons who are relatively removed and immune from the influence and authority of others may show initiative or impassivity, rapid discouragement or persistence, and timidity or assertiveness. What separation does is to remove the individual from the influence of others, but it does not assure any given consequences or have specific behavioral implications.

Previous investigations have indicated a number of conditions associated with the formation of dependence and independence. Though these studies employed broader definitions of independence than we have proposed, there are several features that appear common to both definitions, and enable us to generalize from their results. Among the conditions that have been found to produce dependency are protectiveness,[6,7] intrusiveness, excessive contact, and diminution and exclusion of outside forces. A related and more direct situation[8] is that in which the mother encourages and rewards reliance upon her and allows little opportunity for independent judgments. A second line of studies[9] indicates that parents of dependent boys have low regard for each other, are in considerable conflict with one another, and tend to reject their children. The inference here—that dependency may be a response to feelings of *insecurity*—has been supported by other findings,[10] which indicate that dependency increases when adults are not readily available. The third line of studies suggests that *deprivation* from adult contact can eventuate in greater need for affiliation with them. A fourth and final set of findings[11] indicate that dependency occurs when a need is first established by reward and subsequently *frustrated* or punished. In the particular example cited by this study, severe weaning following favorable experiences of early feeding is related to subsequent dependency in nursery school. These four sets of findings reflect four different theoretical interpretations of the antecedents of

---

[6] J. K. Beller. "Dependence and independence in young children." *J. Genet. Psych.*, 87:25–35 (1955).

[7] A. L. Baldwin, J. Kalhoun, and F. H. Breese. "The appraisal of parent behavior." *Psych. Monogr.*, 63: No. 4 (Whole No. 299) (1949).

[8] D. M. Levy. *Maternal Overprotection.* New York, Columbia University Press, 1943.

[9] W. McCord, J. McCord, and P. Verden. "Familial and behavioral correlates of dependency in male children." *Child Develp.*, 33:313–326 (1962).

[10] F. L. Gewirtz. "A factor analysis of some attention-seeking behaviors of young children." *Child Develp.*, 27:17–36 (1956).

[11] R. R. Sears, J. W. M. Whiting, V. Nowlis, and P. S. Sears. "Some child-rearing antecedents of dependency and aggression in young children." *Genet. Psych. Monogr.*, 47:135–234 (1953).

childhood dependency. The theory of indulgence proposes that children do not venture from the cocoon; the theory of insecurity suggests that uncertain or disturbed children lack confidence; the deprivation theory hypothesizes an unfilled need; and the frustrated-need hypothesis suggests that inconsistent handling results in a sustained expression of the behavior.

We should at this point like to propose an alternative and more general hypothesis of childhood dependency. This theory is related to our previous discussion and proposes a cognitive, information-seeking disposition as its essential component. The general proposition may be stated as follows: dependency behaviors represent an attempt to confirm or establish a definition of one's worth or capacities. This proposition assumes that the dependent individual lacks a stable definition or appraisal in an area salient to him, that only one or few persons are deemed capable of stabilizing the appraisal, and that the failure to achieve stability has distressing consequences. It further assumes that the dependent (that is, information-seeking) behavior will continue until cognitive stability is achieved or until the need loses its importance. According to our interpretation, dependency will be produced by conditions that do not provide clear and stable evaluations. Dependent individuals are persons who are uncertain of their attitudes and opinions and require the reassurance of external confirmation and appraisal.

The four previous theories we have briefly examined manifest conditions that are subsumed under our general proposition. The conditions of indulgence do not provide an opportunity for the child to test his abilities, and he must therefore remain uncertain of his adequacy and effectiveness in the world at large. The uncertainty of worthiness thereby produced is resolved by attending to the appraisals advanced by the indulgent parent. Indulgence, in effect, produces illusions of grandeur and omnipotence but does not permit these illusions to be tested in the broader and more objective arenas of performance. The protective, encompassing parent assumes the role of cocoon and maintains the engulfed object on a selective and supportive diet that is nowhere else available. The insecurity produced by parental conflict produces a sense of uncertainty that is less sheltered but equally unstable. Thus the child is caught between differences in values that make assessments of self-worthiness difficult. In these conditions the child may well be a pawn who is used and abused as a medium of exchange. His environment is unstable, its major figures disagree, and there is an omnipresent threat that the situation may be drastically altered. Any source that could provide a clear and definite assessment would alleviate the distress of uncertainty and provide a stabilizing anchor in the storm of uncertainties.

The proposition applies equally to the inconsistent treatment resulting from needs that are established and then abruptly and severely frustrated. This treatment makes it difficult for the child to comprehend what is actually desired and leaves him uncertain that what is required today will indeed be required in the future. Intermittent and inconsistent treatment has been found to result in behaviors that are more difficult to extinguish, and our proposition provides an explanation of why this may be the case. Where the organism cannot establish a set of clear and stable expectations, it must remain alert to alternative possibilities and must seek to establish a stabilizing interpretation or relationship. Inconsistency interferes with the formation of stabilizing interpretations and leads to an assumption that the environment is relatively unpredictable. The effects of inconsistent treatment may be expected to vary according to the degree of consistency manifested. We would expect that greater inconsistency would produce greater reliance upon others for evaluation and stabilization of oneself and the situation. Such differences in inconsistency might underlie the differing results obtained for the frustration of different needs.[12,13] In any event, it would appear that inconsistent treatment would interfere with ready interpretation of the situation and might induce reliance upon those who determine and control changes.

The fourth theory of dependency relates the early absence of adults to subsequent need for them. Inasmuch as this theory is based on the hypothesis that social deprivation evokes attempts for attention and affiliation, the issue is how to interpret the latter, attention-seeking behaviors. From our proposition we conclude that these behaviors are an attempt to gain a stable frame of reference in an otherwise impoverished environment. Children who are placed in situations in which adults are not present have few bases by which to interpret the situation or their own reactions. Faced with more extreme conditions of sensory deprivation, even adults experience distress and seek to establish an orienting framework.[14] In the case of children without adults, we would interpret their disposition toward affiliation as a similar attempt to gain a stable self-orientation. Dependency in all these cases would appear to stem from a common reliance upon significant individuals to stabilize the personal environment, and, in the process, to provide a reliable assessment of one's worth.

---

[12] See Footnote 11.

[13] R. R. Sears, E. G. Maccoby, and H. Levin. *Patterns of Child Rearing*. Evanston, Ill., Row-Peterson, 1957.

[14] L. Goldberger and R. R. Holt. "Experimental interference with reality contact (perceptual isolation): Method and group results." *J. Nerv. Ment. Dis.*, **127**:99–112 (1958).

TABLE 12.1 *"A child should be protected from jobs which might be too tiring or hard for him"*

| | Subjective self-esteem | | |
| Reply | Low | Medium | High |
| --- | --- | --- | --- |
| Agree | 41.2% (14) | 75.0% (12) | 54.8% (17) |
| Disagree | 58.8% (20) | 25.0% (4) | 45.2% (14) |
| Totals | 100.0% (34) | 100.0% (16) | 100.0% (31) |

$\chi^2 = 5.06$      df $= 2$      $p < .08$

*Source:* Mother's questionnaire.

### SELF-ESTEEM AND INDEPENDENCE TRAINING

In attempting to clarify the relationship between self-esteem and independence training, we shall focus our inquiry upon the following two questions: "What are the independence training practices employed by the parents of our child subjects?" and "How are these practices related to indications of uncertain self-judgments and reliance upon others?" The practices to be considered represent various manifestations of protectiveness and indulgence. Conditions associated with the other theories of dependency previously discussed are not considered in this exposition.

One of the more striking expressions of dependency-inducing behavior is the mother's protectiveness of her child. By such protectiveness, the mother is sheltering the child from events, experiences, and goals that she believes to be overly demanding or dangerous. An actively protective attitude limits the child in his exploration of new areas of experience and new levels of accomplishment. It effectively curtails enterprise and initiative and restricts the range and level of activities to those the parent deems safe, realistic, and appropriate. The underlying theme of restriction apparently represents an exaggerated concern about the dangers to which the child is vulnerable. As we shall see, the child's interpretation of this concern has important implications for the effects of protectiveness. One of our indices of protectiveness was the mother's response to an item included in our parent attitude questionnaire: "A child should be protected from jobs which might be too tiring or hard for him." Mothers who agreed with this statement (see Table 12.1) were expressing an attitude in favor of protectiveness; those who disagreed were advocating greater exposure to environmental demands.

As Table 12.1 shows, the parents of children with medium self-esteem were

TABLE 12.2 *"Some children don't realize how lucky they are to have parents setting high goals for them"*

| | Subjective self-esteem | | |
| Reply | Low | Medium | High |
|---|---|---|---|
| Agree | 67.6% (23) | 37.5% (6) | 48.4% (15) |
| Disagree | 32.4% (11) | 62.5% (10) | 51.6% (16) |
| Totals | 100.0% (34) | 100.0% (16) | 100.0% (31) |

$\chi^2 = 4.70$      df $= 2$      p $< .10$

*Source:* Mother's questionnaire.

more likely to express a protective attitude than were the parents of children with either high or low self-esteem. The distribution is curvilinear, with 75.0 percent of the mothers in the medium esteem group responding in the affirmative and 41.2 and 54.8 percent of the mothers in the low and high esteem groups doing the same. The differences between the groups do not quite achieve customary levels of statistical significance ($\chi^2 = 5.06$, df $= 2$, p $< .08$), but they are nonetheless notable.

Another item of our questionnaire approached this same topic from the vantage of goal setting: "Some children don't realize how lucky they are to have parents setting high goals for them." Parents who agreed with this statement were, in effect, taking a nonprotective attitude, but those who disagreed were assuming a more sheltering position. The results (Table 12.2) again indicate that the parents of medium esteem subjects are more protective than those in either low or high esteem groups. The parents of children with medium self-esteem are more likely to disagree with this statement than are the parents of children with high or low self-esteem.

Thus we find that 62.5 percent of the parents in the medium group see no particular advantage in high goals, but only 32.4 percent of parents in the low group and 51.6 percent of those in the high group express such reservations. Again the distribution is curvilinear and again the result approaches a level that would permit acceptance ($\chi^2 = 4.70$, df $= 2$, p $< .10$). Because of the similarity of results on both items, their closeness to customary levels of acceptability, and their theoretical consistency with subsequent findings, we believe them worthy of consideration. They provide an initial indication that the parents of children with medium self-esteem are most likely to employ protective practices, which other studies have associated with the development of dependency.

TABLE 12.3 *Mother's anxiety about child's sleeping outside of home*

| Degree of anxiety | Subjective self-esteem | | |
|---|---|---|---|
| | Low | Medium | High |
| Little or no anxiety | 36.7% (11) | 11.8% (2) | 57.6% (19) |
| Moderate or considerable anxiety | 63.3% (19) | 88.2% (15) | 42.4% (14) |
| Totals | 100.0% (30) | 100.0% (17) | 100.0% (33) |

$\chi^2 = 10.03$     df $= 2$     $p < .01$

*Source:* Mother's interview.

Another manifestation of training in independence is the parents' willingness to permit independent and exploratory behavior. Parents who encourage such behavior apparently help their children to do things without them and to venture into new, previously unexperienced activities. Presumably, they would be more inclined to prod and stimulate the child when he is not venturesome and would be more likely to expose him to new and demanding situations. They would tend to be relatively nonchalant about the child's excursions and accept his ventures in a favorable and nonthreatening light. At the other extreme we might anticipate that parents who tend to foster dependency would try to restrict the child's activities as much as possible to those which can be carried out under their supervision. They would limit outside activities and try to prevent the development of interests or relationships that would introduce external, nonfamilial forces. Exploratory or demanding tasks would be viewed with alarm and, where they could not be avoided, regarded with dread and anxiety. There were two questions in our interview schedule that dealt with the mother's anxieties aroused by outside activities and pressures toward achievement. The first of these tapped the mother's feelings about her son's sleeping overnight at a friend's or relative's home. The responses were coded according to the amount of discomfort or anxiety the mother reported. Table 12.3 presents the percentage of mothers in each of the self-esteem groups who experienced limited and considerable anxiety. This table again reveals a curvilinear relationship between dependency-inducing behavior and self-esteem.

The percentage of mothers in the medium group who experience considerable anxiety about their children sleeping away from home is markedly greater (88.2 percent) than it is in the high (42.4 percent) or low (63.3 percent) esteem groups. Even more notable is the frequency of mothers who experience little anxiety about such an occurrence. We find roughly one-eighth (11.8 percent) of the medium group mothers to be nonchalant about the problem, and three times as many mothers of the low group (36.7 percent) and almost five times as many mothers of the high group (57.6 percent) are equally casual. The generally greater anxiety expressed by the mothers of the medium group is presumably communicated also to their children. These women gave a variety of reasons for their anxiety and indicated their solicitude and concern for their sons. Their reasons suggested that their children, ten to twelve years of age, were not yet ready to venture beyond their homes to uncertain and strange environments. The mothers suggested that the children would be more at ease where they, the mother, could provide for their needs and assure safety and acceptance.

Analysis of other questions revealed that parental protectiveness was also manifest in attitudes toward present and future achievement. During the interview we asked the mother how she responded when her child did poorly in school. The responses reveal that the mothers of children with medium self-esteem are more inclined to exert limited pressure (35.3 percent) than are the mothers of other children (21.3 percent). Thus, the same tendency to protect and indulge, to limit pressure and accept manifest performance, is more frequently found in the parents of children with medium self-esteem than in the actions and attitudes of parents of children with high or low self-esteem. Our medium self-esteem subjects are not encouraged or required to extend their efforts but are sustained and supported for whatever efforts they do exert.

Parental protectiveness also extends into plans and aspirations for the future as well as procedures for the present. Such protectiveness is not necessarily limited to either parent, but can be expressed by both, thereby providing a more inclusive sheltering home environment in which fathers and mothers are in agreement that their son should be shielded from "unnecessary" pressures. They can establish a comforting retreat that minimizes the influence of external prods and incentives. To determine the father's attitudes toward protectiveness, we included a question on our interview schedule dealing with the father's aspirations for his son. The mother was asked to indicate the occupation her husband wished their child to attain. The occupations chosen were coded according to their social class level and assigned to the five classes designated by Hollingshead and Redlich.[15] The results were divided into two categories (Higher—I and II; Lower—III, IV,

---

[15] A. B. Hollingshead and F. C. Redlich. *Social Class and Mental Illness.* New York, Wiley, 1958.

TABLE 12.4 *Father's aspiration for his son's future work status*

| Level of job | Subjective self-esteem | | |
|---|---|---|---|
| | Low | Medium | High |
| Lower (Classes III, IV, V): lower middle and working classes | 23.3% (7) | 41.2% (7) | 12.2% (4) |
| Higher (Classes I, II): upper middle classes | 76.7% (23) | 58.8% (10) | 87.8% (29) |
| Totals | 100.0% (30) | 100.0% (17) | 100.0% (33) |
| $\chi^2 = 5.45$     df $= 2$ | p $<$ .07 | | |

*Source:* Mother's interview.

V) and the distribution for the various self-esteem groups examined. The aspirations of the fathers in the various self-esteem groups are presented in Table 12.4, which reveals that the fathers of medium esteem boys have lower aspirations for their sons than do the fathers of boys with low or high esteem. Forty-one percent (41.2) of the fathers of children with medium self-esteem designate working or lower middle class occupations for their sons, but only 12.2 percent of the responses of the high esteem and 23.3 percent of the low esteem group are assigned to that category. The lower aspirations that the fathers of children with medium self-esteem hold for their sons might conceivably stem from a wide variety of motives, including ability and performance. However, as we have previously reported in Chapter 7 (Characteristics of the Subjects), children with medium self-esteem are at least average in both these regards. Yet the parents of these children have lower aspirations for them than do the parents of the less competent and failing Low-Low group. Thus, whereas the parents of these medium esteem children have more basis for assigning them to higher occupations than do those parents of low esteem children, they aspire to more modest and limited goals.

Another way in which parents can foster dependence is by the duration and intensity of contact with their children. By monopolizing their children's time, parents effectively limit the possibilities of contact with other persons and are thus assured that their influence will remain paramount. Such a monopoly may be achieved by restricting the child's activities directly or through more devious procedures of control. The mother may take the children with her wherever she goes, forbid friendships, or insist that social activities be carried on solely within the family. In addition to such physical

TABLE 12.5 *Mother's opinion on whether child is entitled to privacy in his own room*

| Degree of privacy | Subjective self-esteem | | |
|---|---|---|---|
| | Low | Medium | High |
| Child has little or no right to privacy | 21.9% (7) | 52.9% (9) | 12.9% (4) |
| Child has considerable or strong rights of privacy | 78.1% (25) | 47.1% (8) | 87.1% (27) |
| Totals | 100.0% (32) | 100.0% (17) | 100.0% (31) |

$\chi^2 = 9.67$     df $= 2$     p $< .01$

*Source:* Mother's interview.

manipulation, she may insist that there be no barriers of privacy between the child and herself. This intrusion upon the thought and ideas of the child represents a direct invasion of the child's privacy and an implicit refusal to recognize his distinctness as a person. It is an extreme manifestation of the desire to remove whatever independence the child may have achieved. Our data provide two indications of parental attitudes regarding the child's physical and psychological privacy. These are presented respectively in Tables 12.5 and 12.6.

The first attitude toward physical privacy (Table 12.5) deals with the mother's belief about her child's right to privacy in his own quarters. We see that the mothers of children with medium self-esteem are more likely (52.9 percent) to believe that their children have little if any rights on this issue than do the mothers of children with either high (12.9 percent) or low (21.9 percent) self-esteem. Over one-half the mothers of children with medium self-esteem believe that they have the right to enter their child's room at their own discretion, but less than one-quarter of the other mothers hold a similar view. This belief presumably reflects a conviction that the child should not be permitted to engage in activities that cannot be shared with his parents and that the parents have full and total right of entry to his room. Inasmuch as the mothers of children with medium self-esteem are relatively accepting, we can infer that the intrusions of these mothers stem from generally favorable rather than malicious intentions. There may be underlying sentiments of rejection[16] but our present study provides no basis for inferring the presence or extent of such sentiments or whether they play

[16] D. M. Levy. *Maternal Overprotection.* New York, Columbia University Press, 1943.

TABLE 12.6 *"An alert parent should try to learn all her child's thoughts"*

| Reply | Subjective self-esteem | | |
|---|---|---|---|
| | Low | Medium | High |
| Agree | 87.5% (28) | 94.1% (16) | 64.5% (20) |
| Disagree | 12.5% (4) | 5.9% (1) | 35.5% (11) |
| Totals | 100.0% (32) | 100.0% (17) | 100.0% (31) |

$\chi^2 = 9.90$     df = 2     p < .01

*Source:* Mother's questionnaire.

an important or determining role in the mother's intrusive behavior. One possibility suggested by other research[17] is that such intrusive parents do not differentiate themselves from their children. According to this interpretation, intrusive parents regard their children as an extension of themselves so that their attempts to control them are but an extended instance of self-control. Speculative as it is, this line of reasoning does suggest that the parents of children with medium self-esteem identify closely with their children and are likely to regard them as extensions of themselves. It further suggests that these parents and children may both have difficulty in delineating the boundary between themselves and others.

The intrusiveness of the medium esteem parent apparently extends to psychological as well as physical privacy (Table 12.6). This is revealed by their responses to the statement, "An alert parent should try to learn all her child's thoughts," which was included in the mother attitude questionnaire. The mothers of children with medium self-esteem are more apt to support such intrusiveness (94.1 percent) than are the parents of children with high (64.5 percent) or low (87.5 percent) self-esteem. The preeminence of the medium group in dependency-evoking behaviors is again expressed in the curvilinear relationship between intrusiveness and subjective esteem.

The over-all pattern of results leads to the surprising finding that it is the parents of children with medium self-esteem who are more protective and intrusive. Their protectiveness is expressed in lower goals, demands, and aspirations than for children with either higher or lower self-esteem and is associated with anxiety about the child's independent actions. Their intrusiveness is expressed by a failure to grant the child either physical or psychological privacy. Children with medium self-esteem are reared under con-

[17] H. A. Witkin, R. B. Dyk, D. R. Paterson, D. R. Goodenough, and S. A. Karp. *Psychological Differentiation.* New York, Wiley, 1962.

ditions that are most likely to eventuate in their becoming dependent. They are kept close to the family, sheltered from demands, and are permitted little freedom of action. It is these children, rather than those high or low in self-esteem, who apparently are least detached from others. In the light of the theoretical analysis of dependency presented earlier in this chapter, we propose that it is this middle group that is most inclined to rely upon others for their self-evaluations. This brings us back to the question regarding the relationship between independence and self-esteem. From our results it appears that this question would best be divided into two parts. "Why is independence training associated with either high or low esteem but not with medium esteem?" and "Why is dependence associated with medium esteem rather than other levels of self-appraisal?" Though our answers to these questions are necessarily speculative, they do elaborate upon one aspect of self-esteem we have not previously considered.

The issue underlying both these questions is how involvement or detachment from others is related to self-appraisal. If we examine our four major explanatory concepts—successes, values, aspirations, and defenses—we find that none appears to be directly or immediately related to dependency. If we employ the term dependency in the sense of differentiation from others, we can find no basis to assume that it should produce more or less frequent successes, different values, higher or lower aspirations, or more or less adequate defenses. Detachment from others may bring more failures as well as successes, and it will certainly not provide the same supportive figures as are present in a dependency relationship. We might propose that dependency is less socially valued in American society, but this general value is not the self-value by which each individual judges his own actions. There is abundant evidence that many ethnic groups[18] reject independence as a value, as do many families and individuals. The aspirations of dependent persons might conceivably be lower than those of independent persons but this will obviously vary according to the person(s) upon whom they rely. Should the dependent person rely on individuals who set high aspirations for them, they could well have higher aspirations than more differentiated individuals. Thus, there does not appear to be any necessary relationship between an individual's level of aspiration and his differentiation from others. Finally, we can see no reason to believe that an individual's ability to define or interpret an event positively is related to his involvement with others. Dependent persons who rely upon strong and supportive figures and who can reject certain non-

[18] A. H. Leighton, J. A. Clausen, and R. N. Wilson (Eds.). *Explorations in Social Psychiatry.* New York, Basic Books, 1957.

personal domains from consideration, such as academic achievement, are in a good position to view the vast bulk of their experiences in a favorable light. They would, in fact, appear to be in a much better position to achieve favorable interpretations than are persons who demand more of themselves in all areas and who stand without social support.

From the foregoing analysis it appears that the relationship between self-esteem and dependency is not readily subsumed under our four major concepts. The curvilinear relationship between self-esteem and dependency suggests that there is a particular, specific effect of dependency and that this effect has a distribution different from the other expressions of esteem we have considered. We propose that the variable that follows this curvilinear relationship, and is associated with training for dependency, is *certainty of esteem*—by which we mean an individual's conviction that his self-appraisal is a reliable estimate of his worthiness, adequacy, and significance. According to this interpretation, dependent persons are unsure but not necessarily demeaning of their worth. They are therefore more apt to be nagged by doubts as to their "true" worth in the broader, less explored, and protected arenas of achievement and social performance. Supported and restricted as they are, dependent children live in a home environment that is markedly different from that which they encounter in the classroom and playground. They do not know how they would fare in the more open competition of that world and cannot resolve their doubts by exploration and confrontation. The dependency-producing environment provides no basis for testing personal adequacy and leaves the individual uncertain of his worth. Uncertainty and instability of self-esteem, rather than low self-esteem, would appear to be the consequences of nondifferentiation.

To say that dependent persons are uncertain of their worth is in effect saying that such persons cannot make independent judgments of themselves as well as other, more external matters. They have learned to place great reliance upon others to determine their opinions and courses of action, and they have also learned to rely upon others to determine their worthiness. Such reliance is present to some extent in all persons, but it is much more marked in the dependent person. The child who is protected and restricted, who is indulged and constrained, is living in an artificial environment. Like a flower developing within a hothouse, he can survive within its shelter but is too unprotected to thrive outside its bounds. He does not know why he is being protected, he does not know what difficulties lurk in the shadows beyond his world, and he does not know whether he can deal with them. Is he being protected because he is incompetent or valued? Would he be able to deal effectively with greater demands or with new or rapidly changing environments? Parents who restrict their child's freedom and limit his enterprise and exploration will prevent their children from developing *personal* answers to these questions. They will produce a child attuned to the needs of his parents, a child who will seek their assurance to determine the significance of his own views. The result is self-doubt (rather than negative appraisal) and an extreme reliance upon other persons' definitions of one's worth.

With this interpretation as a guide we are in a position to answer our questions and clarify the relationship between dependency and self-esteem. Applying our hypothesis that training in independence results in more certain judgments of one's worth, we conclude that persons high and low in self-esteem are relatively certain of their self-appraisals. Both have been given latitude to explore, to move outside the family circle, and to develop private worlds of their own; both have been able to free themselves of reliance upon others, and, given this detachment, have reached different conclusions. The detachment of the child with high self-esteem has been accompanied by experiences of success and acceptance, and a favorable independence is achieved. This child has been given the opportunity to test his mettle and he has found that he can be successful on his own. The child with low self-esteem has been given the same opportunity but, lacking competence and support, has reached generally negative conclusions. The differentiation of the person with high self-esteem is accompanied by a series of personally achieved successes, which lay the foundation for a stable and lofty self-esteem. He is accepted or successful within the broader social context, yet is not reliant upon their appraisals. The differentiation of the person with low self-esteem is accompanied by a series of failures, which cannot be readily or wholly attributed to other persons. These individuals with low self-esteem are differentiated, and, without recourse or justification, they are convinced of their inferiority. Differentiation, in effect, exposes the individual and makes it possible for his capacities to be demonstrated more clearly. It may result in any level of self-esteem and it will provide the individual with a self-appraisal in which he has confidence.

The parents of children with medium self-esteem provide little opportunity for the children to achieve successes they can call their own. They interfere with attempts at autonomous activity and reduce the likelihood of their achieving private and personal experiences. These parents provide an environment in which only their own goals are espoused and rewarded, with little presentation or explanation of alternatives. In time the child comes to assume opinions that are very much attuned to theirs and seeks their assurance when deviant opinions or ambiguous situations arise. The parent is the source of assurance and confirmation of worthiness; where he does not express a judgment, the child has difficulty achieving an independent judgment of his own. From other analyses of dependency-inducing conditions,[19,20] it appears that the parents of children with medium self-esteem identify closely with them. They presumably derive gratification from their child's successes and sorrow from his failures. This identification makes it difficult for the parent to expose his child, since he would, in effect, be exposing himself. The result is reduced risk-taking, which minimizes the possibilities for extreme failures and at the same time minimizes the possibilities of notable success. These dependency-producing parents are frequently self-indulgent, somewhat helpless persons who lack fulfillment in their own lives and seek to gain it vicariously through their children.

Another basis for the uncertainty of the person with medium self-esteem may be in the medium position itself. Such persons are not outstanding in being either very good or very bad in the academic and social activities we have considered. Given their abilities and personality characteristics, it is likely that they are in the same middle position in other unexamined activities. These persons evaluate themselves as moderate in esteem—an appraisal that is supported by the appraisals of their teacher and borne out by the records of their performance. This medium position, which they apparently accept, poses greater uncertainties than do either of the extreme positions. Persons who are at the bottom or top of their group can place themselves with relative confidence. Their position in the scheme of things is relatively unambiguous and they can appraise themselves accordingly. The man in the middle range is in the much more uncertain situation of not knowing how well he has met the criteria of judgment. The middle part of the range extends from close to the top to close to the bottom, but the top and bottom are more limited areas. The person with medium self-esteem, who is generally average in performance, may be less certain of just where in this middle range he really belongs. This uncertainty may be expressed in less confident self-appraisals and in the need for external confirmation.

That persons with medium self-esteem are uncertain of their worth as a result of dependency training suggests that they may be distinct in other

---

[19] H. A. Witkin, R. B. Dyk, D. R. Paterson, D. R. Goodenough, and S. A. Karp. *Psychological Differentiation.* New York, Wiley, 1962.

[20] G. Heathers. "Acquiring dependence and independence: A theoretical orientation." *J. Genet. Psych.,* 87:277–291 (1955).

respects. We have previously noted (Chapter 7) that such persons are most likely to be value-oriented and supportive of general social values. Dependent as they are upon others, they may also be most eager to be liked and most desirous of attention. Lacking stable internal frames of reference, they may seek external sources of support and confirmation. Being person-oriented, they may well feel little intrinsic involvement in their work and tend to be ego- rather than task-oriented in their approach to tasks. Less venturesome, they may be more inclined to enter safer occupations and take fewer risks. Undifferentiated from others, they would presumably have a relatively poor and diffuse body image,[21] and show little ability to plan and anticipate. This could be expressed in global, undifferentiated thinking rather than in a more precise and analytic variety.[22]

As is evident from this discussion, our findings on the medium self-esteem group raise a host of theoretical and empirical questions. That the medium group is distinct in certain important regards raises questions on the distribution of other, related personality characteristics that may also be distributed in curvilinear fashion. The hypothesis that medium self-esteem is associated with uncertain self-worth and derives, at least in part, from dependency-inducing experiences raises issues on the meaning of dependency and on how much trust an individual places in his (self) appraisals. These hypotheses clearly require more direct and extended study before they can be accepted with confidence. Until that time they provide an alternative interpretation of the significance of dependency, the conditions that produce it, and the uncertainty of the man in the middle.

---

[21] S. F. Fisher and S. G. Cleveland. *Body Image and Personality*. Princeton, N.J., Van Nostrand, 1958.
[22] See Footnote 19.

*Chapter thirteen*

# SUMMARY AND PERSPECTIVE

T he findings of this study provide new and basic knowledge about the conditions associated with the formation of self-esteem. They reveal not only the sets of circumstances that are most likely to result in favorable self-attitudes and those most likely to result in unfavorable ones, but also provide increased understanding of how and why these circumstances have the effects they do. We have, in effect, examined the various major determinants of self-esteem proposed by other researchers and ourselves and have decided which of them can be considered trustworthy. This examination focused upon the dimensions of capacity and treatment that are presumably related to formation of self-esteem as well as on the ages and areas of experience that seemed salient to that formation. Such discrete analyses did not provide a ready appreciation of the over-all pattern of our findings nor did they indicate the extent to which our findings substantiated the conceptual analyses that centered attention upon successes, aspirations, values, and defenses. In this concluding chapter I shall attempt to summarize, integrate, and evaluate our findings, and indicate some of their implications for the process and study of personality development. In accord with these aims, this chapter is divided into four sections: Summary and Integration, Theoretical Reformulation, Consequences of Parental Treatment, and Issues and Implications.

## SUMMARY AND INTEGRATION

What summary statements and conclusions can we make about the conditions associated with the development of high self-esteem? Or, more exactly, what differentiates the antecedent conditions and personal characteristics associated with the occurrence of high self-esteem from those associated with less favorable self-appraisals? The most general statement about the antecedents of self-esteem can be given in terms of three conditions: total or nearly total *acceptance* of the children by their parents, clearly defineɗ and enforced *limits,* and the *respect* and latitude for individual action that exist within the defined limits. In effect, we can conclude that the parents of children with high self-esteem are concerned and attentive toward their children, that they structure the worlds of their children along lines they believe to be proper and appropriate, and that they permit relatively great freedom within the structures they have established. Examination of this combination of conditions reveals some general relationships between childrearing practices and the formation of self-esteem. The most notable of these deal with parental behavior and the consequences of the rules and regulations that parents establish for their children. These relationships indicate that definite and enforced limits are associated with high rather than low self-esteem; that families which establish and maintain clearly defined limits permit *greater* rather than less deviation from conventional behavior, and freer individual expression, than do families without such limits; that families which maintain clear limits utilize *less* drastic forms of punishment; and that the families of children with high self-esteem exert greater demands for academic performance and excellence. Taken together, these relationships indicate that, other things being equal, limits and rules are likely to have enhancing and facilitating effects and that parental performance within such limits is likely to be moderate, tolerant, and generally civilized. They suggest that parents who have definite values, who have a clear idea of what they regard as appropriate behavior, and who are able and willing to present and enforce their beliefs are more likely to rear children who value themselves highly. Parents who can act this way apparently have less need to treat their children harshly, and, from all indications, are viewed with greater affection and respect by their offspring.

There is, of course, an underlying question about the nature and enforcement of the limits and rules espoused by the parents of children with high-esteem. Two sources of evidence lead us to believe that the limits established are reasonable, rational, and appropriate to the age of the child, and are not arbitrary and inflexible. The first basis for this belief is the consistent and marked acceptance of their offspring that these parents express. They are concerned for their welfare, are willing to exert themselves on their behalf, and are loyal sources of affection and support. They express their acceptance in a variety of ways, with expressions of interest and concern being perhaps the major underlying feature of their attitudes and behaviors. The second reason for believing that the limits are moderate and reasonable comes from our evidence concerning the parents. Our study indicates that the parents of children with high self-esteem are themselves active, poised, and relatively self-assured individuals who recognize the significance of childrearing and believe they can cope with the increased duties and responsibilities it entails. The parents generally appear to be on relatively good terms with one another and to have established clear lines of authority and responsibility. Both father and mother lead active lives outside the family and apparently do not rely upon their families as the sole or necessarily major sources of gratification and esteem. The concern that these parents show for their children, the attention they give them, and their calm, realistic, and assured demeanor lead us to believe that they would be unlikely to impose harsh or extreme restrictions, or to behave in a capricious manner; firm, clear, but extensive limits appear to be much more consistent with their personalities. There are no indications —and several contraindications—that these (high self-esteem) parents are harsh, vindictive, emotional, or power seeking. They apparently believe strongly in the validity of their perceptions and values and guide the lives of their children accordingly, yet at the same time accept and tolerate dissent within the limits that they have established.

Why well-defined limits are associated with high self-esteem can be explained in several ways. First and foremost we should note that well-defined limits provide the child with a basis for evaluating his present performance as well as facilitating comparisons with prior behavior and attitudes. The limits serve to define the social geography by delineating areas of safety and hazards, by indicating means of attaining goals, and by pointing out the landmarks that others use to judge success and failure. When the map drawn by the parents is a realistic and accurate depiction of the goals accepted by the larger social community and the means used to reach them, it serves as a guide to the expectations, demands, and taboos of that community. As such, the map clarifies the ambiguities and inconsistencies of social behavior and also endows such behavior with a sense of meaning and purpose. If provided early, and accurately enough, and if it is upheld by behavioral as well as verbal reinforcement, limit definition gives the child the conviction that there is indeed a social reality that makes demands, provides rewards, and punishes violations. Imposition of limits is likely to give the child, on a rudimentary nonverbal and unconscious level, the implicit belief that a definition of the social world is possible and that the "real" world does indeed impose restrictions and demand compliance with its norms. On this level limits result in differentiation between one's self and the environment and thus serve to increase self-definition. In sum, imposition of limits serves to define the expectations of others, the norms of the group, and the point at which deviation from them is likely to evoke positive action; enforcement of limits gives the child a sense that norms are real and significant, contributes to self-definition, and increases the likelihood that the child will believe that a sense of reality is attainable.

That persons with high self-esteem come from homes notable for their definition of limits raises the question whether persons with positive self-attitudes are likely to be more rigid, submissive, and insensitive. In more neutral and descriptive terms the question is whether persons reared under clear, enforced limits are likely to comply automatically with the desires of others, lose their initiative, and assume a pedestrian and simple way of perceiving and thinking. The issue, in effect, is whether the gains of self-esteem that flow from definite standards may be offset by inflexible opinions, sanctimonious convictions of personal correctness, and a closeminded insensitivity to possibilities and alternatives. From the evidence available to us, the response to this question would appear to be generally negative. We find that individuals with high self-esteem who are reared under strongly structured conditions tend to be more, rather than less, independent and more creative (Table 3.5) than persons reared under more open and permissive conditions. From other indications (see Chapters 3 and 7) it appears that children reared within definite limits are also more likely to be socially accepted as peers and leaders by their associates and also more capable of expressing opinions and accepting criticism. Thus many of the presumably negative effects of limit definition are not supported by empirically derived evidence. Once the loaded terms and value judgments are cast aside and specific behavioral indices are employed, it appears that parents who are less certain and attentive of their standards are likely to have children who are more compliant to the will of their peers and less likely to perceive alternatives—as well as lower in self-esteem.

Psychologically, the distinctive feature of the home in which limits are clearly defined is that the standards, information, and cues it provides are cognitively clear. This clarity enables a child to judge for himself whether he has attained a desired goal, made progress, or deviated. In a home where standards are ambiguous, a child requires the assistance of others to decipher its cues, recognize its boundaries, and understand its relationships. In the cognitively clear world he learns to rely upon his own judgments and interpretations of events and consequences; the locus is internal and personal rather than external and social. Detailed definition of standards, and their consistent presentation and enforcement, presents the child with a wealth of information that he himself can employ to appraise and anticipate the consequences of his actions. A psychological world that provides sparse, ambiguous, or inconsistent information makes it difficult for the child to make rational decisions—that is, decisions with predictable outcomes—and increases the likelihood that he will either continually seek aid in interpreting his environment or will gradually withdraw from it: in neither case will he come to believe that he can, by himself, interpret his environment and guide himself through the thickets of its ambiguities.

Despite the benefits that they confer, would cognitively clear limits have beneficial effects upon children without the warmth and respect expressed by their parents? In more specific terms we may ask whether our results indicate that a *pattern* of conditions is necessary to produce high self-esteem, whether any single condition or set of conditions plays a greater role than others, and whether the self-esteem of the parents is invariably related to the child's self-esteem and to parental patterns of behavior. Although our results do not permit a definitive empirical answer to all of these questions they do provide the basis for a tentative response. First, and foremost, we should note that there are virtually no parental patterns of behavior or parental attitudes that are common to all parents of children with high self-esteem. Examination of the major indices and scales of acceptance, limit definition, respect, and parental self-esteem provides explicit support for the view that not all of these conditions are essential for the formation of high self-esteem. Thus, we find that 21.2 percent of mothers of children with high self-esteem rate low on acceptance (Table 9.1), 12.1 percent of them do not enforce limits carefully (Table 10.3), 19.4 percent do not believe that children should be permitted to dissent from their parent's views (Table 11.3), and 24.3 percent are themselves rated as below average in self-esteem (Table 6.1). The other side of this analysis—that is, examination of the attitudes and actions of parents whose children have low self-esteem—is equally revealing: 56.7 percent of them rate high on acceptance (Table 9.1), 60.0 percent enforce definite limits (Table 10.3), 50.0 percent tolerate dissent and expression (Table 11.3), and 56.7 percent have high self-esteem (Table 6.2). These findings apparently indicate that although we have established the general conditions associated with producing high self-esteem, not all of these conditions (or others) are essential to its development in any given individual nor is any single one of them sufficient to produce marked enhancement. Even though errors of measurement, scaling, and so on may contribute to the distribution of responses in any single analysis and the distributions differ for different analyses, it nonetheless appears that the apparent basic conditions of parental treatment and personal characteristics are not individually necessary nor sufficient to produce high self-esteem. This would suggest that combinations of conditions are required—more than one but less than the four established by this study (acceptance, limit definition, respect, and parental self-esteem). In addition it is likely that a minimum of devaluating conditions—that is, rejection, ambiguity, and disrespect—is required if high self-esteem is to be attained.

At least in theory, two combinations are likely to occur with considerable frequency: high parental self-esteem is likely to be associated with acceptance; firm limit definition is likely to be found in concert with respect for individual expression. The rationale for the relationship between high parental self-esteem, acceptance, and the child's high self-esteem stems from the findings of other investigators of the process of identification.[1,2,3] Their general conclusion appears to be that the child's identification with his parents is markedly increased and to a great extent derives from parental acceptance. A close affective tie apparently establishes the desire to emulate, and also the likelihood that parentally approved behaviors will be expressed. In effect, the child is more likely to follow in the footsteps of his parents and accede to their desires if they indicate their approval of him than if they disapprove of him and treat him in a punitive, rejecting manner. Doll play, used as an index of underlying attitudes, reveals that parental nurturance is positively associated with preference for adult dolls:[4] a child is less likely to adopt an adult role when he is physically punished or rejected. Studies of institu-

---

[1] G. Bateson. "Cultural determinants of personality." In J. McVickers Hunt (Ed.). *Personality and the Behavior Disorders, Vol. II,* New York, Ronald Press, 1944.

[2] R. R. Sears. "Identification as a form of behavioral development." *In* D. B. Harris (Ed.). *The Concept of Development.* Minneapolis, University of Minnesota Press, 1957.

[3] J. W. Whiting. [Symposium paper.] *In* J. M. Tanner and B. Inhelder (Eds.). *Discussions on Child Development II.* New York, International Universities Press, 1954.

[4] H. Levin, "Permissive child rearing and adult role behavior in children." (Paper delivered at Eastern Psychological Association, Atlantic City, March 28, 1952.)

tionally reared children[5,6] suggest that persons who have not had a history of nurturant experience with a parental figure tend to be socially immature and shallow in their emotional responses. Our own results indicate that children with high self-esteem are more likely than others to be close to their parents, to confide in them, to respond to the punishments they administer, to be socially skilled and emotionally responsive. This leads us to the initial conclusion that, to the extent that identification plays a role in the formation of self-esteem, children with high self-esteem are more likely to identify, as well as more likely to have a favorable model with which to identify.

The second suggestion—that clear, enforced limits are related to respect for individual expression—stems from the observation that openly expressed rules and restraints provide a framework for discussion and hence require less supervision and restriction. From a purely structural viewpoint, rules that are fixed and accepted make it possible, although not certain, that persons exercising authority will be less concerned and threatened by differences of opinion. If such rules of conduct do not exist, persons in authority are more likely to consider that differences of opinion threaten their position. An external code of specified practices and rights that is enforced provides those governed by it with at least some degree of assurance against arbitrary actions and also permits those who exercise authority to be more casual in their treatment of dissent; it engenders a more relaxed attitude for those who must administer social organizations as well as for those who must live within them.

The relation between parental self-esteem and the child's self-esteem indicates that unconscious identification and conscious modeling may well underlie the self-evaluations of many individuals. These processes need not contribute equally to the history of each person but there does appear to be a general relationship between the parent's self-esteem and the manner in which he treats his children. Parents with high self-esteem are generally more accepting of others, decisive, inclined to lead active personal lives, and convinced of their powers. They presumably have less need to gain vicarious successes from the accomplishments of their children and are able to provide their children with a definite idea of what they expect and desire. The parent with low self-esteem who is accepting of his child may provide a negative model for esteem building but at the same time the pattern of his actions may well lead the child to a higher level of self-appraisal than he has himself

---

[5] W. Goldfarb. "Psychological privation in infancy and subsequent adjustment." Am. J. Orthopsychiat., **15**:247–255 (1945).

[6] J. Bowlby. *Maternal Care and Mental Health.* World Health Organization Monograph No. 2, 1951.

attained. The combination of a high self-esteem model and an enhancing pattern of treatment should provide the highest and most stable levels of positive self-evaluation. Some recent attempts[7] to modify the antisocial actions of adolescents suggest that an effective, rewarding model establishes the motivation for change and provides the specific cues for desirable action patterns.

### THEORETICAL REFORMULATION

With this summary of the conditions associated with the formation of self-esteem, we now consider whether our findings support or refute the conceptual analysis presented in Chapter 2. There we proposed that the specific, determining variables of self-esteem be subsumed under the concepts of successes, values, aspirations, and defenses. According to that formulation, the process of self-judgment derives from a subjective judgment of success, with that appraisal weighted according to the value placed upon different areas of capacity and performance, measured against a person's personal goals and standards and filtered through his capacity to defend himself against presumed or actual occurrences of failure. The degree of self-esteem an individual actually expressed would thus reflect the extent to which his successes approached his aspirations in areas of performance that were personally valued, with his defenses acting to define and interpret what is "truly" valued, the "actual" level of aspiration, and what is regarded as "successful." To achieve a positive self-evaluation, he would have to reach a level of performance in valued areas that met or exceeded his aspirations, and he would have to be able to diminish and reject the derogatory implications of any differences and deficiencies. What follows will provide us with an indication of how the findings bear out our conceptual analysis and indicate how each concept is actually employed in the process of self-evaluation.

*Success.* Widely accepted public notions of the potency of status, or physical appearance as influences in personal judgments of worthiness appear to be wide of the mark. To take but a few examples, self-esteem is not related to height and physical attractiveness, two widely respected attributes in middle-class American society, and it is only rather weakly related to social status and academic performance. The limited, though significant, relationship between self-esteem and indices of material wealth, education, and achievement are all the more surprising because of the great weight publicly

---

[7] A. Bandura and R. H. Walters. *Adolescent Aggression.* New York, The Ronald Press, 1959.

placed upon these conditions and the general conviction that they are among the major foci and motives of contemporary American life. They indicate that the communal acceptance and respect associated with status, the increased knowledge and skills that derive from education, and the greater material comforts and security that accompany wealth are not sufficiently salient determinants to generally result in favorable self-appraisals. Such results reveal the limited utility of general public standards for understanding and predicting individual subjective appraisals of success, and underscore the importance of a person's immediate, effective interpersonal environment in making such judgments. It is from a person's actions and relative position within this frame of reference that he comes to believe that he is a success or failure, and *not* in the far broader and more abstract context of general sociocultural standards. Since all capacities and performances are viewed from such a personal context, we must know, for example, conditions and standards within a given classroom, a group of professionals, or a family before making any conclusions about any individual's feelings of worthiness. All other things being the same, a bright, competent child in a classroom of equally capable children is likely to be lower in self-esteem than a less competent child who is markedly superior to his classmates. The absolute, objective appraisal of capacity, performance, or possession does not have, for the individual, the significance of the psychological appraisal made in a personal context.

The recognition that definitions of success occur within a personal frame of reference does not mean that we cannot make some general statements regarding the conditions generally associated with favorable self-appraisals. What it does suggest is that such statements are indeed general rather than individually relevant, that these general statements have relevance to the extent that common dimensions and standards are employed in different frames of reference, and to the extent that the terms employed (such as acceptance or respect) have similar connotations and importance. Given these conditions, we can make some general statements on the attributes and treatment that lead middle-class American preadolescents to view themselves as successes or failures. The most notable bases for judgments of success are acceptance, the possibilities of individual expression and dissent (within limits), and academic performance. Acceptance is generally manifested by parental care, concern and attention; individual expression, by open discussion within well-defined limits; and academic performance, by competence relative to the members of one's group. Taken as a whole the results do indicate that favorable attitudes and treatment by persons significant to an individual, be they parents or peers, are likely to have enhancing effects on self-judgments. It is, however, important to note that the most favorable self-judgments are not associated with uncritical, unrestricted, and totally favorable attitudes and treatment. For in the families of children with high self-esteem there are greater and more definite limits to behavior, parents are more apt to lead active lives outside their families, and there is a clear expression of parental authority. In addition, we find that the parents in these families spend no more time with their children than do the parents in other families, nor are they any less inclined to punish their children for transgressions. The child in these families nonetheless concludes that he is indeed significant to his parents, which is evidenced as much by their restrictions as by their attention and concern.

*Values.* The conceptual analysis developed in Chapter 2 proposes that persons weight their success and failure experiences according to the values they espouse. Persons who fail in areas that are of no great importance to them are unlikely to attribute much significance to their lackluster performance, and those who succeed in valued areas are likely to assume that deficiencies in other areas are relatively unimportant. The hypothesis that persons place different weights upon various areas of performance and capacity suggests that possibly persons place greatest weight on those areas in which they excel. Such a weighting would have the most enhancing consequences and could—under conditions of free value selection and emphasis—result in everyone's having high self-esteem. Our own findings indicate that such conditions of free value selection and emphasis do not, in fact, prevail, but that persons at all levels of self-esteem tend to employ very similar standards to judge their worth. Despite limitations in ability, performance, and social skills, persons with low self-esteem are just as likely to attach importance to intelligence, achievement, and social success as are individuals with high self-esteem who tend to be superior in these regards. The similarity of value preferences in spite of manifest differences in capacity and achievement suggests that the value preferences that people actually employ in judging their worthiness are those that are generally espoused by their group rather than those that they may dwell upon in their private and fantasy experiences. Thus, although individuals are theoretically free to select their values, the years spent in home, school, and peer groups generally lead to acceptance of group standards and values. Individuals may well obtain some relief and gratification by employing different and more restricted standards, but it is unlikely that they will employ these standards as the *principal* bases for judging their worthiness. The general social norms of one's group become internalized as self-values, so that self-judgments are made in regard to them rather than in regard to more private and more independently derived standards.

The compelling nature of social norms places marked restrictions on the selection and weighting of self-values, so that in actual practice members of a group will tend to place similar importance on various capacities and behaviors. Although shared standards make it very likely that persons will emphasize and value the same goals, they may differ in how they appraise their attainment of those goals. Thus, two students who place a high value on a muscular, coordinated physique, and who are actually similar in their body builds and athletic ability, may come to quite different conclusions on how closely they come to achieving their standards. One may conclude that he is an Adonis and regard himself with marked favor; the other may conclude he is a runty weakling. Apparently interpretation and weighting come into play in judging whether one attains the value, and not in focusing upon any particular value. This process may more properly be considered as part of the defensive capacities of the individual than his self-value preferences. Perhaps the most notable impression that emerges from our examination of self-values is that personal norms are likely to be far less influential in judging worthiness than group norms. Indeed, such private norms appear relatively unimportant factors in over-all assessments of personal worthiness.

*Aspirations.* According to the model presented in Chapter 2, self-judgments involved a comparison of one's actual performance and capacities with one's personal standards and aspirations. If standards have been met or exceeded, particularly in valued areas of behavior, the person is likely to conclude he is worthy; if it falls below those standards, he is likely to conclude he is insufficient. Since this process involves a comparison of goal and performance, it suggests that "objective" success, as manifest publicly, is not as psychologically significant as is the personal conclusion that is reached. On theoretical grounds we might anticipate that persons with high self-esteem might set lower (and more attainable) goals for themselves (and hence conclude they are successful); thus they would be more likely to live up to their standards. Our results, however, suggest that there is a major and essential distinction between the goals that are socially espoused and the self-significant goals that persons set for themselves. Individuals who differ in self-esteem do not differ in the public goals they espouse, even though they differ markedly in the personal ideals they set for themselves. They will thus tend to select much the same occupational levels and strive for approximately the same targets when asked to play a toss game. Apparently they believe that their choices in these tasks have little, if any, personal significance for their future behavior and actual self-judgment, so that the goals they select are likely to represent wishful choices rather than standards to which they are committed. When we turn to more personal goals, we find that persons with high self-esteem set significantly *higher* goals for themselves than do persons with medium and low self-esteem. These individuals with high self-esteem seemingly expect more of themselves than do persons with less self-esteem and presumably maintain their esteem by meeting their expectations rather than lowering their standards. In effect, it appears that more favorable self-attitudes are not associated with lowered personal standards that permit judgments of success at lower levels of performance but rather with higher standards that are then objectively attained. Persons with high self-esteem generally conclude they are closer to their aspirations than are the individuals with low self-esteem who have set lower goals.

The results on the importance of limits and the rules of family conduct add another dimension to this discussion of aspirations. The findings in these areas suggest that explicit, enforced standards of conduct make it easier for the child to know when he has failed, by how much, and what he must do to achieve success. The absence or limited presence of such defined standards apparently leaves the child uncertain of his success and failure and lessens the likelihood that he will judge his performance as successful. Uncertain, shifting, ambiguous standards are likely to be associated with uncertain or lessened feelings of worthiness rather than with self-enhancing judgments. Another implication of the results is that persons are likely to employ their *expectations* of success rather than their private hopes in setting personally significant standards. Persons with low self-esteem are as desirous of success as those with loftier esteem, but they are less likely to believe that such success will occur. The pessimism that results is an expression of anticipated failure, which in itself decreases motivation and probably contributes to the occurrence of such failure. Personal aspirations, in short, reflect personal expectations rather than more general standards or vague secret hopes.

*Defenses.* Just as individuals differ in their aspirations and values, so also do they differ in their ability to deal with failure and uncertainty. Two individuals encountering the same stresses may respond in drastically differing ways, depending on their interpretation of the stresses and their ability to tolerate and minimize their consequences. The general paradigm for understanding the psychological bases for resistance and vulnerability revolves around the concepts of threat, anxiety, and defense. The process is seen as one in which a threatening stimulus or situation arouses anxiety, which evokes defenses, which in turn act to remove or curtail both the anxiety and its sources from conscious awareness. Persons who have defenses that are effective, varied, and flexible—without being massive—are presumably able to reduce the personal distress attendant upon anxiety without isolating themselves from their inner experiences or the external environment. Such persons are able to eliminate or reinterpret noxious stimuli and thereby are able to maintain equanimity and effective behavior. On theoretical grounds it would appear that persons with high self-esteem are better able to defend themselves against inner and external sources of distress. The major basis for this proposal was the assumption that the expression of a highly favorable, validated self-attitude pointed not only to a notable history of personal successes but also to an ability to handle the stresses and strains that all persons necessarily encounter.

Although the results presented in this report do not include any of the traditional indices of defensive ability (such as Rorschach scores or responses to the TAT), they do provide other indications of how well our subjects dealt with threat. At a relatively overt level manifest anxiety is negatively associated with self-esteem; that is, persons with positive self-attitudes tend to have low anxiety scores (Table 7.9). Another related index of anxiety expression is the significantly fewer number of psychosomatic symptoms among persons high in self-esteem (Table 7.12). In the same vein, ratings indicate that children with high self-esteem are more effective (Table 7.3) and are less likely to display marked problems (Table 7.11). Within a more limited sphere we find that children with high self-esteem are less sensitive to criticism (Table 3.8), more willing to speak up when their responses are likely to evoke anger (Table 3.7), and less likely to be distracted from public affairs by personal concerns (Table 3.10). The unanimous direction of these findings strongly suggest that children with high self-esteem are less likely to display distress and anxiety and are better able to deal with threats when they do arise than are children who think less well of themselves. The only limitation in these findings is that they are based upon the reports of the subjects and the appraisals of their mothers rather than upon indices derived from projective material. Inasmuch as defenses are assumed to be largely unconscious, this limitation is of considerable importance. Without entering at this point into the details of the scoring and results of the projective tests, we should note that they generally indicate that persons with high self-esteem are better able to deal with anxiety than are those who rank low in their own estimation.

On a more abstract and theoretical level it is essential to explicate the meaning of the terms "threat," "anxiety," and "defense" and to relate them more specifically to self-esteem. Turning to each of these in order, let us first inquire as to what is threatened when a failure or other stress occurs. As noted in a prior publication,[8] the significance of the threat that disturbs the individual lies in its negative implications for his self-esteem, and the attendant experience of anxiety is marked by feelings of inadequacy and helplessness that are generally reported by persons low in self-esteem. Viewed in this context the term threat applies to a stimulus or situation which the individual is uncertain of handling effectively; this raises doubts as to his powers and capacities, with consequent lowering of self-esteem. Defenses represent the ability to resist or reject devaluating stimuli and events and hence permit the individual to maintain the conviction that he is powerful, capable of dealing with adversity, and successful. In this formulation defenses may be made manifest after the threat has been presented or they may occur in the initial recognition and interpretation of the threatening situations and stimuli. Whether they occur post hoc in response to stimulation or as a priori interpretations, self-attitudes and other attitudes that enable the individual to maintain esteem defend him against the debilitating effects of temporary or long-term feelings of helplessness. Persons with positive self-attitudes apparently start from the initial position of assurance that they can deal with adversity; such attitudes may themselves be considered a form of defense or perhaps of immunity. Inasmuch as the definition, interpretation, and response to a stimulus play an essential role in determining what is deemed to be a threat, the prevailing level of self-esteem would appear to be an important determinant of whether, how, and how well an individual will defend himself. Meaning is, after all, imposed upon a situation and persons who feel powerful and adequate to deal with threat are less likely to have their confidence shaken than are persons who are fearful and unsure of their abilities.

Two other findings appear notable. The first is the relative frequency with which subjective self-esteem is affected by parental treatment and personal attributes. Subjective self-esteem is far more likely to be related to parental behavior and attitudes than are behavioral or discrepant indices of self-esteem. There are, over all, only a handful of findings that indicate any relationships between behavioral indices of self-esteem and parental treatment or attributes. These relationships are scattered over the range of dimensions and categories discussed and do not appear to fall into any meaningful

---

[8] S. Coopersmith. "A method of determining types of self-esteem." *J. Abn. Soc. Psych.*, **59**:87–94 (1959).

pattern. There are more frequent instances of relationships between discrepant self-esteem—that is, subjective and behavioral differences—and parental attitudes and practices. These relationships appear to center around parental stability and stability in the family's living conditions. By and large, the relatively limited findings for discrepant and behavioral self-esteem serve to accentuate the pervasive and significant relationships obtained with subjective self-esteem. The relative frequency of relationships with subjective self-esteem strongly suggests that parental attitudes and treatment have far greater influence upon the individual's self-attitudes than upon his behavioral expression. This is borne out by the agreement between child and parental reports, both of which are generally related to subjective self-esteem, as well as by the projective material, which is generally concordant with the subjective reports. Taken as a whole, the results suggest that self-attitudes may well be a more reliable and sensitive index of parental treatment than are more overt behavioral expressions of esteem.

Finally, we should note the surprising and theoretically important findings regarding persons with medium self-esteem. From the results presented in these pages it would appear that persons with medium self-esteem have had a family background that is most likely to result in dependency upon their parents. These persons of medium self-esteem are also inclined to take strong value positions on a wide and relatively indiscriminate array of values. This generalized value orientation, their greater dependency, and their intermediate and hence ambiguous position of worth suggest that there may well be particular, distinguishing characteristics associated with medium self-esteem. Rather than being a mere pivotal, intermediate part of the range of self-esteem, the middle portion may well reflect the consequences of uncertain self-appraisal.

### CONSEQUENCES OF PARENTAL TREATMENT

Although this monograph has not focused upon the consequences of different levels of self-esteem, it has revealed several of the feeling states and behaviors associated with positive, moderate, and negative self-attitudes. Without dwelling on the details of these findings the general patterns into which they fall will be summarized. Persons with high self-esteem, reared under conditions of acceptance, clear definition of rules, and respect, appear to be personally effective, poised, and competent individuals who are capable of independent and creative actions. Their prevailing level of anxiety appears to be low, and their ability to deal with anxiety appears to be better than that of other persons. They are socially skilled and are able to deal with external situations and demands in a direct and incisive manner. Their social relationships are generally good and, being relatively unaffected or distracted by personal difficulties, they gravitate to positions of influence and authority. Persons with medium self-esteem appear to be relatively similar to those high in esteem—with a few major exceptions. They are relatively well accepted, possessed of good defenses, and reared under conditions of considerable definition and respect; they also possess the strongest value orientation and are most likely to become dependent upon others. From the context of other evidence, it appears that they are uncertain of their worth and inclined to be unsure of their performance relative to others. Persons with low self-esteem, reared under conditions of rejection, uncertainty, and disrespect, have come to believe they are powerless and without resource or recourse. They feel isolated, unlovable, incapable of expressing and defending themselves, and too weak to confront and overcome their deficiencies. Too immobilized to take action, they tend to withdraw and become overtly passive and compliant while suffering the pangs of anxiety and the symptoms that accompany its chronic occurrence.

An important consequence of the different patterns of social treatment associated with various levels of self-esteem are the expectations that these treatments establish with regard to oneself and the situations one encounters. Persons with high self-esteem, conditioned and fortified by favorable treatment and by performance they believe to be successful, appear far more likely to expect successes in their social and academic encounters than are the individuals with low self-esteem who have previously experienced rejection, disrespect, and failure. In general, we may assume that an individual arrives at a crude ratio of his successes and failures and employs that ratio in estimating future possibilities of success. An individual who achieves below-average performances or encounters rebuffs in the majority of his experiences is unlikely to believe he will lead the pack in his future encounters; a person who has led his class in performance and has been its social leader is quite likely to believe that his future actions will be equally successful and well received. With our knowledge of the conditions of treatment prevailing in families of children differing in self-esteem and of the psychological states associated with various levels of esteem, we would anticipate marked differences in what these children expect of themselves and other persons. Examining each level in turn we may note differences in parental expectations, the child's self-expectations, and the expectations brought to specific tasks and interpersonal situations. The parents of high self-esteem children apparently expect their children to strive and comply with the standards they establish. These expectations represent a belief in their child's adequacy and a conviction that he has the ability to perform in whatever way is required to succeed. Such convictions are supportive and encourage the child to believe that success is indeed attainable. When set at reasonable levels, they represent a parental vote of confidence. To the child they provide a clear indication that what is desired is attainable, thereby giving courage as well as direction. Implicit in parental expectations and the child's expectations of himself is the conviction that one's personal behaviors will indeed affect what happens, with a corresponding feeling that one can control his destiny. This confidence that one can deal with adversity, realize personal strivings, and gain respect and attention is likely to be self-fulfilling by the persistence and poise it engenders and by the demands it imposes on other persons. Self-expectations of success are likely to be expressed as assertiveness, urges toward exploration, and self-trust—qualities that are apt to have invigorating and stabilizing consequences. In social situations persons who are accustomed to acceptance and expect to be successful are likely to believe that they will be treated with due appreciation of their worth. They will probably insist upon their rights and prerogatives and resist any treatment that even suggests they are not equal to others. Where parents are realistic and knowledgeable about their children, we would expect that a beneficent cycle of parental expectations of success leads to a child's confidence and more frequent successes, which in turn leads to greater expectations of success on his part.

The parental, self, and social expectations of individuals with low self-esteem are marked by lack of faith, expectations of failure, and the anticipation of rejection. Relating to their children in a distant and rejecting manner, these parents lead the children to believe that they cannot learn, are not important, and have no powers and privileges. These children come to believe that this is their due and that they may expect similar treatment from other persons. Such anticipations of rejection and failure are likely to result in passivity and withdrawal in the belief that they deserve no better and are incapable of improving their lot. Expectations of failure and rejection by parents thus engender doubts of adequacy in the child, which are made self-fulfilling by the manner in which the parent treats them and the self-image of weakness and inferiority they develop. By virtue of the treatment he receives and the self-attitudes he develops as a consequence, the child with low self-esteem is unlikely to believe that his personal actions can have a favorable outcome, that he can effectively cope with adversity, or that he is worthy of love and attention. These anticipations of failure are likely to sap his motivation, reduce his personal vigor, and leave him little hope or courage for dealing with the people and problems he must inevitably confront.[9]

In considering the relationship between self-attitudes and expectancies, we should note that these attitudes are self-fulfilling by their very effects upon motivation and action. The person who believes, realistically or not, that he is likely to succeed and that he deserves respect and attention will present a posture of confidence and thereby increase the likelihood of his success and of the respectful attention of others. Such a person's expectations become a reality to others as well as to himself, both by virtue of his overt actions and statements and by the energizing effects that positive expectations for the future are likely to have upon the present. These positive expectations should be differentiated from the vague positive anticipations of success that are experienced at all levels of self-esteem. Expectations of success reflect a confident belief that a given (favorable) event will occur; positive anticipations reflect the person's prior hope or belief of what may occur without indicating how confident the person is in this belief. Expectancies reflect a high degree of certainty and are therefore more likely to have affects or motivation and behavior; anticipations represent generalized notions and wishes and are likely to be transitory and illusory in their affects as well as in their occurrence. Anticipations may provide some transitory pleasure and are likely to be associated with hope, as in entertaining the idea that what one longs for will come true; expectations are likely to be associated with courage—that is, firmness of mind and purpose—which enables the person to meet danger and difficulties.

There are two other consequences of parental treatment that need to be considered before concluding this section. The first of these concerns the level of stimulation within families that produce children who differ in self-esteem; the second deals with the question of whether the concepts of adjustment and adaptation are appropriately applied to children with high self-esteem. From the findings obtained in this study it appears that the treatment associated with the formation of high self-esteem is much more vigorous, active, and contentious than is the case in families that produce children with low self-esteem. Rather than being a paradigm of tranquillity, harmony and open-mindedness, we find that the high self-esteem family is notable for the high level of activity of its individual members, strong-minded parents dealing with independent, assertive children, stricter enforcement of more stringent demands, and greater possibilities for open dissent and disagree-

---

[9] C. N. Cofer and M. H. Apley. *Motivation: Theory and Research*, Chap. 16. New York, Wiley, 1964.

ment. This picture brings to mind firm convictions, frequent and possibly strong exchanges, and people who are capable and ready to assume leadership and who will not be treated casually or disrespectfully. The parents apparently start with many of these characteristics as part of their personality structure and by early adolescence their children are well on the way to being assertive persons in their own right. The interchanges between parents and child— necessitated by limit definition and enforcement, by expressions of concern, by greater latitude for discussion—are likely to result in a more active and stimulating social environment. The child reared under these conditions would have a good deal of experience with adults, particularly strong-minded ones who would help him achieve his own self-definition. In addition, the procedure of establishing limits within which discussion and disagreement can occur increases the possibility of communication and the development of mutual knowledge and respect. In sum, the conditions of treatment associated with the formation of high self-esteem are likely to be marked by high levels of activity, strong and independent convictions, and differences of opinion that contribute to self-definition, provide social stimulation, and lead to increased communication between family members.

The second consequence of parental treatment bears upon some prevailing notions of adjustment and mental health. From all indications, children who are high in self-esteem are apt to manifest independence, outspokenness, exploratory behaviors, and assertion of their rights; children with low self-esteem are likely to be obedient, conforming, helpful, accommodating, and relatively passive. The child with high self-esteem is likely to be a considerable source of travail and disturbance to his parents, teachers, and other persons in authority, and the child with low self-esteem is more inclined to be overtly submissive and accepting. We should note, however, that persons who are low in self-esteem have higher levels of anxiety, more frequent psychosomatic symptoms, are rated as less effective, and are likely to be more destructive than persons who regard themselves with considerable worth. The frequently raised question of whether the criteria of adjustment to one's social group is a suitable basis for judging psychological health is re-evoked by the finding that children with high self-esteem are at least as aware as other persons of their social world but they are inclined to pay greater attention to their personal beliefs and convictions than are persons who are less sure of themselves. The relation between inner convictions and social values, like the relation between the individual and his society, cannot be assumed to operate best when the individual negates his own views and merges harmoniously into the group. This latter is a rather parochial view of psychological health, and judging by our findings it is likely to be associated with lessened creativity and social participation as well as with more frequent indications of anxiety. What we do find is that persons whose behavior may be viewed by those in authority as disruptive are likely to possess greater interpersonal skills and are generally more capable of protecting their interests and opinions than are persons who take a less favorable view of themselves.

## ISSUES AND IMPLICATIONS

The findings reported in this monograph, interesting in their own right, answer questions of both a theoretical and practical nature, and inevitably raise others. These questions pertain to the concepts and results of other studies of personality development and, perhaps more practically, to the assumptions and procedures employed in forming and strengthening self-esteem. To the extent that researchers, child clinicians, and parents believe that self-esteem contributes significantly to personal happiness and effective functioning, they may find in these results some clues to guide their own thoughts and actions. This section will underscore some of these clues, examine some of the assumptions on which they are based, and indicate their significance and implications. My discussion will proceed from the theoretical research-oriented implications to those that apply more directly to the procedures employed to develop and alter self-esteem.

At its most general level the findings affirm the significance of self-esteem and its importance for varied and more overt forms of behavior. Far from an epiphenomenon, self-esteem appears significantly associated with specific antecedents on one end and behavioral consequences on the other. The questions of response sets and defensive postures, which have long clouded the acceptance of studies of self-esteem, appear to be more critical in theory than in the relationships that actually prevail. In terms of validation this study provides not only laboratory and projective evidence generally confirming the operational significance of self-attitudes but also reveals an internally consistent pattern. The measurement problems and theoretical issues associated with response sets remain[10] but the findings do reveal that the response styles associated with self-attitudes are valid, reliable, and theoretically consistent. Far from closing the issue of genuine and spurious responses, this criticism and that of experimenter-induced biases[11] compel a reappraisal

---

[10] Jack Block. *The Challenge of Response Sets.* New York, Appleton-Century, 1966.
[11] Robert Rosenthal. "Experimenter outcome orientation and the results of the psychological experiment." *Psych. Bull.,* 61:405–412 (1964).

of the attitudinal and situational influences on responses to psychological investigations. Although the presence and importance of these influences appear to be beyond question, they underscore the need for tighter controls, extended validation, and more specific theories rather than generalized doubt and skepticism. These strictures apply to all manner of responses as well as self-attitudes, with scientific acceptability determined by procedure and proof rather than the nature of the variable.

In this same context of response sets and validity we should note the implications of our findings for the concept of defensiveness. As determined by our procedure of comparing subjective, behavioral, and projective indications of esteem, it would appear that the great majority of respondents are nondefensive in their evaluative behaviors. This result may be partially a function of our sample, partially of the procedure itself and partially a function of indeterminate sources, but it nonetheless remains the case. Insofar as we seek to make general statements about the validity of self-attitudes we may say that they are generally associated with overt behaviors and unconscious attitudes and are far more likely to have motivational and behavioral consequences than are either behavioral or projective indices of the same variable. This generalization obviously does not apply in every case but our evidence supporting general concordance of subjective, behavioral, and projective esteem appears far more powerful and persuasive than general arguments to the contrary. This conclusion gives us reason to seek more effective procedures for identifying those who make, consciously or otherwise, spurious statements about their internal states without leading us to believe that all or most such statements are spurious.

The results of the study also provide some intriguing addenda regarding the bases and significance of defensive reactions. Though the concept of defensiveness is interpreted in a variety of ways, it is generally assumed that defensive reactions stem from the individual's desire or inclination to present a public response that differs from his private attitudes and convictions. The responses that are publicly expressed are assumed to be generally supportive of socially accepted norms and thereby gain or maintain group or self-acceptance that would be lost if the genuine attitudes were expressed. Defensive reactions are thus assumed to provide a façade that gains acceptance or at least nonpunitive responses by denying public expression of private, generally antisocial attitudes. This denial may be either conscious or unconscious and stems from the individual's inability to tolerate the anxiety aroused by group disapproval and self-condemnation and an unwillingness to publicly dissent from group norms. Defensive reactions would thus appear to reflect a denial of subjective experience as a basis for public action, a condition which we have previously associated with low self-esteem (Chapter 3). The results confirm the hypothesis that individuals with low self-esteem are likely to be defensive, and reveal that such reactions are likely to be associated with either discrepant or medium self-esteem. In persons with discrepant esteem (High-Low and Low-High) we find indications that contradictory bases of action associated with an unstable home background are likely to reduce public effectiveness; in persons with medium self-esteem we find greater support for social values and the likelihood of dependence upon other persons. The nature and pattern of our findings suggest that low self-esteem (passive acceptance), medium self-esteem (active espousal), and discrepant self-esteem (lessened social effectiveness) are associated with different defensive reactions. Defensiveness, in short, is not a single phenomenon associated with low self-esteem but appears to consist of a variety of reactions reflecting different deficiencies of esteem. The marked social desirability set that many investigators have imputed to those low in self-esteem appears to be more rightly assigned to those who are medium in self-esteem, who are uncertain of their worth, rather than those low in self-esteem, who have already judged themselves to be unworthy.

The study also suggests that present conceptualizations of parental behaviors are insufficient to describe the parental attitudes and treatments that produce high self-esteem. The concepts of control, puermissiveness, strictness, discipline, and domination suggest a simple, single-dimensional concept relating to power and authority in the family; such concepts as acceptance, love, and affection refer to the parents' basic approval of their child. Some analyses of parental behavior[12,13] have, in fact, concluded that these behaviors are organized along two major conceptual dimensions: love-hostility and control-autonomy. These conceptualizations are intended to provide a framework for organizing detailed and varied research findings. They do provide a model of parental behavior, and they suggest that the concepts of control and love are both simple and readily identified. However, as our results have repeatedly indicated, the control and love expressed by the parents of children with high self-esteem are more complex than they appear on the surface, and are likely to contain what may be construed as contradictory components. Thus we find that the parents of children with high self-esteem who are more attentive and concerned about their children

---

[12] E. E. Schaefer. "Converging conceptual models for maternal behavior and for child behavior." *In* J. C. Glidewell (Ed.). *Parental Attitudes and Child Behavior.* Springfield, Ill., Charles C. Thomas, 1961.
[13] E. S. Schaefer. "A circumplex model for maternal behavior." *J. Abn. Soc. Psych.,* **59**:226–235 (1959).

are also more demanding and are inclined to lead active lives outside their families; they are no more likely to spend time with their children than the parents of children with less self-esteem. Similarly, if we turn to the concept of control, we find that the families of children with high self-esteem are marked by well-defined limits of behavior and clear statements of rights and privileges, coexisting with greater tolerance for individual expression and less drastic forms of punishment. It may be possible to resolve these apparent contradictions by assuming that limits are inimical with "true" democratic practices, or that the "truly" accepting mother does not find satisfaction in activities outside her home. Such a resolution is not logically necessary, nor is it borne out by their children's perceptions and responses nor by the consequences upon their children's attitudes and performances. From the analysis here it appears that the requirements for maintaining and protecting the child and reconciling the needs of the various members of the family make some (minimum) regulations and restrictions inevitable. To call parents who establish such regulations rejecting, undemocratic, or punitive is to disregard the realities of childrearing.

Similarly, we cannot assume that mothers who work and who enjoy working are necessarily rejecting or are ruining their children. This study reveals that such mothers are likely to have children who are high rather than low in their self-esteem and who are less likely to manifest anxiety and psychosomatic symptoms. The significance of the mother's absence from home apparently depends upon how she, her child, and the other members of the family view such absence; that is, it is not the treatment but how the treatment is perceived in the family context that determines its effects upon the child. A mother may well regard certain duties and conditions associated with childrearing as onerous without making the child feel that she does not care for him.[14] Her negative attitudes toward many of the events and conditions of childrearing man reflect direct and realistic thinking rather than the rejection of her child. Clinical studies have indicated that persons who are normal and psychologically healthy are better able to express negative statements about themselves and their life circumstances. To generalize from the mother's attitudes toward the conditions of childrearing to her acceptance for her child appears unwarranted and, from our evidence, false. The patterns of parental behavior we find associated with the favorable consequences of high self-esteem suggest that the concepts of love and autonomy present a much simpler picture of parental behavior than exists in reality.

---

[14] J. Kagan. "On the need for relativism." *Am. Psychologist,* **22**:131–142 (1967).

Not only must the dimensions be combined in the right amounts to describe how a given parent behaves, but the specific operational referents of each dimension must be given more explicit definition.

Further consideration of the concepts applied to childrearing and of our results suggests that interpretation of these concepts are often idealized versions of parent-child interaction. Such terms as democracy and domination, which deal with authority within the family, appear to have been taken over full-blown from the analyses of other social groups. Originating in the arena of public politics, they apparently were generalized to the smaller and markedly different group of the family. Idealized, ambiguous, and inappropriate in that context, these generalizations dwelt upon the rights and privileges of family members without equal attention to the importance of regulations and restrictions, checks and balances, and executive leadership. The general notions of family democracy and permissiveness failed to consider that children have less knowledge and foresight than their parents, that discussions based on ignorance tend to be aimless, and that parents are ultimately responsible for the conduct of their young children. In attempting to counter the abuses of prior generations, to maintain contact with their children, to gain personal gratification, and presumably to rear more secure and adjusted children, many parents accepted a redefinition of parental authority. Authority was equated with authoritarianism, discipline was associated with punishment, and restrictions were thought to indicate rejection. From the results obtained in this study it appears that parents who accepted this redefinition were not very confident of their own beliefs and were also more likely to produce anxious rather than confident children. The parents of children with high self-esteem have continued to assert their authority, presumably relating it to experience, knowledge, seniority, and responsibility, while at the same time permitting open discussion and dissent. They have thus provided a framework that may be viewed as either guiding or restricting —depending on one's convictions—but a framework that nevertheless has demonstrably favorable consequences for their children's esteem.

Thus, although certain expressions of parental authority appear to have favorable consequences, our concepts and understanding of such authority are still relatively crude, as well as burdened with surplus meaning. In applying the ideas and concepts of social philosophies to family practices, many parents have proceeded on vague assumptions, with little confirmation, toward utopian goals. The laissez-faire tradition of American society, the change in social values and norms, and the increasing isolation of nuclear family units from their extended families have all tended to lessen the force of authority within the modern families in our society. An additional influence may well have been the redefinition of the male role, traditionally one of authority, to one which shared powers and privileges with his spouse. The female may well have had equal authority in the past, but the public acceptance of these changes may have caused members of both sexes to be chary of publicly exercising their authority. Another factor undermining parental authority may have been the expansion of psychological, psychiatric, and pediatric knowledge about developmental processes. Faced with scientific knowledge and experts, many parents probably concluded that their own inclinations and traditional means of treating children should be put aside in favor of more advanced and tested information. Because of all these factors, a closer look at the power distribution and decision-making that occurs in the normal, effective family is in order. It may well be that we shall need a new language to describe what actually occurs in a modern family and the types of parental treatment that produce favorable or unfavorable consequences.

Another issue raised by our findings concerns the relationship between restriction—manifested in limits and rules—and self-initiated activities. The indication that children with high self-esteem reared under well-defined rules are likely to be more creative, assertive, and independent runs counter to expectations and raises some interesting theoretical questions. Although the relations between early treatment and subsequent initiative are far from clear, it has often been proposed that initiative and self-reliance are likely to be associated with early freedom. According to this view the child learns how to respond to himself and how to organize situational ambiguities in ways that keep him relatively free of the authoritative views and demands of others. The lack of restrictions, in effect, permits self-expression and a broad exploration of possibilities, whereas restrictions tend to emphasize the convictions of other persons and the goals and procedures *they* endorse. Judging by the pattern of our findings, the opposite is actually true: early external restrictions are likely to be associated with greater self-knowledge and expressiveness as well as more assertive and enterprising actions. Of the several possible bases for this apparently reversed relationship we should first note that firm clear external limits are likely to result in clearer, internal definitions of one's convictions, beliefs, and attitudes. Self-attitudes are likely to reflect the clarity and incisiveness of the environmental attitudinal system as well as its content. Clear statements by those in the environment makes for clearer self-definition, which is likely to result in more definite bases of action. Such action is not necessarily similar or congruent with that which is publicly espoused and may be contrary or deviant as well as exploratory. Ambiguous or nonexistent limits make it incumbent upon the child to develop and impose his own definitions and restrictions, a task for which he is not culturally or conceptually equipped. Limits provide the child with an interpretation of acceptable behavior that markedly reduces the range of permissible alternatives and provides a context that is more concrete and manageable. Because of the child's limited symbolic and conceptual capacities, restrictions are likely to provide a greater sense of order and meaning and to offer more frequent occasions for manifesting mastery than are unstructured, criterion-free conditions. The child may be more inclined to explore in broader fields if he has previously proved his prowess in environments that were cognitively clear and manageable and if he believes that there is indeed an underlying order and structure. In addition, and most critical to this discussion, is the finding that families in which limits are set—families that produce creative and assertive children—are also families that accept and respect their children. It is thus not possible to say that it is the restrictions rather than the other conditions that result in personal assertiveness. An alternative hypothesis would be that limits and rules provide a concrete, manageable environment and a belief in an orderly universe, whereas respect and acceptance lead to self-respect and self-valuation that enable the individual to venture new and personally satisfying interpretations. The child who has come to value himself by virtue of favorable reflected appraisals is likely to attend to his own perceptions and reactions while being guided by environmental feedback on his effectiveness. Poorly structured environments would appear to provide little feedback, particularly for the younger child whose symbolizing capacities are limited and who does not yet possess a stable assessment of his powers.

We shall briefly comment on the implications of our findings for the prevention and treatment of low self-esteem. Turning first to their implications for prevention, we may note that our results can be employed to describe how treatment destructive to self-esteem can be limited or eliminated, or conversely, indicate those conditions that are likely to result in high self-esteem. Thus, depending on whether we are dealing with the concerns of younger or older parents, school administrators or directors of resident institutions, we may focus upon the elimination of particular methods of punishment, specific "democratic" practices, or disrespectful treatment, or we may seek to establish those conditions of acceptance, limit definition, and respect associated with positive self-attitudes. The range of possible applications is a wide one: parent education regarding our general findings; examination of classroom practices to determine how destructive conditions can be reduced without interfering with learning; specific advice to a given set of parents on how they may implement enhancing practices; and generally increasing the confidence of parents regarding the use of limits and rules.

Whichever of these procedures is employed, it seems clear that we are now in a position to provide relatively well-established information of the kind of treatment that is likely to eventuate in high self-esteem. Since low self-esteem has in this report been associated with anxiety and neurotic symptoms, and in other studies with neuroses and psychoses, this is no mean achievement. We should restate in this context of prevention that higher levels of self-esteem are associated with greater demands, firmer regulation, and parental decisiveness rather than with a tension-free, permissive, and otherwise idealized environment. Children with high self-esteem appear to learn quite early that they must respond to the challenges and troublesome conditions they encounter. It may be the model of decisive parents and the clear demands that are enforced and thus provide solutions, or it may be that parental acceptance and respect makes them more responsive to themselves and more expressive and assertive in their actions. Whichever of these prevails in a given case, our study provides clear indications that the individual with high self-esteem feels capable of coping with adversity and competent enough to achieve success, and that the individual with low self-esteem feels helpless, vulnerable, and inadequate. Such convictions of helplessness are learned reactions to self-responses and the responses of others, and preventive measures should therefore seek to reduce such learning and replace them with situations that result in feelings of control, adequacy, and competence. Some recent studies with infra human subjects point to the importance of self-initiated activities in developing competence[15] and suggest that early experiences of control may provide immunity against subsequent noxious experiences.[16,17] Self-initiation apparently increases under conditions of sensory enrichment,[15] a condition we might assume occurs more generally in the energetic, frequently interacting family of high self-esteem. The child with high self-esteem is likely to be enterprising, active, and exploratory and this might well lead him to become more personally involved in his self-discovered tasks and more competent in their execution. Although this generalization is speculative at this point—more valid at a conceptual than at an empirical

---

[15] R. Held and B. L. White. "Competence and sensory-motor development." Paper presented to Committee on Socialization and Social Structure, Social Science Research Council, April 30, 1965.

[16] J. B. Overmeier and M. E. P. Seligman. "Effects of inescapable shock on subsequent escape and avoidance learning." *J. Comp. Phys. Psych.* (in press).

[17] M. E. P. Seligman and S. F. Maier. "Failure to escape traumatic shock." *J. Exp. Psych.* (in press).

level—there is evidence that the child with high self-esteem is more active, enterprising, and competent. The studies[16,17] that indicate the immunizing effects of early experiences of control suggest that helplessness is learned in much the same way that feelings of power and adequacy are learned. Animals that were shocked under conditions where they could escape subsequently behaved quite differently under conditions of inescapable shock than did animals who were always treated to inescapable shock. Those who had learned that active responding produced relief sought to escape and were able to maintain effective functioning; those who had previously experienced only inescapable shock seemed to give up, to passively accept noxious treatment, and to manifest aberrant behavior. Early experiences of control apparently lead the individual to believe he may have some influence over his environment, so that he believes in his capacity to obtain relief by his own efforts. Learning how to cope with adversity is apparently acquired quite early by the child with high self-esteem; learned helplessness is the set established for those low in self-esteem.

In considering the implications of our findings for treating disturbances in self-esteem, we should first underscore the speculative nature of our discussion. Although there is an empirical basis for our suggestions on how self-esteem may be increased and stabilized, there is a clear difference between personality formation within the family and treatment carried out in a therapeutic situation. Nonetheless, the issues and procedures suggested by our findings do, in many ways, differ from those frequently espoused in psychological treatment, and they appear worthy of extended consideration. We shall limit ourselves to a brief consideration of three specific therapeutic implications, derived from our theoretical formulations and results. First, the conceptual analysis (Chapter 2) posed four major bases of esteem: competence, significance, virtue, and power. That is, persons come to evaluate themselves according to how proficient they are in performing tasks, how well they meet ethical or religious standards, how loved and accepted they are by others, and how much power they exert. We believe that determining the basis or bases a given individual employs in judging his worth may well be a crucial step in determining the source of his difficulties and in guiding therapeutic efforts. It may be, for example, that an individual may employ a basis in which he is markedly deficient—for example, he may be woefully incompetent—instead of employing a basis in which he is indeed worthy—such as his significance to others. Another individual may employ two bases that are mutually incompatible, thereby leading him to believe he has failed to live up to one of them. An example of this would be the person who judges his worthiness on the basis of whether he is competent and significant. This combination of conditions might gain him a greater sense of his worthiness from his parents but in subsequent life he is likely to find that outstanding competence that leads to public success and acclaim may also lead to the envy and disaffection of his peers. Appreciating and adjusting such incompatibilities between the bases of self-esteem themselves, and between the bases and the individual's capacities, afford a way of conceptualizing the sources of low self-esteem and may thus serve as a guide for treatment.

A second therapeutic implication is that the conditions for gaining positive self-attitudes are considerably more structured, specific, and demanding than generally prevail in traditional therapeutic settings. The clarity and firmness of the limits and rules that prevail in families of high self-esteem presumably establish standards and expectations that facilitate self-judgments. If these rules are set at a level that is appropriate to the environment and is realistic for the individual, the possibility for favorable self-judgments is markedly increased. It may be claimed that structuring the therapeutic situation, and possibly the life situations, of an individual may retard independence and self-expression, but our results suggest that this consequence is not inevitable. The result may depend, in part, upon the age of the individual, the life circumstances in which he lives, or the nature of his difficulties, but the indications are that more definite structure (plus other conditions) is associated with higher self-esteem and greater creativity.

A third implication is that the patient may benefit quite markedly by modeling his behavior after an effective, assured, and competent individual. The exact behavior that an individual may require or seek to follow undoubtedly varies with each person, but it may be that the style of response is more critical than the particular action. Thus the individual may observe how an effective individual deals with anxiety, resolves ambiguities, and makes decisions. He may observe how the person deals with insults and failures, handles money, and makes friends; the individual may thus learn alternative ways of action that confer a greater sense of power and control than he has previously experienced. Providing advantageous behavioral alternatives in their specific expression is a more parsimonious procedure than waiting for their self-discovery, and even more parsimonious than awaiting their recurrent use. Defining the world, dealing with it, and handling its difficulties are learned in much the same way as are other responses. Individuals with low self-esteem lack the capacity to define and to deal with their environment, but they may learn to do so more rapidly and efficiently if they are exposed to persons who are themselves confident and effective.

# APPENDIX A  SELF-ESTEEM INVENTORY (SEI)

Please mark each statement in the following way:

If the statement describes how you usually feel, put a check (√) in the column, "*Like Me.*"

If the statement does not describe how you usually feel, put a check (√) in the column "*Unlike Me.*"

There are no right or wrong answers.

|  | *Like Me* | *Unlike Me* |
|---|---|---|
| 1. I spend a lot of time daydreaming. | ___ | ___ |
| 2. I'm pretty sure of myself. | ___ | ___ |
| 3. I often wish I were someone else. | ___ | ___ |
| 4. I'm easy to like. | ___ | ___ |
| 5. My parents and I have a lot of fun together. | ___ | ___ |
| 6. I never worry about anything. | ___ | ___ |
| 7. I find it very hard to talk in front of the class. | ___ | ___ |
| 8. I wish I were younger. | ___ | ___ |
| 9. There are lots of things about myself I'd change if I could. | ___ | ___ |
| 10. I can make up my mind without too much trouble. | ___ | ___ |
| 11. I'm a lot of fun to be with. | ___ | ___ |
| 12. I get upset easily at home. | ___ | ___ |
| 13. I always do the right thing. | ___ | ___ |
| 14. I'm proud of my school work. | ___ | ___ |
| 15. Someone always has to tell me what to do. | ___ | ___ |
| 16. It takes me a long time to get used to anything new. | ___ | ___ |
| 17. I'm often sorry for the things I do. | ___ | ___ |
| 18. I'm popular with kids my own age. | ___ | ___ |
| 19. My parents usually consider my feelings. | ___ | ___ |
| 20. I'm never unhappy. | ___ | ___ |
| 21. I'm doing the best work that I can. | ___ | ___ |
| 22. I give in very easily. | ___ | ___ |
| 23. I can usually take care of myself. | ___ | ___ |
| 24. I'm pretty happy. | ___ | ___ |
| 25. I would rather play with children younger than me. | ___ | ___ |

|  | Like Me | Unlike Me |
|---|---|---|
| 26. My parents expect too much of me. | | |
| 27. I like everyone I know. | | |
| 28. I like to be called on in class. | | |
| 29. I understand myself. | | |
| 30. It's pretty tough to be me. | | |
| 31. Things are all mixed up in my life. | | |
| 32. Kids usually follow my ideas. | | |
| 33. No one pays much attention to me at home. | | |
| 34. I never get scolded. | | |
| 35. I'm not doing as well in school as I'd like to. | | |
| 36. I can make up my mind and stick to it. | | |
| 37. I really don't like being a boy—girl. | | |
| 38. I have a low opinion of myself. | | |
| 39. I don't like to be with other people. | | |
| 40. There are many times when I'd like to leave home. | | |
| 41. I'm never shy. | | |
| 42. I often feel upset in school. | | |
| 43. I often feel ashamed of myself. | | |
| 44. I'm not as nice looking as most people. | | |
| 45. If I have something to say, I usually say it. | | |
| 46. Kids pick on me very often. | | |
| 47. My parents understand me. | | |
| 48. I always tell the truth. | | |
| 49. My teacher makes me feel I'm not good enough. | | |
| 50. I don't care what happens to me. | | |
| 51. I'm a failure. | | |
| 52. I get upset easily when I'm scolded. | | |
| 53. Most people are better liked than I am. | | |
| 54. I usually feel as if my parents are pushing me. | | |
| 55. I always know what to say to people. | | |
| 56. I often get discouraged in school. | | |
| 57. Things usually don't bother me. | | |
| 58. I can't be depended on. | | |

# APPENDIX B BEHAVIOR RATING FORM (BRF)

1. Does this child adapt easily to new situations, feel comfortable in new settings, enter easily into new activities?

   ____always ____usually ____sometimes ____seldom ____never

2. Does this child hesitate to express his opinions, as evidenced by extreme caution, failure to contribute, or a subdued manner in speaking situations?

   ____always ____usually ____sometimes ____seldom ____never

3. Does this child become upset by failures or other strong stresses as evidenced by such behaviors as pouting, whining, or withdrawing?

   ____always ____usually ____sometimes ____seldom ____never

4. How often is this child chosen for activities by his classmates? Is his companionship sought for and valued?

   ____always ____usually ____sometimes ____seldom ____never

5. Does this child become alarmed or frightened easily? Does he become very restless or jittery when procedures are changed, exams are scheduled or strange individuals are in the room?

   ____always ____usually ____sometimes ____seldom ____never

6. Does this child seek much support and reassurance from his peers or the teacher, as evidenced by seeking their nearness or frequent inquiries as to whether he is doing well?

   ____always ____usually ____sometimes ____seldom ____never

7. When this child is scolded or criticized, does he become either very aggressive or very sullen and withdrawn?

   ____always ____usually ____sometimes ____seldom ____never

8. Does this child deprecate his school work, grades, activities, and work products? Does he indicate he is not doing as well as expected?

   ____always ____usually ____sometimes ____seldom ____never

9. Does this child show confidence and assurance in his actions toward his teachers and classmates?

   ____always ____usually ____sometimes ____seldom ____never

10. To what extent does this child show a sense of self-esteem, self-respect, and appreciation of his own worthiness?

    ____very strong ____strong ____medium ____mild ____weak

11. Does this child publicly brag or boast about his exploits?

_____always  _____usually  _____sometimes  _____seldom  _____never

12. Does this child attempt to dominate or bully other children?

_____always  _____usually  _____sometimes  _____seldom  _____never

13. Does this child continually seek attention, as evidenced by such behaviors as speaking out of turn and making unnecessary noises?

_____always  _____usually  _____sometimes  _____seldom  _____never

# APPENDIX C  MOTHER'S QUESTIONNAIRE

*The PARI scales.* The 80 items are arranged in cyclical order. There are 14 sub-scales, two of which (Equalitarianism and Acceleration of Development) contain 10 items. The other 12 subscales contain 5 items each. The subscales are divided into three units, corresponding to three factors found by both Baldwin and Shoben to be the major underlying parental attitudinal and behavioral determinants.

*Democracy–Domination* (25)          *Item locations*
   1. Encouraging verbalization (5)    1, 17, 33, 49, 65
   2. Excluding outside influence (5)   2, 18, 34, 50, 66
   3. Equalitarianism (10)          3, 4, 19, 20, 35, 36, 51, 52, 67, 68
   4. Comradeship and Sharing (5)    5, 21, 37, 53, 69

*Acceptance–Rejection* (25)
   5. Breaking the will (5)          6, 22, 38, 54, 70
   6. Irritability (5)             7, 23, 39, 55, 71
   7. Rejecton of homemaking role (5)   8, 24, 40, 56, 72
   8. Avoidance of communication (5)   9, 25, 41, 57, 73
   9. Dependency of mother (5)     10, 26, 42, 58, 74

*Indulgence–Autonomy* (30)
  10. Acceleration of development (10)  11, 12, 27, 28, 43, 44, 59, 60, 75, 76
  11. Strictness (5)             13, 29, 45, 61, 77
  12. Intrusiveness (5)          14, 30, 46, 62, 78
  13. Fostering dependency (5)    15, 31, 47, 63, 79
  14. Approval of activity (5)     16, 32, 48, 64, 80

*The questionnaire.* Indicate your opinion by drawing a circle around the "A" if you strongly agree, around the "a" if you mildly agree, around the "d" if you mildly disagree, and around the "D" if you strongly disagree. If you have any ideas which you feel should be included jot them down at the end. We would appreciate having them. Others who have given us their ideas say that it is best to work rapidly. Give your first reaction. If you read and reread the statements, it tends to be confusing and time-consuming.

There are no right or wrong answers, so answer according to your own opinion. It is very important to the study that all questions be answered. Many of the statements will seem alike but all are necessary to show slight differences of opinion.

|  | Agree | | Disagree | |
|---|---|---|---|---|
| 1. Children should be allowed to disagree with their parents if they feel their own ideas are better. | A | a | d | D |
| 2. It's best for the child if he never gets started wondering whether his mother's views are right. | A | a | d | D |

|  |  | Agree | | Disagree | |
|---|---|:---:|:---:|:---:|:---:|
| 3. | Parents should adjust to the children some rather than always expecting the children to adjust to the parents. | A | a | d | D |
| 4. | Parents must earn the respect of their children by the way they act. | A | a | d | D |
| 5. | Children would be happier and better behaved if parents would show an interest in their affairs. | A | a | d | D |
| 6. | Some children are just so bad they must be taught to fear adults for their own good. | A | a | d | D |
| 7. | Children will get on any woman's nerves if she has to be with them all day. | A | a | d | D |
| 8. | One of the worst things about taking care of a home is a woman feels that she can't get out. | A | a | d | D |
| 9. | If you let children talk about their troubles they end up complaining even more. | A | a | d | D |
| 10. | There is nothing worse for a young mother than being alone while going through her first experience with a baby. | A | a | d | D |
| 11. | Most children are toilet trained by 15 months of age. | A | a | d | D |
| 12. | The sooner a child learns to walk the better he's trained. | A | a | d | D |
| 13. | A child will be grateful later on for strict training. | A | a | d | D |
| 14. | A mother should make it her business to know everything her children are thinking. | A | a | d | D |
| 15. | A good mother should shelter her child from life's little difficulties. | A | a | d | D |
| 16. | There are so many things a child has to learn in life there is no excuse for him sitting around with time on his hands. | A | a | d | D |
| 17. | Children should be encouraged to tell their parents about it whenever they feel family rules are unreasonable. | A | a | d | D |
| 18. | A parent should never be made to look wrong in a child's eyes. | A | a | d | D |
| 19. | Children are too often asked to do all the compromising and adjustment and that is not fair. | A | a | d | D |
| 20. | As much as is reasonable, a parent should try to treat a child as an equal. | A | a | d | D |
| 21. | Parents who are interested in hearing about their children's parties, dates, and fun help them grow up right. | A | a | d | D |
| 22. | It is frequently necessary to drive the mischief out of a child before he will behave. | A | a | d | D |

|  |  | Agree |  | Disagree |  |
|---|---|:---:|:---:|:---:|:---:|
| 23. | Mothers very often feel that they can't stand their children a moment longer. | A | a | d | D |
| 24. | Having to be with children all the time gives a woman the feeling her wings have been clipped. | A | a | d | D |
| 25. | Parents who start a child talking about his worries don't realize that sometimes it's better to just leave well enough alone. | A | a | d | D |
| 26. | It isn't fair that a woman has to bear just about all the burden of raising children by herself. | A | a | d | D |
| 27. | The earlier a child is weaned from it's emotional ties to its parents the better it will handle it's own problems. | A | a | d | D |
| 28. | A child should be weaned away from the bottle or breast as soon as possible. | A | a | d | D |
| 29. | Most young mothers are bothered more by the feeling of being shut up in the home than by anything else. | A | a | d | D |
| 30. | A child should never keep a secret from his parents. | A | a | d | D |
| 31. | A child should be protected from jobs which might be too tiring or hard for him. | A | a | d | D |
| 32. | Children who don't try hard for success will feel that they have missed out on things later on. | A | a | d | D |
| 33. | A child has a right to his own point of view and ought to be allowed to express it. | A | a | d | D |
| 34. | Children should never learn things outside the home which make them doubt their parents' ideas. | A | a | d | D |
| 35. | There is no reason parents should have their own way all the time, any more than that children should have their own way all the time. | A | a | d | D |
| 36. | Children seldom express anything worthwhile; their ideas are usually unimportant. | A | a | d | D |
| 37. | If parents would have fun with their children, the children would be more apt to take their advice. | A | a | d | D |
| 38. | A wise parent will teach a child early just who is boss. | A | a | d | D |
| 39. | It's a rare mother who can be sweet and even-tempered with her children all day. |  |  |  |  |
| 40. | [Omitted.] |  |  |  |  |
| 41. | Children pester you with all their little upsets if you aren't careful from the first. | A | a | d | D |
| 42. | A wise woman will do anything to avoid being by herself before and after a new baby. | A | a | d | D |

|  | Agree | | Disagree | |
|---|---|---|---|---|

43. Children's grades in school are a reflection of the intelligence of their parents.     A    a      d    D

44. It is more effective to punish a child for not doing well than to reward him for succeeding.     A    a      d    D

45. Children who are held to firm rules grow up to be the best adults.     A    a      d    D

46. An alert parent should try to learn all her child's thoughts.     A    a      d    D

47. Children should be kept away from all hard jobs which might be discouraging.     A    a      d    D

48. Parents should teach their children that the way to get ahead is to keep busy and not waste time.     A    a      d    D

49. A child's ideas should be seriously considered in making family decisions.     A    a      d    D

50. The child should not question the thinking of the parents.     A    a      d    D

51. No child should ever set his will against that of his parents.     A    a      d    D

52. Children should fear their parents to some degree.     A    a      d    D

53. When you do things together, children feel close to you and can talk easier.     A    a      d    **D**

54. Children need some of the natural meanness taken out of them.     A    a      d    D

55. Raising children is a nerve-wracking job.     A    a      d    D

56. One of the bad things about raising children is that you aren't free enough of the time to do just as you like.     A    a      d    D

57. The trouble with giving attention to children's problems is they usually just make up a lot of stories to keep you interested.     A    a      d    D

58. Most women need more time than they are given to rest up in the home after going through childbirth.     A    a      d    **D**

59. A child never sets high enough standards for himself.     A    a      d    **D**

60. When a child does something well we can start setting his sights higher.     A    a      d    **D**

61. [Omitted.]

62. It is a mother's duty to make sure she knows her child's innermost thoughts.     A    a      d    D

63. I liked my child best when I could do everything for him.     A    a      d    D

|  |  | Agree | | Disagree | |
|---|---|---|---|---|---|
| 64. | The sooner a child learns that a wasted minute is lost forever, the better off he will be. | A | a | d | D |
| 65. | When a child is in trouble he ought to know he won't be punished for talking about it with his parents. | A | a | d | D |
| 66. | Parents should be careful lest their children choose the wrong friends. | A | a | d | D |
| 67. | A child should always accept the decision of his parents. | A | a | d | D |
| 68. | Children should do nothing without the consent of their parents. | A | a | d | D |
| 69. | Children should have a say in the making of family plans. | A | a | d | D |
| 70. | It is sometimes necessary for the parent to break the child's will. | A | a | d | D |
| 71. | It's natural for a mother to "blow her top" when children are selfish and demanding. | A | a | d | D |
| 72. | A young mother feels "held down" because there are lots of things she wants to do while she is young. | A | a | d | D |
| 73. | Children should not annoy their parents with their unimportant problems. | A | a | d | D |
| 74. | Taking care of a small baby is something that no woman should be expected to do all by herself. | A | a | d | D |
| 75. | Some children don't realize how lucky they are to have parents setting high goals for them. | A | a | d | D |
| 76. | If a child is pushed into an activity before he is ready, he will learn that much earlier. | A | a | d | D |
| 77. | Unless one judges a child according to strict standards, he will not be industrious. | A | a | d | D |
| 78. | It is a parent's business to know what a child is up to all the time. | A | a | d | D |
| 79. | Children are better off if their parents are around to tell them what to do all the time. | A | a | d | D |
| 80. | A child should be rewarded for trying even if he does not succeed. | A | a | d | D |

# APPENDIX D  MOTHER'S INTERVIEW

1. How old is [child's name] [at time of interview]?
   - 1a. How old are you?
   - 1b. How old is your husband?

2. Where was [child's name] born?
   - 2a. Where were you born?
   - 2b. Where was your husband born?

3. How many generations has your family been in U.S.?
   - 3a. And your husband's family?

4. Was your childhood or adolescence spent for the most part in urban or rural backgrounds?
   - 4a. And your husband?

5. What is your religious affiliation?
   - 5a. And your husband?
   - 5b. To what extent are you involved in religion? And your husband?

6. How many years of schooling have you completed?
   - 6a. And your husband?

7. What is your husband's occupation?
   - 7a. What was his father's occupation?
   - 7b. What is your occupation? Did you ever plan to have a career? What was that? Have you been able to continue in this line at all?
   - 7c. What was your father's occupation?

8. What is the approximate combined family income of your husband and yourself?

9. How many years have you been married? Were you previously married? Have you and your husband ever been separated for any length of time? Does his job require that he be away from home any length of time?

10. Does your husband's work make it necessary for you to move fairly often? How many times have you moved in the past 5 years? Do you have a feeling of permanence about your present home situation or are you contemplating any moves?

11. How many children do you have? Tell me their names and ages.
    - 11a. What ordinal position does [child's name] have?

12. Were you working before your first child was born? How much have you worked since then? How did you feel about stopping? (if did): Would you like to stop working in the near future? (if still working): What do you do? How many hours a week do you work?

13. As far as either you or your husband were concerned, was there anything which made [name of firstborn]'s coming slightly inconvenient? What was that?

14. What are some of the reasons you wanted to have children? Did most of your friends have children when [first child's name] was born?

15. In what ways have you found family life different from what you expected?

16. Do you find you have ample time to do the things you want to do outside of the home?

    16a.   Is there anything which you would especially like to do which you find you don't have time for? What would you like to do if you had more time?

17. What changes did having children bring into your life? How did you feel about these things?

18. What sort of pregnancy did you have with [child's name]?

19. What sort of delivery did you have with [child's name]?

20. To what extent has [child's name] been taken care of and/or trained by other persons? Both at present and in the past. What has been the nature of the care—i.e., has he lived with them for a year, month, weekends; eaten with them, been read to, received gifts? (This question includes grandparents as well as others. In all cases the agent should be described.)

21. Now we'd like to get some information about [child's name] growth and development. Could you tell me at what age he first stood up? When did he begin to walk with support? Without support? When did he start talking, using his first real words?

22. Could you tell me when you started toilet training? How did it go? How old was he when he was bowel-trained? When was he bladder-trained? What did you do about it when he had accidents after he was mostly trained?

    22a.   At what age do you feel children *can* be toilet-trained?

    22b.   At what age *should* they be trained?

23. Were there any feeding problems? Are there any feeding problems at present?

    23a.   Did you breast feed? For how long? When did he go to the bottle? When did he go to the cup?

    23b.   What was the schedule of feeding (permissive-disciplined)?

24. Did [child's name] suck his thumb? How long did this last? How did you feel about it? What was the frequency of thumbsucking?

25. Could you tell me at what age [child's name] was allowed to dress himself? to bathe himself? to cross the street alone? to use public transport? to go to store on errand? to sleep at friend's home?

26. At what age did you enjoy [child's name] most?

    26a.   Would you call him a pretty affectionate child?

    26b.   Was there any age at which it was especially easy to be affectionate with [child's name]?

27. How does your child respond to affection now? Do you still hug and kiss him? How do you think he feels about this?

28. In raising [child's name], what periods were especially difficult for you?
    28a. What kind of problems arose then?
    28b. How were they solved?

29. Many children go through phases during which they damage and break things around the home. Could you tell me some of the things [child's name] has done which you consider destructive? What have you done about his doing things like that?

30. How important is discipline in raising children? What do you think is the basic purpose of punishment?

31. Before he was in school, how did you punish [child's name] when he misbehaved? How did he react when you punished him? What did you do about this? How effective was punishment? What was child's reactions to punishment?

32. How did he react when he was naughty?

33. How much do you think a child should be encouraged to try new things?

34. At what age do you think that children should have jobs around the home?
    34a. Does [child's name] have any jobs? What are they?
    34b. Why do you think it's important for him to have jobs to do?
    34c. How do you go about getting him to do them?
    34d. How did you set up what he should do?

35. What do you think is the best way of rewarding a child? Do you think it is a good idea to show your feelings at such times?

36. Did you think it is more important that the child solve the problem successfully, perhaps under the supervision of the parents, or that he gain the experience of working it out for himself?

37. Before [child's name] started kindergarten, did you teach him anything like reading words, or writing the alphabet, or drawing, or telling time, or things like that?
    37a. How did you happen to teach him these things?
    37b. When did you start?
    37c. What could he do when he went to kindergarten?
    37d. At what age do you think mothers can start teaching their children nursery rhymes?
    37e. Mother's attitude towards pre-school accomplishments of child.

38. Has [child's name] had any severe illness or injuries? Which ones? When?
    38a. Has he had any operations? Which ones? When?

39. Have there been any instances where [child's name] has been emotionally upset?
    39a. Has he ever required treatment for such upsets by school personnel or your family doctor?

39b. How would you describe his general state of emotions and ability to get along with other people?

39c. Has he ever been involved in any serious scrapes with school authorities or public officials? Were there such incidents in the past which have disappeared?

40. Has [child's name] always been pretty easy to get along with?

40a. How would you say he compares in this respect with your other child (children)?

41. In what respects do you believe [child's name] to be different from your other children?

42. Do you think it is easier for mothers to understand girls than boys?

43. Could you give me some examples of things you and [child's name] frequently enjoy together? How frequently do you do these kinds of things?

43a. How much time do you or your husband spend playing with [child's name]?

44. How do you think your husband behaves towards [child's name]?

44a. Do you think he's taking as much interest as he could and doing what he can for the boy?

45. What is your husband's attitude towards your son? Does he spend much time with him, express affection readily, and respect his feelings?

46. Do you think children enjoy spending time with adults? What do you think they like most about doing things with their parents?

47. Most boys have worries and problems which they won't talk about. How difficult is it to find out what is bothering [child's name]?

47a. Why does he keep things to himself?

47b. How do you find out what's bothering him?

47c. Does he confide in his father?

48. How do you feel when you find out that [child's name] has been keeping things secret from you? What sort of things do you believe he should be allowed to keep private?

49. In what situations do you most often express approval to [child's name]?

50. Could you give me some examples of when you have been especially proud of [child's name]?

51. How is [child's name] about doing what you ask him to do?

51a. Do you think a child should usually act right away when the parent asks or makes a request?

51b. Why do you feel this way?

52. How are rules and restrictions decided in your home? If he didn't want to study, how would you handle it?

53. How do you usually get [child's name] to act as you want him to? What kind of rewards do you use?

    53a. Would you tell me about some of the restrictions which are placed on [child's name] behavior and activities?

54. How do you punish [child's name] now? Could you give me a couple of specific examples? How does he react to this sort of thing? How do you feel about punishment in general?

55. If [child's name] does something which is wrong, does he come and tell you about it? Does he do this generally or only if something unusually bad happens? When he is asked about doing wrong things, does he admit or deny them?

    55a. Would you say [child's name] is hard on himself, i.e., judges himself severely and demands high levels of performance and morality?

56. Some children get angry with their parents on occasion and shout at them. Has this ever happened in your home with [child's name]?

    56a. Why do you think children do this sort of thing? Do you think that is why [child's name] did it?

    56b. How have you handled the problem?

57. Can you remember any times when you have punished [child's name] when he probably should have been punished less severely or not at all?

    57a. What have you done when you found you were wrong? Do you think many parents apologize to their children? Do you think this is a good idea?

58. How do you feel about [child's name] questioning things you tell him? For instance, if you told him he couldn't have any of your alcoholic beverage and he asked why, what would you tell him?

59. Most mothers find that children playing around them get on their nerves after a while. Do you find that you have to get away from them or take a breather? How often? Any particular occasions?

60. If the door is closed to [child's name] room, would you always knock before you went in? Do you think it is all right for a child to expect a parent to knock? Do you expect your child to knock before entering your room?

61. Do you allow [child's name] to play with children of whom you don't approve? Why have you disapproved of certain of his acquaintances? How have you handled the problem of keeping him from playing with such children?

62. What is your policy about [child's name] letting you know where he is? What would happen if he didn't do this?

63. What time is he supposed to go to bed? How is he about going to bed on time? Are there regular exceptions to this bedtime? How do you handle it when he wants to stay up late? What do you consider reasonable grounds for letting him stay up later?

64. Does [child's name] try to do things which are beyond him? Could you give me some examples?
      64a. How do you feel about children trying to extend themselves?

65. What do you want [child's name] to be when he grows up?
      65a. Do you have any particular educational plans for him?
      65b. What do you think he will be?
      65c. What are your husband's ideas about [child's name] future?
      65e. How do you think any differences between you and your child should be resolved?

66. Do you think [child's name] can do as many things without help or supervision as most children his age? Would you like him to be more self-reliant and independent?

67. Do you think most parents help their children with homework or assist them with school projects? Do you think this is a good idea? Why do you feel this is good? How much of this sort of thing do you do? Why is this?

68. Do you feel [child's name] works up to his ability at school? If he doesn't, how do you handle it?
      68a. What have you done in school situations where [child's name] has not done as well as expected? What are the reasons this may have occurred (i.e., poor study habits, not interested, play, etc.)?

69. Do you think [child's name] considers himself generally better, worse, or about average in respect to his friends? What makes you say that? Is he generally confident and self-reliant?

70. Have you noticed any changes in [child's name] personality during the past few years?
      70a. Has he become more interested in girls; serious about career, boisterous or silly?
      70b. Has there been much physical growth in the past few years? Has he during this period experienced an extreme spurt of growth, or period of uncoordination and gawkiness?

71. How would you rate your child's intelligence and general ability in comparison with other children his age? In what ways is he better than the average? In what ways does he need to develop?

72. Despite his problems, do you think that [child's name] is generally a happy, normal child?

what would you change

# INDEX

Esteem
  certainty of, 231
  experience of, 46
  four bases of, 38, 262
Expectations, 147, 246, 251
Experimental behaviors, 15
Exploratory behavior, 225

# F

Family
  as group, 200
  size, 149, 151
Father, 87–90, 108, 227
Feeding, 154, 156
Friendships, 50, 172
Fromm, E., 27, 34

# G

Goal setting, 224
Grade point average (GPA), 128

# H

Happiness, 133
Height, 122
Horney, K., 27

# I

Ideal self, 145
Ideal self–self discrepancy, 146
Idealized image, 33
Identification, 241
Illnesses, 158
Independence, 52, 54, 209, 217
  training for, 216–234
Inferiority, 33
Intelligence, 126
Isolation, 34

# J

James, W., 27, 29
Judgmental process, 7

# L

Learned helplessness, 261
Limits and rules, 204, 236, 259
Love, 3
Lowy, D. G., 78

# M

Management practices, 191
Marital history, 101

Maternal role, 103–106
Mead, G. H., 27, 29
Medium self-esteem, 141, 229, 249
Modeling, 241, 263
Mother's Interview, 74, 75, 275
Mother's Questionnaire, 74, 269
Mother's self-esteem, 97, 240

# O

Occupation, 87, 144
Ordinal position, 150, 152

# P

Parent Attitude Research Instrument
    (PARI), 74, 269
Parental acceptance, 164–180
  compromise, 210
  conflict, 112
  consistency, 185
  contact, 227
  control, 190, 205
  demands, 184
  interactions, 111
  self-esteem, 240
  strictness, 183
  values, 100
Paternal role, 108
Pathology, 134
Permissiveness, 35, 181–189
Physical activities, 121
Physical attributes, 120
Popularity, 49
Power, 38
Preadolescence, 8
Preoccupation with failure, 69
Preparatory set, 23
Prevention of low self-esteem, 260
Previous marriages, 101
Privacy, 228
Problems, childhood, 158
Protectiveness, 223–226
Psychosomatic symptoms, 134
Punishment, 191–194

# R

Rapport, maternal, 169
Reflected appraisal, 31
Regulations, 186, 205
Religion, 36
Response set, 2, 25, 254
Reward, 190

Rogers, C., 27, 34
Rosenberg, M., 35, 82, 85, 101

# S
Sample size, 17
Self
    concept of, 19–25
    extensions, 30
Self-appraisals in different areas, 6
Self-consciousness, 68
Self-consistency, 6
Self-esteem
    divergent groups, 12
    four sources of, 38
    of mother, 97, 240
    theoretical context, 27
    types, 12
Self-Esteem Inventory (SEI), 5, 9, 265
Self-image, 34
Self-values, 138
Sensitivity to criticism, 67
Siblings, 151, 161
Significance as basis of esteem, 38, 258
Social class, 82
Social participation, 48
Stimulation level, 252
Strictness, 183
Subject selection, 9

Success, 29, 37, 38, 242
Sullivan, H. S., 27

# T
Testing procedures, 72
Thematic Apperception Test (TAT), 77, 173
Therapy, 260
Tolerance of dissent, 209
Trauma, 156

# U
Unconscious appraisals, 26

# V
Values, 26, 29, 37, 41, 244
Virtue, 38

# W
Withdrawal of love, 191
Work history of father, 88–90
    absence from home, 90
    job stability, 90
    occupations, 87
    unemployment, 88
Work history of mother, 90–92
Wylie, R., 3